WRITING IN REAL TIME

From Walt Whitman to the contemporary period, the long poem has been one of the more dynamic, intricate, and yet challenging literary practices of modernity. Addressing those challenges, *Writing in Real Time* combines systems theory, literary history, and recent debates in poetics to interpret a broad range of American long poems as emergent systems, capable of adaptation and transformation in response to environmental change. Due to these emergent properties, the long poem performs essential cultural work, offering a unique experience of history that remains valuable for our rapidly transforming digital age. Moving across a broad range of literary and theoretical texts, *Writing in Real Time* demonstrates that the study of emergence can enhance literary scholarship, just as literature provides unique insights into emergent properties, making this book a key resource for scholars, graduate students, and undergraduate students alike.

PAUL JAUSSEN is an assistant professor of literature at Lawrence Technological University in Southfield, Michigan. His research covers nineteenth- and twentieth-century literature, with a particular focus on poetics and literary theory. His essays and reviews have appeared in *New Literary History, Contemporary Literature, Journal of Modern Literature, William Carlos Williams Review, Jacket2*, and *The Volta*.

Recent Books in This Series

WRITING IN REAL TIME

Emergent Poetics from Whitman to the Digital

PAUL JAUSSEN

Lawrence Technological University

CAMBRIDGE
UNIVERSITY PRESS

CAMBRIDGE
UNIVERSITY PRESS

University Printing House, Cambridge CB2 8BS, United Kingdom

One Liberty Plaza, 20th Floor, New York, NY 10006, USA

477 Williamstown Road, Port Melbourne, VIC 3207, Australia

4843/24, 2nd Floor, Ansari Road, Daryaganj, Delhi - 110002, India

79 Anson Road, #06-04/06, Singapore 079906

Cambridge University Press is part of the University of Cambridge.

It furthers the University's mission by disseminating knowledge in the pursuit of education, learning and research at the highest international levels of excellence.

www.cambridge.org
Information on this title: www.cambridge.org/9781107195318
DOI: 10.1017/9781108163989

First published 2017

Printed in the United States of America by Sheridan Books, Inc.

A catalogue record for this publication is available from the British Library

ISBN 978-1-107-19531-8 Hardback

Contents

v

Acknowledgments

Writing a book is a journey. In my case, the adventure began at the University of Washington, where my dissertation was a first attempt to think about the long poem, form, and history. I was directed in this process by the wise, rigorous, and inimitable Herbert Blau. He is sorely missed. Leroy Searle has also been a valued mentor. Other faculty refined, supported, and challenged my thinking; in particular, I thank Henry Staten, Jeanne Heuving, Brian Reed, and Marshall Brown.

The journey continued at Case Western Reserve University, where intelligent colleagues pressed me to expand my arguments. Michael Clune has been more than generous with his time and suggestions; this book owes much to him. I am also grateful to my fellow lecturers in the English department for creating a supportive and stimulating community, particularly Joshua Hoeynck, Mark Pedretti, Megan Swihart Jewell, Erika Olbricht, and Eric Chilton.

In the final stages of writing, I was cheered on by colleagues at Lawrence Technological University. Although most of them come from disciplines other than literary criticism, they have graciously suffered through my enthusiastic speeches about emergence and poetic form. There are too many to name here, but I am particularly grateful to Franco Delogu, Giulia Lampis, Phil Vogt, Melinda Weinstein, Dan Shargel, Corinne Stavish, Jason Barrett, and Hsiao-Ping Moore.

Along the way, I have had the support of a wonderful network of scholars and poets. A special thanks goes to Rachel Blau DuPlessis and Nathaniel Mackey, who have inspired and encouraged me in so many ways. The relationship between living writers and their critics can be complex; they have been both generous and respectful. I thank Marjorie Levinson for inviting me to share this work with her graduate students and for her ongoing enthusiasm for the project. Steven Gould Axelrod, Jeffery Gray, Matthew Levay, James Searle, and Jason Hoelscher have been supportive correspondents and commentators.

Three readers for Cambridge University Press offered remarkably insightful, thorough, and generous reports. Their suggestions showed me how to bring the work to its full potential. I thank Ray Ryan and Ross Posnock for their early faith in the project and for their encouragement and patience during the writing process.

An early version of Chapter 4 appeared as "Charles Olson Keeps House: Rewriting John Smith for Contemporary America" in *Journal of Modern Literature*, reproduced courtesy of the Indiana University Press. An early version of Chapter 5 appeared as "The Poetics of Midrash in Rachel Blau DuPlessis's *Drafts*" in *Contemporary Literature*, © 2012 by the Board of Regents of the University of Wisconsin System, reproduced courtesy of the University of Wisconsin Press.

I did not journey alone; two people walked with me at every step. When the destination became obscure, the road challenging, and my spirits low, they offered me vision, companionship, and enthusiasm. For their support and love, I dedicate this book to my wife, Capria, and to my son, Ransom.

CHAPTER I

Introduction
The Poetry of Emergence

In 1861, six years after Walt Whitman first published a volume titled *Leaves of Grass*, America erupted into civil war. Whitman the person responded to the war in a variety of ways, leaving Brooklyn to search for his injured brother and spending his days caring for wounded soldiers. Whitman's poem also responded to the war. The structure and tone expanded, adapting to the new events in surprising ways even as the text remained *Leaves of Grass*. In 1945, Ezra Pound would be confined to a prison camp in Pisa, Italy, having been captured by Allied forces. Fifteen years before, Pound had published a *Draft of XXX Cantos*, one of the first collected volumes of his long poem. Like *Leaves of Grass*, *The Cantos* would transform themselves to process this new event. In 1948, Pound published *The Pisan Cantos*, deploying the resources of the earlier work to imaginatively engage his time in the prison camp, an event he could not have anticipated at the outset of the project. A third example: in 2005, Hurricane Katrina raged through the Mississippi delta, leaving New Orleans residents, particularly those who were black and poor, stranded in desperate conditions. Twenty-five years earlier, Nathaniel Mackey had begun two twinned long poems, *"mu"* and *Song of the Andoumboulou*, both of which represented postcolonial diaspora through the imagery of deadly and inhospitable seas. In *Nod House*, his 2012 addition to these works, scenes from the flooded Ninth Ward of New Orleans entered the poem, transforming the hostile waters of the earlier work. It was as if Mackey had been writing a Katrina poem since the 1980s.

Each of these poems responds to changes in its environment, a more or less empirical fact of literary history. But what constitutes the poetics of this adaptability? Is there a theoretical model that can more accurately describe *how* these poems change? This book is an attempt to answer these questions. Drawing on the interdisciplinary framework of systems theory, I argue that these texts exemplify "emergent poetics," functioning as complex adaptive systems. John Holland's basic definition of emergence is a useful place to begin thinking about complex adaptive behavior. For Holland, emergence is "much coming from little": the idea that small, local actions or actors can produce large, global, and unexpected effects.[1] Emergence is visible in a variety of complex adaptive systems, including "ant colonies, networks of neurons, the immune system, the Internet, and the global economy."[2] In each of these systems, first-order actions produce unexpected second-order effects. These higher order patterns, in turn, redirect the behavior of the first order, transforming the system as a whole and shaping its encounters with the environment.

One of the most elegant illustrations of emergence is a flock of birds moving across a landscape. Made up of individual agents and guided by no central consciousness, the flock nevertheless exhibits a definite shape; at any given moment, the birds exist within a recognizable form. This form, however, is constantly fluctuating in response to both environmental and systemic shifts; more precisely, the system shifts with the environment. The birds encounter a tree or a sudden gust of wind, changing the trajectory or speed of their flight. This movement cascades through the entire flock, producing an emergent formation. We could say that the flock as a whole, through this continuously unfolding process, is interpreting a landscape in its form. The flock presents us with an emergent structure embedded within a changing world, change that, somewhat paradoxically, the flock itself, through its movement, is making visible. The flock's performance across the sky reveals the world anew.

Akin to a flock of birds, emergent long poems develop through the ongoing activity of writing in real time. Poetic form, far from being determined in advance, arises as a dynamic second-order pattern out of first-order activities, prompting the poem to further evolution. Over the past decades, emergent systems have been theorized and studied in a range of disciplines, from biology to cognitive science. However, few critics have studied the long poem in these terms, as a textual practice capable of interpreting a changing world. *Writing in Real Time* seeks to address that critical gap, combining systems theory with literary criticism. As I hope the following chapters demonstrate, the implications of such an approach are wide-ranging, providing insight into difficult, unwieldy long poems while also contributing to critical discussions of literary form, the relationship between form and history, and the creative agency of literature. Indeed, I would hazard a bolder claim: that literary texts may be a neglected yet crucial site for apprehending the concepts of scientific discourse, including systems theory.

What makes a poem peculiarly "emergent"? I argue that emergent poems are characterized by several interacting elements. First, such texts enact *provisional closure*, creating a poetic form or structure (closure) designed specifically for engagement with the environment, capable of future rearticulations and transformations (provisionality). In the poems I take up here, moments of provisional closure are often given a name, whether as "Canto," "Draft," "Song," or "Letter." Through provisional closure, the text establishes and then redefines itself in response to an ever-changing present. This provisional closure is shaped by way of *feedback loops* with the environment: as the poem interacts with its cultural, social, and historical world, the form of its provisional closure is adapted, and these modifications, in turn, produce new possibilities for engagement or *structural coupling*, whereby the operations of one system are entangled with another. To return to our analogy, the flock of birds is structurally coupled to the system of weather fronts and wind patterns. Similarly, the emergent text is structurally coupled to the life of the author, the conditions of composition and publication, the historical events that unexpectedly appear – in other words, an extensive network of relationships. These texts are further characterized by *iteration*, which is the deployment of single, repeatable, and yet variable structures, and *recursion*, wherein elements from one structure are self-referentially used as a model for generating subsequent structures. Through these processes, *emergent* effects arise: formal, thematic, and aesthetic properties that could not be anticipated by the poet nor predicted from the outset of the poem. Emergent poems thus generate surprises through their form while also registering surprises in their world.

The basic characteristics of emergent poetics are evident in the three examples with which I began. Whitman's use of the bound volume, poetic cluster, or individual "leaf" functions as a mode of provisional closure, producing a formal space whose boundaries are constantly being negotiated and expanded in response to historical events like the Civil War. Whitman's practice is also profoundly iterative and recursive. Each edition of *Leaves of Grass* is an iteration of the poetic system that in turn recursively expands that system into new historical and linguistic territory. *Leaves of Grass* repeats itself in order to register changes in its world. Similarly, Pound's work illustrates the principle of a feedback loop. As a poetic practice, *The Cantos* establish an intertextual network that incorporates primary texts, paratexts, typography, speech, and marginalia. When confronted with the radically unfamiliar environment of the detention center at Pisa, the poem's practice of textual appropriation is extended and modified, drawing the speech of Pound's guards into the poem and shifting to a more autobiographical register. As with Whitman, this iteration in *The Cantos* transforms the total field of the poem, enabling an unanticipated and yet continuous structure to unfold. A similar effect can be seen in Mackey's *Nod House*, where the language of diasporic seas from the earlier volumes is extended to the new historical context of post-Katrina New Orleans. Suddenly, the earlier iterations of the poem, where castaways and shipwrecks indicated forced migration and slavery, take on a new meaning made visible by the poem itself. The poem's vocabulary now bridges the past and the present, allowing an unexpected cultural memory to emerge through the complex adaptive process of poetic composition.

In what follows, I develop this conceptual framework of emergent poetics through readings of several long poems, all of which clearly enact an adaptive form through writing in real time. Alongside Whitman, Pound, and Mackey, I dedicate close attention to works by A. R. Ammons, Lyn Hejinian, Charles Olson, Rachel Blau DuPlessis, and Juliana Spahr, texts that clearly demonstrate the properties of complex adaptive systems. Alongside my primary case studies, I offer commentary on works by William Wordsworth, T. S. Eliot, Wallace Stevens, Robert Lowell, Ron Silliman, Derek Walcott, and M. NourbeSe Philip, demonstrating how emergent practices relate to other forms of long poetry. Approaching the long poem through the framework of emergence extends and complicates general concerns in modern and contemporary poetics with openness and closure, formal identity and social context. In many of the poems I consider here, one cannot cleanly separate formal adaptation from unexpected historical events because the poem's provisional closure makes visible the new event within its environment. The poem's form becomes the framework through which the environmental event is experienced *as* an event. Whitman set out to write America; Pound, the relationship between art and economics; Mackey, the cultural complexities of postdiasporic experience. The practice of writing the poem thus focuses attention, shaping the poet's perception of the world and allowing the world, in turn, to shape the poem. As the scope of a particular subject matter changes (often through wars, disasters, revolutions, and other unexpected occurrences), so too must the structure of the poetic text. As a self-reflexive, self-organizing system, the poem extends its terms and reevaluates its initial aesthetics, providing continuity within change, as we will see with Whitman's shifting definition of "democracy," the expanding sense of Ammons's "storm," or Spahr's self-reflective "I speak."[3] The emergent poem, like T. S. Eliot's notion of the "really new" work of art,[4] retrospectively transforms everything that preceded it without abandoning those prior elements – indeed, without the earlier poetic moves, the later additions wouldn't be possible at all, just as the individual birds are a necessary component of the entire flock.

A skeptic might object that the language and concerns of systems theory are an artificial imposition on poetry, an unnecessary proliferation of concepts foreign to literature. I would counter that long poems persistently reflect on the challenges of transformation within time, quite often anticipating the discourse of complex adaptive systems. Systems theory and the long poem may be not-so-distant cousins, sharing a family resemblance of concerns. For example, consider how A. R. Ammons draws time into form through the initiating act of provisional closure at the beginning of his self-consciously emergent *Tape for the Turn of the Year*. Here are Ammons's opening lines:

> 6 Dec:
> today I
> decided to write
> a long
>   thin
>   poem[5]

Ammons's initial artistic move is what Ted Gioia calls the "retrospective method" of artistic practice, which he heuristically contrasts with the "blueprint method." Where architects typically create a blueprint as a model for the construction of the work, the improvising musician "may be unable to look ahead at what he is going to play."[6] Instead, "he can look behind at what he has just played [and] thus each new musical phrase can be shaped with relation to what has gone before."[7] For Gioia, the retrospective artist "can start his work with an almost random maneuver – a brush stroke on a canvas, an opening line, a musical motif – and then adapt his later moves to this initial gambit."[8] In Ammons's case, the act of writing a long, thin poem becomes the "initial gambit" of provisional closure explicitly stated at the poem's outset, to which he continually responds *by way of time*, generating a feedback loop between poem and environment. To be sure, the range of emergence in *Tape* is limited at the outset due to a material constraint: the poem is composed on a single roll of receipt tape fed into a typewriter, a strategy that guarantees the text will have a predetermined length. Still, formal decisions must continually be made in the process of writing, and so the poem constantly varies, as the occasion demands, between short lines, single words or phrases, adaptive spacing, and enjambment. The tape's predetermined constraints may appear to be a blueprint but are in fact closer to an initiating gesture. To blend the models, it is an adaptive structure responding to the unpredictable present.

Ammons calls this contingent interplay between environment, experience, artistic practice, and imagination "the stream," placing faith in its processes over "facts," "arrangements," or "any shore":

> only the stream is
> reliable: get
> right up next to the
> break between
> what-is-to-be and
> what-has-been and
> dance like a bubble
> held underwater by water's
> pouring in: (TTY 19)

The speaker's immersion into the stream grounds his epistemological faith in that which is "reliable," not least because time itself, figured as the stream, is presented as both an active force and a duration. Indeed, duration as the space between events, the "break between," makes an artistic response possible because the stream's flow produces the air bubble's dancing motion, "dance" being the only word for artistic practice in the passage. We can read the bubble as the poet or reader integrated into the bubble-stream-water system, not least because Ammons admonishes himself and his reader to occupy the break: agency comes through the decision to inhabit time in a responsive, creative way. The resulting art, the "dance," is generated by an external force pressing against and shaping the generally passive air bubble – the dancer, in this case, does not know where he will be moving next. Generally passive, yet not entirely so, for the bubble must also be resilient, maintaining its identity against the stream for the dance to emerge. We might say that the persistence of provisional closure in the poem makes time visible.

By offering emergence as a new framework for understanding the relationship between the "dance" and the "stream" in the long poem, *Writing in Real Time* also seeks to intervene in a larger critical debate about the nature of literary form. The modern long poem has always been treated as a formal misfit. Consequently, it should come as no surprise that most theoretical reflections on form start with more conventional examples, most often the lyric poem. We can see this neglect of the long poem and the privileging of the lyric in classic texts of New Criticism, structuralism, deconstruction, and Frankfort school criticism,[9] but it is also an implicit value in the latest revival of critical interest in literary form. These "new formalisms" have come in many stripes, as Marjorie Levinson carefully argues in her 2007 review essay dedicated to the topic, and yet most have had little to say about the long poem.[10] Levinson's piece represents a broader critical moment, where literary scholars have been reevaluating (and revaluing) concepts like the literary, the formal, or, most recently, the descriptive. Within this moment we might place works like Derek Attridge's *The Singularity of Literature*, Rita Felski's *Uses of Literature*, and Gayatri Spivak's *An Aesthetic Education in the Era of Globalization*, all of which attempt to rethink literary value, either on the grounds of the text's irreducible singularity, in the multiple readerly responses that literary texts provoke, or in literature's capacity for imaginative training.[11] Such arguments share common cause with movements like Sharon Marcus and Stephen Best's "surface reading," itself affiliated with what has been called the "descriptive turn" in literary scholarship.[12]

This latest reevaluation of form has not simply neglected the long poem – it originally offered very little new insight about form *as such*, as Levinson pointed out in 2007, with many critics relying more or less on form as a received concept.[13] Recent work has revisited the matter of form, and some critics have begun to deploy frameworks like systems theory, complexity, and actor-network theory.[14] But here, too, the focus often remains on the lyric. For example, Cary Wolfe's analysis of Niklas Luhmann's theory of poetic form, while sharing an intellectual family resemblance to the arguments I offer here, uses the lyrics of late Stevens to exemplify his argument.[15] Similarly, Levinson's recent work on recursion also seeks to respond to debates over the lyric.[16] These interventions are not entirely surprising, given the developments in lyric studies, where scholars like Virginia Jackson argue that the lyric is a product of the theoretical models used to read it.[17]

In such a critical climate, a reassessment of the long poem on the level of form seems timely. Whether valorized (Wolfe) or critically historicized (Jackson), the theory of form in literary criticism is more often than not a theory of lyric form. My purpose is not to dismiss lyrical models of form but simply to suggest that a different set of formal coordinates, like the long poem and the discourse of complex systems, might allow us to rearticulate these questions. Perhaps by beginning with the long poem, a practice caught up at the intersection of form and time, far removed from the lyric's purported capacity to cross or transcend time, we may be able to read other literary forms, including the lyric, in a new light.

But my concern here is not simply formalist. The discourse of form is itself entangled with other issues, such as the concept of literary autonomy, one of the master narratives of modernist criticism. To be sure, complex adaptive textual systems are not unique to modernity – indeed, as I suggest in Chapter 5, emergent properties can be found in ancient literary practices, such as the Jewish textual tradition of midrash. Nevertheless, emergence is particularly useful for thinking about the critical commonplace of modernist art's autonomy. A tradition of thought running from Immanuel Kant to Theodor Adorno has claimed formal self-sufficiency for modern art, freeing it from the demands of rhetoric, religion, pedagogy, or the market. However, autonomy always came at a cost, namely art's ability to speak to that which is outside itself, and the most productive accounts of autonomy have struggled to reconcile autonomy with political or social meaning. Autonomy thus presents something of a dilemma: the aesthetic theories of the European Enlightenment may have freed art to its own devices, and yet, as a consequence, art was unable to entirely move beyond itself; its independence diminished its communicability.

This narrative of art's autonomy is well known to the point of becoming an ideology, as Frederic Jameson has argued. In *A Singular Modernity*, Jameson claims that accounts of modernist autonomy emerged around World War II; the "classical moderns" themselves (Jameson's term) understood their work in quite different terms. Jameson cites Clement Greenberg's formalism as the exemplar of this ideology of autonomy; for Greenberg, modernist painting established autonomy through a self-reflective attention to the medium.[18] Against this account, Jameson suggests that modernist writing was characterized less by the establishment of autonomy through self-reflection and more by the "experience of contingency," "the shock of the existence of a real world of noisy and chaotic urban daylight."[19] In language that echoes theories of emergence, Jameson argues that high modernism was born not of a will to autonomy but through the adaptations that come from environmentally entangled form:

> But was not Cubism already an attempt to confront such an experience, by multiplying the shards of form into which the old stable everyday object began to shatter? And does not every line of *Ulysses* bear witness to an ever-changing empirical reality which Joyce's multiple forms (from *The Odyssey* parallel on down to chapter form and sentence structure themselves) are unable to master? What I want overhastily to argue here is that, in the moderns, such form is never given in advance: it is generated experimentally in the encounter, leading on into formations that could never have been predicted (and whose incomplete and interminable multiplicities the innumerable high modernisms amply display).[20]

Picking up on Jameson's "overhasty" argument, the following chapters trace a poetic practice that is born of those experimental encounters. Approaching the long poem as a complex, adaptive system supplements Jameson's core insight, offering a more precise account of literary form as it engages experimentally with an unpredictable world.

In other words, emergence offers an alternative to standard accounts of modernist autonomy while also respecting the radical formal energy of the last two centuries and the "singularity," as Derek Attridge puts it, of poetic practice. Instead of autonomy, "medium as content," or negation, emergent texts offer provisional closure, structural coupling, and environmental entanglement, a distinctive openness that comes precisely from the work's formal adaptation. Ultimately, the emergent long poem represents a literary wager, the risky bet that writing in real time could generate the capacity to interpret the world. The poets I examine in this book seek to develop a writing practice independent *and* structurally coupled, formally precise *and* hermeneutically rich, a uniquely poetic mode of immanent historiography. Emergent poetics is thus a literary practice that seeks to overcome autonomy's threat of isolation, an artistic historiography of the present that eschews narrative mastery, and a mode of writing that shapes the subjectivity of poet and reader through the adaptive forms of an imagination fully embedded in time.

By drawing a link between the long poem and the broader experimental energies of modernism, experiments that encompass Picasso's Cubism and Joyce's *Ulysses*, I also want to suggest that complex, adaptive properties may be detected in a wide variety of literary practices and aesthetic fields. In the chapters that follow, I present the long poem as an essential case study in what could be a much more extensive critical project. Once we begin analyzing structural coupling, feedback loops, iteration, recursion, and emergence, new models of literary history may be possible. These concepts are much larger than a single textual tradition. By looking closely at one distinctively emergent literary practice, such as the long poem, *Writing in Real Time* points to a way of analyzing and understanding literature that, hopefully, will be of value to critics working in other domains.

Literary form, aesthetic autonomy, the role of literature within modernity: these are large, unwieldy problems. Approaching them at a high conceptual level runs the risk of abstracting one away from the rough ground of literary practice itself, the texture and challenges of the poems. Nevertheless, if the readings that follow are successful, I hope that this success is in part measured by their contribution to these methodological and theoretical issues, opening new vistas for reading and criticism. For now, let us return to that rough ground. To better establish the immediate critical context for my own argument, we must survey the history of the long poem's formal deviance.

I   The Strange Form of the Long Poem

The long poem does not exist. At least that was the claim made by Edgar Allan Poe in his 1850 essay "The Poetic Principle," an argument that rested entirely on time's relationship to human perception. For a text to count as a poem, according to Poe, it must "excite," thus "elevating the soul," and yet "all excitements are, through a psychal [sic] necessity, transient."[21] The long poem exceeds the brief and transitory, and so it fails to achieve the status of poetry. Because Poe is primarily concerned with the capacity of poetic form to elevate the soul, his critique of the long poem implicitly becomes a critique of the long poem's form within time – the long poem is *too much form*. We are not fully capable of perceiving the long poem's form and thus not capable of experiencing it as pleasure; our emotional attention is overwhelmed. The realization that formal pleasure is dependent on our time- and space-bound senses can be found as early as Aristotle, who similarly argued that a creature of vast size could not be perceived as beautiful.[22] Aristotle's point clarifies Poe's argument. If the long poem has form, that form is inaccessible to us on the level of aesthetic pleasure. Perhaps Poe should have been more precise: it is *as if* the long poem does not exist . . . at least for us.

Poe's argument inaugurated nearly two centuries of critical trouble with the form of the long poem. These formal problems have often been registered on the level of genre, with critics deploying various generic models to contain the long poem's formal mutability. As I will demonstrate, this approach has proven to be of limited value; the long poem, to paraphrase Jacques Derrida, tends to be a work without a single genre.[23] Consequently, genre trouble – and, by implication, form trouble – is evident in the two major clusters of literary criticism dedicated to the long poem. The first of these clusters is a series of studies published between the late 1970s and the early 1990s, written out of the critical consensus that *The Cantos*, William Carlos Williams's *Paterson*, and *The Maximus Poems*, when coupled with works like Stevens's "Notes Toward a Supreme Fiction," H. D.'s *Trilogy*, Hart Crane's *The Bridge*, or Eliot's *The Waste Land*, constituted a tradition of modernist long poetry. A more recent group of criticism focuses on post–World War II long poetry, which is often (although not always) read in contrast to the modernist predecessors. Although both critical traditions have offered valuable insight into the long poem, there are obvious limitations. If, as I argue here, the emergent long poem is characterized by iterative and recursive adaptations, feedback loops, and unpredictable developments, such generic accounts will inevitably confront their own impossibility. Displacing the form of the long poem onto genre thus ends up solving neither formal nor generic questions.

The criticism of the 1970s through the 1990s, while admitting that the modern long poem was distinctive, often relied heavily on the rubric of traditional poetic genres. In the case of those texts that I am calling emergent, critics discovered a number of genres in the text, often after some highly selective reading. For instance, some critics characterized the modernist long poem as fundamentally lyric in nature. Perhaps the most extreme example of this view can be found in M. L. Rosenthal's and Sally M. Gall's *The Modern Poetic Sequence: The Genius of Modern Poetry* (1983). The authors argue that these poems liberate and maximize "lyrical structure," what they call the fundamental characteristic of all poetry.[24] The modern poetic sequences of individual lyrics "tend to interact as an organic whole," as an organization of "centers of intensity."[25] In this way, the sequence functions as a lyric poem writ large: *"A poem depends for its life neither on continuous narration nor on developed argument but on a progression of specific qualities and intensities of emotionally and sensuously charged awareness."*[26] Each individual lyric within the sequence functions as one of these "intensities," playing off of and organized alongside the intensities of the other verses in the sequence.

In keeping with their affect-centered theory of emotional intensities, Rosenthal and Gall's readings of emergent poems highlight lyrical aspects of the text at the expense of other elements. The authors place *The Pisan Cantos* at the center of Pound's work, suggesting that the less "emotionally and sensuously charged" moments of the poem – presumably the many didactic, rote, or encyclopedic elements that make up a substantial portion of *The Cantos* – could have been expunged without much of a loss.[27] Similarly, the multiple volumes of *The Maximus Poems* are relegated to the first volume of more confessional lyrics, with the exception of the highly lyrical *"Maximus to Gloucester, Letter 27* [withheld]," which they rescue from its placement in the second volume of the work.[28] In effect, the authors' theoretical commitment to "lyrical structure" forces them to edit the actual poems, even though they can find lyrical moments embedded in these (often mechanical and mundane) texts. Although such expurgations may produce a collection of compelling poems, such an approach cannot be considered an adequate account of the work's entire structure, let alone its moments of self-transformation and change.

In contrast to the lyric approach, more critics emphasize the epic elements of the long poem, particularly as the epic functions as a form of public address. Michael André Bernstein's influential study *The Tale of the Tribe: Ezra Pound and the Modern Verse Epic* (1980) best represents this critical lens. While Bernstein admits that the "modern verse epic" does not strictly adhere to the traditional conventions of the genre, he frames his analysis of Pound, Williams, and Olson through the following definition of epic:

> a) The epic presents a narrative of its audience's own cultural, historical, or mythic heritage. . . . b) The dominant voice narrating the poem will, therefore, not bear the trace of a single sensibility; instead, it will function as a spokesman for values generally acknowledged as significant for communal stability and social well-being. . . . c) Consequently, the proper audience of an epic is not the *individual* in his absolute inwardness but the *citizen* as participant in a collective linguistic and social nexus. . . . d) The element of instruction arguably present, if only by implication, in all poetry, is deliberately foregrounded in an epic which offers its audience lessons presumed necessary to their individual and social survival.[29]

In these public and political terms, Bernstein analyzes *The Cantos, Paterson*, and *The Maximus Poems*, admitting that none of these poems will entirely fit his generic definition. While Bernstein's focus of study is decidedly narrower than Rosenthal and Gall's, the differences between their approaches are striking. Where the latter emphasize lyric interiority and affective intensity, Bernstein reads many of the same poems as rhetorically motivated forms of public address, an avowedly impersonal conversation about shared values addressed to equally abstract citizens.[30] Nevertheless, as with the lyric approach, the epic reading of the long poem requires editorial trimming. For example, Bernstein also sticks to the first volume of *The Maximus Poems*. He confesses that he has "virtually ignored the two subsequent volumes, *Maximus IV, V, VI* and *The Maximus Poems Volume Three*," because he sees these volumes as "only peripherally relevant to an analysis of [Olson's] contribution to the modern verse epic."[31] Neither as lyric nor epic do the latter *Maximus* volumes fare very well; both approaches subject the poem to a literary-critical version of Procrustes's bed.

The public and political are not the only characteristics of epic, of course, and some critics walk the generic middle ground of what James E. Miller, Jr. calls the "personal epic" (with Whitman as the exemplar though not the originator), defined as "a long poem whose narrative is of an interior rather than exterior action, with emphasis on successive mental or emotional states . . . focusing not on a heroic or semidivine individual but on the poet himself as a representative figure, comprehending and illuminating the age."[32] Miller's "personal epic" brings together the public, rhetorical emphasis of traditional epic as well as the interiority and affectivity of lyric. Crucially, however, Miller ultimately discovers coherence and formal identity not in the text but in the individual consciousness of the poet. The personal epic is a type of psychological narrative, remaining in the form of an autobiographical *story*, even though narrative form simply does not exist in most of these texts. Thus, where Rosenthal and Gall or Bernstein must expunge from the work's messy reality, Miller must add a virtual subject to give the work (generic) shape.[33]

These early critical readings of the long poem, while shedding light on a number of important aspects, are often forced to admit that certain texts exceed, lack, or otherwise resist the necessary characteristics of the generic model being employed. Whether in Rosenthal's and Gall's willful dismissal of sections of *The Maximus Poems* or in Miller's "personal epic," each of these studies indirectly reveals what Rachel Blau DuPlessis sees as the inevitable generic mutability of the modern long poem, a transformative tendency brought to its fullest expression in emergent works. After proposing one possible taxonomy for the long poem, DuPlessis immediately calls that tentative organization into question:

> The more interesting question is whether this taxonomy can possibly be plausible even if it is a little inexact. The answer? – maybe, but only as a pedagogic instrument. The poems, angry as revenants, contestatory and explosive, are already crawling, creeping, rising, and popping out of my boxlike, over-generalized categories, arguing and fulminating, offering alternative ideas of what they are doing. . . . The solemn critical rectitude of some division like this, the modal and generic definitions that keep poems in category cannot ignore the facts that some works disturb this taxonomy, and if anyone thinks too hard . . . the whole schemata goes up in smoke.[34]

As soon as one posits a possible generic schema for the long poem, problems emerge. One can uncover any number of genres within the works, and yet, even as one does so, obvious and numerous violations of the genre appear. This mutability radically challenges the sufficiency of genre as a critical approach to the long poem. Indeed, DuPlessis concludes that the "long poem may be said to have multiple genres without having a single genre."[35]

In response to this generic multiplicity, later critics of the American long poem shifted the focus to questions of historical context and periodization. Lynn Keller's *Forms of Expansion: Recent Long Poems by Women* (1997), Joseph M. Conte's *Unending Design: The Forms of Postmodern Poetry* (1991), and Brian McHale's *The Obligation toward the Difficult Whole: Postmodernist Long Poems* (2004) helped to distinguish the modernist from the postmodern long poem. The latter two studies, in particular, focus on the relationship between formal practices and periodization, attempting to define a uniquely postmodern poetics. Consequently, Conte and McHale's reflections on boundedness, seriality, and the relationship between openness and closure offer a valuable precursor to my claims for emergence, despite our many differences in focus, method, and argument.

Conte explicitly seeks to generate a "systematic typology of postmodern poetic forms."[36] The motivation behind this typology is twofold: first, to offer critical support for the significant innovations of post–World War II poets and, second, to demonstrate that those developments occurred on the level of form. As Conte puts it, the postmodernists "have given a verifiable identity to the shape of poetry in the latter half of the twentieth century," an identity distinct from their romantic and modernist predecessors (UD 5). This identity is manifest in two signature practices, namely "serial" and "procedural" form. In the serial poem, poetic unity is replaced by multiplicity, difference, and disunity, reflecting "the discontinuous and often aleatory manner in which one thing follows another" (UD 3). Serial poets, like Robert Creeley, George Oppen, and Jack Spicer, "[discern] a serial order that is 'protean' and provisional," one that "incorporates random occurrences without succumbing to formlessness" (UD 11). Serial poetry is complemented by procedural poetics, in which the poet follows "predetermined and arbitrary constraints" to generate form (UD 3). Procedural projects range from John Ashbery's adaptation of traditional forms like sestinas to the complex, even hermetic generative processes adopted by someone like John Cage (UD 40, 43).

While Conte does emphasize contingent and surprising elements that shape the poetic practice, his largest formal claim for the long poem is its capacity to represent an ultimately chaotic, centerless, incomprehensible postmodern reality. Serial texts, for example, articulate "both the indeterminacy and the discontinuity that the scientist discovers in the subatomic world" while proceduralism "constrains the poet to encounter and examine that which he or she does not immediately fathom, the uncertainties and incomprehensibilities of an expanding universe in which there can be no singular impositions" (UD 19, 16). Given this emphasis on epistemological uncertainty, seriality as Conte theorizes it never moves beyond itself: in such poems, there is "no initiation, climax, or terminus precisely because there can be no development. . . . The reader does not require the information of any one section in order to comprehend the others" (UD 23). The knowledge generated by the poem is at best snatches of minimal connection, discrete linkages that cannot offer more than simply metonymic juxtaposition because, under Conte's characterization of postmodernity, there are few prospects for knowledge – or form – other than the aleatory and the discontinuous. The form of the long poem, in this case, is the dramatization of its own formlessness.

Conte's typology clarifies the way some postmodern poets conceptualized form, and, given his deliberately constrained focus on the contemporary period, his account of postmodern epistemology, ontology, and poetics is important. However, as I suggest in my later discussion of emergence, the poetic practices that Conte identifies can be reinterpreted in the service of a larger, more robust interpretive practice. More precisely, Conte's categories do not go far enough in considering the development of new structures and second-order, emergent forms through the poetic process itself. Far from simply responding to a postmodern world of chance, centripetal forces, entropy, and indeterminacy, emergence allows us to conceive of a poem generating through its form a real and evolving, albeit limited, knowledge of the world; in the language of neocybernetic theorists Bruce Clarke and Mark B. N. Hansen, the "chaotically complex" reality of the world becomes "manageably complex" through the processes of meaning-making systems.[37] If we recognize that certain long poems function as adaptive systems navigating a "chaotically complex" environment within time, emergence allows us to understand how poets can use serial structures and procedures – like iteration and recursion – to generate larger structures of form and fields of knowledge in response to apparently random occurrence. At the same time, emergence can also clarify how poets use such formal strategies to *recognize and register* the contingencies of the present. Formal change, in this sense, is both a response to environmental change and a mechanism for comprehending such change.

In contrast to seriality and proceduralism, McHale examines the narrative and architectural tendencies of the long poem in order to detect "the *difference* of the postmodernist long poem relative to its modernist precursor."[38] The two models he offers to conceptualize that difference are the postmodernist novel and postmodern architecture (ODW 3). Drawing on his influential interpretation of postmodern fiction, McHale sees in postmodernist poetry the ontological concern with modes of being, world-making, and the relationship between fiction and reality, in contrast with the modernist epistemological emphasis on "perception, knowledge, [and] reliability" (ODW 4–5). Additionally, the return to narrative in a number of postmodern poets, from Melvin Tolson to Ed Dorn (ODW 6), gives McHale's novelistic paradigm particular strength. Turning to the link between postmodern architecture and poetry, McHale finds two shared aesthetic tendencies: a light-handed eclectic historicism and a concern with deconstruction (ODW 9–11). For McHale, Susan Howe's *Europe of Trusts* "[builds] with visual voids" or even "[*builds*] *ruins*," while other postmodern poems "burst through . . . textual enclosures and overrun . . . boundaries" (ODW 15, 16). The "difficult whole" of the postmodern long poem is born not of a sense of difficulty, as in high modernism, but from a compulsion to struggle with the "puzzles of inside and outside, inclusion and exclusion" (ODW 17), from the poem exploring the complex grounds of its own identity.

Clearly, both Conte and McHale share an interest in the role of boundary or enclosure in postmodern poetry, a crucial concept for systems theorists. Instead of genre, Conte and McHale anticipate DuPlessis's characterization of long poems as "crawling, creeping, rising, and popping."[39] These critics thus reflect, but do not fully address, the central question of *Writing in Real Time*: how, exactly, do the poems develop this capacity for transformation and change? Conte's seriality is one attempt to grapple with the production of a porous boundary, while McHale's "difficult whole" is another. My study extends and complicates Conte and McHale's focus, arguing that provisional closure and emergent properties exist within a feedback loop, allowing the poem to generate an adaptive account of its environment.

Along with clarifying these formal problems, emergence allows me to read across conventional literary periods. Unlike Conte and McHale, I am not attempting to offer a single definition of the modern, postmodern, or American long poem. Instead, reading for emergence allows us to see how individual poems reconfigured the key concerns of their period, whether that be Whitman's romantic organicism, Pound's mechanical aesthetics, or Spahr's post-9/11 digital imaginary. When I speak of the poem's "environment," I include that nexus of material, aesthetic, and intellectual forces we call a literary period. At the same time, emergence does not bind us to any particular period, as the model allows us to compare many instances of writing in real time, whether in the United States of the 1850s or the Italy of the 1940s. In this sense, the chapters of this study reflect the diverse aesthetic of Ammons's "stream": the dynamic interaction between poem, poet, and environment. Neither genre nor postmodern concepts of form fully account for that dynamism. An alternative model is required.

II Form in Systems Theory

If the long poem and its critics are preoccupied with questions of form, environment, time, and order, so, too, is systems theory. I use "systems theory" to designate a broad intellectual tradition that spans cybernetics, neocybernetics, and complexity theory, with applications in computer science, engineering, biology, neuroscience, sociology, cultural theory, and other fields.[40] Having surveyed the critical history of form in long poetry, I now offer a similar overview of form in systems theory, with a particular focus on how form becomes emergent. After examining systems theory on its own terms, I will then turn to the applications of systems thinking to art, synthesizing these concepts into a model of emergent poetics. I proceed with caution, as my genealogy is necessarily limited. A complete intellectual history of systems thinking would be far more involved; as Luhmann points out, there is no single "general systems theory."[41] This intellectual diversity creates a situation in which theoretical misconceptions are common, if not inevitable. As Bernard Dionysius Geoghegan argues, cybernetics (to take but one example) has often been misrepresented, not least because of the different variations of the theory found in the natural sciences and the humanities.[42] Nevertheless, Geoghegan suggests that these differences were an asset in the dissemination of the theory, as "it was disunity and heterogeneity – discursive, conceptual, material, artifactual, ideological – that constituted cybernetics's peculiar strength and attraction in diverse contexts."[43] Indeed, as Lydia H. Liu has demonstrated, cybernetics shaped the development of semiotics, structuralism, and poststructuralism, an intellectual relationship that continues to be explored.[44]

With those warnings in mind, I begin with cybernetics, an intellectual movement of the 1950s and 1960s derived from the Greek *xubernetes* or "steersman." According to Norbert Wiener, one of its leading theorists, the term was developed to describe "the entire field of control and communication theory, whether in the machine or in the animal."[45] In an attempt to span the many subfields of "control and communication," the Macy Foundation Conferences dedicated to cybernetics, held in the years following World War II,[46] brought together mathematicians, computer scientists, engineers, and biologists, among others, in the hope of developing a unified theoretical discourse. Wiener's point to include the "machine" as a realm of control and communication is fundamental to the cybernetic moment, emerging, as it did, out of the technological advances of World War II, where problems in machine intelligence, adaptability, and autonomy took on a new urgency. At the same time, cybernetics sought to cross organic/inorganic binaries, as the term "cyborg," derived from "cybernetic organism," suggests.

N. Katherine Hayles divides cybernetics into three phases of conceptual development, a useful schema that I borrow here (HBP 16). For Hayles, the first phase, grounded in the Macy Conferences, was characterized by an emphasis on homeostasis or "self-regulating stability through cybernetic corrective feedback" (HBP 298). The concept of equilibrium in a complex system has much earlier precursors, of course. Luhmann argues that as early as the seventeenth century, the concept of equilibrium within a system "was already taken for granted and used in the idea of the 'balance of trade,' . . . [and] by the end of the century it also motivated the idea of an international, specifically European, balance of power between nations."[47] Adam Smith's invisible hand of the market fits within this tradition, where individual agents accumulatively produce meaningful patterns within the entire economic system without centralized guidance. The focus on "self-regulating stability" in cybernetics led to other important concepts, most notably the feedback loop, wherein a system's own output becomes one of its inputs, thus shaping its subsequent behavior. In the first stage of cybernetic discourse, the feedback loop was used to maintain stasis within a system, a concept most clearly illustrated in the homeostat, an electrical device that, when receiving "an input changing its state, . . . searched for the configuration of variables that would return it to its initial condition" (HBP 65). A thermostat is the classic illustration of homeostasis: combining a switch and a thermometer, the thermostat gathers information from the environment that it regulates.

The homeostatic model, while relatively simple on its own, opened the pathway for more complex feedback loops. In the case of engineering and computer science, such feedback loops were deployed to solve technical problems, where the form and function of a mechanism required it to adapt. Wiener described feedback in explicitly engineering terms: "when we desire a motion to follow a given pattern[,] the difference between this pattern and the actually performed motion is used as a new input to cause the part regulated to move in such a way as to bring its motion closer to that given by the pattern."[48] The feedback loop is a corrective device within a machine whose operations within the unpredictable complexity of the world – its "actually performed motion" – will cause it to deviate from that intended pattern. These deviations are further complicated in devices coupled to their environment. Taking the new technologies of industry, military, and computing as his examples, Wiener argues that "the many automata of the present day are coupled to the outside world both for the reception of impressions and for the performance of actions."[49] The form of a system, for early cyberneticians, was thus inseparable from the relationship among a system's function, its environmental interactivity, its design, and its human users.

To take a detour into poetics: the notion of homeostatic form is a suggestive way to reconceptualize conventional "closed" forms, like that of the sonnet. As a mechanism for composition, the sonnet's strict rules have regulated and stabilized poetic practice over centuries of cultural change. New subject matter, topics, diction, or occasions are brought back into the structural homeostasis of the sonnet. Even in those many instances of innovation or apparent rule-breaking – say, in the development of the Shakespearean sonnet or in Bernadette Mayer's contemporary experimental, multigeneric sonnets[50] – the existence of the sonnet form serves as an invisible regulation capable of measuring the deviation from the norm. In other words, for the sonnet to maintain its existence as such, it must maintain its regulatory function. This is not to deny the evolution of closed or conventional forms over time, but to suggest that the very definition of a form *as* closed is analogous to the stabilizing function of a homeostat.

Simple self-regulation was complicated in Hayles's second stage of cybernetic discourse, characterized by the concept of autopoiesis. Developed by Humberto Maturana and Francisco Varela as an application of cybernetic principles to the philosophy of science, autopoiesis defined a living system as a machine that "continuously generates and specifies its own organization," a process that requires "an endless turnover of components under conditions of continuous perturbations and compensation of perturbations."[51] Every living organism, for Maturana and Varela, must perpetually maintain itself within an intrusive environment. Thus, an organism's life was characterized by autopoietic self-maintenance. Significantly, Maturana and Varela's theory clarified the organism's capacity for environmental interaction. The autopoietic organism requires input, sustaining a metabolic relationship with its world. At the same time, this environment is actively brought into appearance by the organism's own processes; the organism is giving interpretive shape to its world. As Hayles puts it, "[reality] comes into existence . . . for all living creatures . . . through interactive processes determined solely by the organism's own organization" (HBP 136). The world of the ant is produced by its distinctive autopoiesis, while the world of the human is produced by another. Each

"living system . . . constructs its environment through the 'domain of interactions' made possible by its autopoietic organization. What lies outside
that domain does not exist for that system" (HBP 137). Thus, the autopoietic system is identifiably "closed" even as it is "structurally coupled" to its
environment, caught within a "circular interplay of processes" (HBP 139).
According to this account, the world as it appears to the organism exists
because of its autopoietic process.

    With autopoiesis, the discourse of cybernetics and complex systems
becomes increasingly dynamic. Form, in the autopoietic account, is inter-
nally adaptive and self-replicating, dependent upon an environment that
it makes appear through its processes. These processes in turn allow the
system to observe or interact with the world. The autopoietic organism
makes the world visible and meaningful, even as what is visible is only
that which is relevant for any given organism's autopoiesis. An additional
layer of complexity arises when the autopoietic system "recursively interacts" with its own representations, "enlarging the domain of interactions
that specify the world for that autopoietic unity" (HBP 143–4). As later
theorists of neocybernetics would argue, the "closure" of the autopoiesis
becomes the condition for a kind of environmental "openness."[52]

    While autopoiesis complicated systems theory's account of self-
reflexivity and environmental interactivity, the theory itself had limited
applications. As Luhmann points out, a system is either autopoietic or it
is not – there is no partially autopoietic system. In its earliest formulation,
autopoiesis is like a leap, the differential between a living and a nonliv-
ing organism.[53] However, the concept of autopoiesis did not remain static.
Varela's later development of the theory shifted the focus from autopoietic
closure to the more elastic process of "enaction," "the active engagement of
an organism with the environment" (HBP 155). While his analysis is limited to biological organisms, Varela's account has important implications
for thinking about interactive form. As Hayles summarizes:

> Whereas autopoietic theory emphasizes the closure of circular pro-
> cesses, . . . enaction sees the organism's active engagement with its surround-
> ings as more open-ended and transformative. A similar difference informs
> the views of cognition in the two theories. For autopoiesis, cognition
> emerges from the recursive operation of a system representing to itself its
> own representations. Enaction, by contrast, sees cognitive structures emerg-
> ing from 'recurrent sensory-motor patterns.' Hence, instead of emphasizing
> the circularity of autopoietic processes, enaction emphasizes the links of the
> nervous system with the sensory surfaces and motor abilities that connect
> the organism to the environment. (HBP 156)

Enactive cognition emerges as the system is transformed by its engagement with the environment. At the same time, the system must already possess certain capacities to make this engagement possible. A simple illustration of enaction is what cognitive scientists call neuroplasticity, the brain's ability to adapt itself in response to environmental inputs. Imagine a child who, due to a minor neural defect or injury, is unable to grasp small objects. Through sufficient stimulation and interaction, new neural pathways will be activated, allowing her to reclaim this function.[54] She is soon able to hold small toys, her dinner fork, even a crayon. Eventually, she will be able to write with a pencil, a capacity that will open up further areas of linguistic and cognitive competency. Without the environmental stimulation, those neural pathways will not fully develop, and her functions may atrophy further. Coupling the cognitive and the material, then, we can say that the environmental interactions of the organism are made possible by its formal organization even as those interactions can produce new, future organizations, which, in turn, make possible further modes of environmental interaction. Autopoiesis introduces the idea of a dynamic system that is structurally coupled to its environment, while enaction shows us how the organism and its environment are engaged in an adaptive feedback loop, adding a new dynamic element to our understanding of the organism's form.

Turning from biology to mathematics, another influential model of form as system was developed in the 1960s by George Spencer Brown. Published in 1969, Spencer Brown's *Laws of Form* offers a calculus that uses a single operation to develop complex, evolving formal structures. Spencer Brown initiates his calculus with the dictum that one "[draw] a distinction," which he indicates by drawing a right-angle line on a blank piece of paper.[55] Such a distinction designates a "world" by producing an inside and an outside, a boundary that can then be crossed, recrossed, and integrated into other boundaries, producing an entire network of complex patterns based on a single recursive operation. Spencer Brown's elegantly simple calculus significantly influenced Luhmann's work in social systems. For Luhmann, Spencer Brown transforms our understanding of form: "When the boundary between the two sides of a distinction is marked, [Spencer Brown] also names this boundary 'form.' . . . A 'form' has two sides. It is not just a beautiful shape or object that can be presented free of all context."[56] Form is thus characterized by the difference marked by the boundary, a distinction that generates a minimal system; as Luhmann puts it, "a system is a form with two sides."[57] At the same time, this basic formal operation does not remain as a simple binary. Instead, a form with two sides can generate unfolding patterns of increasing complexity through the application of a simple rule.

Distinction, then, gives us a theory of provisional closure. The Spencer-Brownian calculus operates according to a closure that makes possible new openings for further articulations, developments, additions, or affordances.[58] As distinction makes a space available, so too another distinction within that space multiplies the possibilities within the system, as the recursively embedded spaces interact. This concept of distinction creating space has important correlatives in poetics, as we might think of the foot, the line, and the stanza in these terms. Indeed, DuPlessis has argued that segmentation as such may be the constitutive element of poetic composition, "the kind of writing that is articulated in sequenced, gapped lines and whose meanings are created by occurring in bounded units precisely chosen." Consequently, "*segmentivity* – the ability to articulate and make meaning by selecting, deploying, and combining segments – is the underlying characteristic of poetry as a genre."[59] From this light, poetic practice produces complex meaning through segmentation, a capacity that the long poem (particularly those I am calling emergent) exploits to a remarkable degree.

The movement from a simple formal operation to a complex system brings us to emergence, which characterizes Hayles's third phase of cybernetics. Emergence synthesizes many of the concepts we have explored thus far, including feedback loops, structural coupling, and enaction. Hayles offers the following definition:

> "Emergence" . . . refers to properties that do not inhere in the individual components of a system; rather, these properties come about from interactions between components. Emergent properties thus appear at the global level of the system itself rather than at the local level of a system's components. Moreover, emergences typically cannot be predicted because the complex feedback loops that develop between components are not susceptible to explicit solution.[60]

Expanding Holland's definition of "much coming from little," emergence arises from phenomena with at least two levels or orders. Activities on the first order generate *unpredictable* patterns and events in the second order. A classic example of these interactive properties is cellular automata, explored at length by Varela, Evan Thompson, and Eleanor Rosch in *The Embodied Mind*.[61] The authors ask us to imagine a simple circular network of individual cells, each of which "receives inputs from two immediate neighbors and communicates its internal state to the same immediate neighbors."[62]

Each cell functions in one of two states, such as 1 or 0, or on or off. The state of the cell is determined by simple operators, such as "and" or "exclusive or," taking as inputs the cells immediately adjacent to it.[63] In other words, the state of the cell is determined entirely by local rules and conditions – there is no larger, global pattern programmed into the system. However, by running this network of simple operations over time, the cells will produce many higher order emergent patterns: waves, arrows, triangles, pyramids, bars, and dots.

This simple emergence is only half of the story, however. Varela et al. go on to propose another level of environmentally embedded emergence, which I call "interactive emergence." In this second model, the system of cellular automata is structurally coupled to a simulated "environment" of random 1s and 0s, an environment capable of stimulating new patterns within the system.[64] In response to these random inputs from the environment, new patterns emerge, diverging from those within the closed model of cellular automata. Taking the system as a whole, these new patterns can be understood as an interpretive procedure: "on the basis of its autonomy (closure), [the system] performs an interpretation [of its environment] in that it selects or brings forth a domain of significance out of the background of its random milieu."[65] In other words, the system of cellular automata is placed within a world of overwhelming information, an unpredictable soup of 1s and 0s that bombard the system. Through its own internal structures, the automaton generates meaningful patterns from that chaos; and yet these patterns are not simply subjective creations on the part of the system. The inputs do in fact exist within the world, autonomous of the system. At the same time, the system is essential for making that pattern visible *as a pattern* – the system "brings forth a domain of significance," as Varela puts it.

Interactive emergence is what enables our flock of birds to respond to its changing world. The environmental inputs – wind, structures, threats, prey, even the seasonal shifts that prompt birds to gather for migration – are essential for generating the emergent patterns that are visible within the flock as a whole. Nevertheless, the flock's own internal network of operations are equally significant in the production of its form. The poetics of the flock, as it were, emerges at the intersection of internal and external change, where local actions, global patterns, and unexpected realities converge. In turn, we might say that the form of the flock of birds is making its environment visible in a new way, creating a unique representation of the environment. The flock of birds is thus an apt image for a systems-theoretical model of form, which we have traced from the relative stability of the homeostat to the unpredictable dynamism of complex, adaptive, and emergent systems. But another question remains: how, outside of theoretical models like cellular automata and symbolic calculus, are such complex systems produced? Or, to return us back to the literary, how might such a *poetic* system be generated?

One way to develop a complex system is through processes of *iteration* and *recursion*. Recursion has played a major role in linguistics, most notably in Noam Chomsky's work on syntax; for Chomsky, recursion is what allows a language with a finite number of units to produce an infinite number of possible sentences.[66] Another linguist, Fred Karlson, suggests that recursion and iteration are fundamentally "cognate concepts": "Their basic common feature is plain structural repetition: 'keep on emitting instances of the current structure, or stop'. Their main difference is that recursion builds structure by increasing embedding depth whereas iteration yields flat output structures which do not increase depth."[67] An iterative structure appears as a series of repeating units – I . . . I . . . I . . . I . . . – whereas a recursive structure is an embedded series of similar functions. One can build a recursive structure by beginning with a given function or unit, such as A, and then continuing to add new predications, thus expanding the total meaning of $A = (((A+1)+1)+1)$. We might think of iterative elements as the formal condition for continuity, while recursive elements provide the formal condition for change, adaptation, modification, and evolution.

To turn to a poetic example of iteration and recursion used to generate structure, consider Allen Ginsberg's *Howl*. Here are the first lines of the poem:

> I saw the best minds of my generation destroyed by madness, starving
>   hysterical naked,
> dragging themselves through the negro streets at dawn looking for an
>   angry fix,
> angelheaded hipsters burning for the ancient heavenly connection to
>   the starry dynamo in the machinery of night,
> who poverty and tatters and hollow-eyed and high sat up smoking in
>   the supernatural darkness of cold-water flats floating across the tops
>   of cities contemplating jazz,
> who bared their brains to Heaven under the El and saw Mohammedan
>   angels staggering on tenement roofs illuminated,
> who passed through universities with radiant cool eyes hallucinating
>   Arkansas and Blake-light tragedy among the scholars of war,[68]

After the initial exposition of the first three lines, the poem presents an iterative form through the anaphoric repetition of "who." Taken abstractly, "who" offers a paratactic form that does not change in levels of complexity or depth, a chain capable of additional links. "Who" as an iterative form here is essentially a container or space, a Spencer-Brownian distinction. This iterative space is the precondition for a more complex recursive level, the ever-expanding meaning of *Howl*'s initial term, "the best minds of my generation." If we take Ginsberg's initial term as M, with each line as a predication of M, then the recursive form of *Howl* appears something like $M = (((M+L_1) + L_2) + L_3) \ldots)$. The total meaning or poetic construction of "the best minds of my generation" is the accumulative network of these recursive operations, a network capable of expansion and adaptation.

If we were to structurally couple that complex network to a changing environment, the result would be an interactive emergent poem, the literary equivalent to our flock of birds. Such a poem would be performing remarkable cultural work through its formal processes, by generating a "domain of significance" that changes with time and yet tracks real relationships through time, a poetic memory of the present generated through the past operations of the system. As I have demonstrated throughout this discussion, systems theory offers us a powerful alternative for thinking about the relationship between form and context, poiesis and history, creativity and change. Although this tradition of thought has had little to say about the long poem, systems theory has crossed over into more general discussions of art, aesthetics, and art practice. I now move from systems theory to the world of art, synthesizing the concepts outlined in this introduction into a critical practice of reading for emergence.

III   System Aesthetics and the Emergent Art of the Long Poem

While the long poem has been conspicuously absent in systems-theoretical discourse, notions of emergence, complexity, and environmental interaction have shaped art criticism since the advent of cybernetics. As early as 1949, Muriel Rukeyser indicated the possible directions for literary criticism coming out of the cybernetic movement, arguing that concepts such as feedback, information, and systemic change had immediate and far-reaching implications for poetry: "What are imaginative information and imaginative feedback in poetry? What are the emotional equivalents for these relationships? How far do these truths of control and communication apply to art?"[69] Although Rukeyser raised these questions, she did not offer a full answer, and in many respects her challenge was not picked up by the literary criticism of her day, which was dominated by New Critical models of form. Several decades after Rukeyser, Jack Burnham's essay "System Esthetics," published in *ArtForum*, offered a manifesto for art in the techno-informational culture of the future. "In the automated state," Burnham argues, "power resides less in the control of the traditional symbols of wealth than in information," a statement that echoes Wiener's cybernetic "control and communication."[70] As a result of this new power of information, Burnham argues that we "are now in transition from an object-oriented to a systems-oriented culture."[71] In responses to this evolving social situation, Burnham advocates a "systems esthetic," where there are "no contrived confines" or proscribed forms but rather a "conceptual focus" where the artist takes on the mantle of "perspectivist."[72] Despite his advocacy, Burnham does not fully articulate a model of the artwork itself as a complex adaptive system; instead, he calls attention to the ways both artwork and artist function within larger systemic processes and informational flows.

It was the work of a later theorist, Niklas Luhmann, to offer a theory of art as a complex system. A sociologist, Luhmann applied systems theory to a variety of phenomena, including science, the economy, and law. His 1995 book *Art As a Social System* begins by distinguishing between communicative systems, like language, and perceptual systems, like the human senses. For Luhmann, art makes perception available for communication – that is, it takes our somatic, embodied experience and turns it into a medium for communication.[73] Building off this initial insight, Luhmann goes on to suggest that art then establishes its own system of distinctions in Spencer Brown's sense, creating spaces of formal discovery that require further elaboration and exploration. Within the individual work, Luhmann argues that the "formation of the work creates surprise and assures variety, because there are many ways in which the work can take shape and because, when observed slowly, the work invites the viewer to contemplate alternate possibilities and to experiment with formal variations."[74] The art work actualizes one of many immanent possibilities, thus becoming a framework for experimental reading. Moving beyond the individual work, Luhmann argues that the art practice as a whole is this series of possibilities and adaptations: "[each] formal determination functions simultaneously as an irritation that leaves room for subsequent decisions" within the entire field of art.[75] The boundary or distinction drawn by a given work creates a new space of possibility that provokes other possible works. The history of art is thus the history of system evolution and adaptation, one that generates the condition for future operations through its current processes.

The art system, one might say, improvises. This is the argument presented by Edgar Landgraf, whose analysis of improvisation approaches my own reading of the long poem as a complex adaptive system. Landgraf's central claim is that improvisation, far from being an instance of pure invention, is the result of an artistic system creating the possibility for the new within its own terms. "Improvisation," Landgraf writes, "is not about the absence of rules and structures, nor about the advent of a true Otherness, but rather can be understood as a *self-organizing process* that relies on and *stages* the particular constraints that encourage the emergence of something new and inventive."[76] Without such self-organization, the creativity of an improvised performance would be invisible, or simply noise; it is only within the interpretive framework or domain of significance constructed by a system that the new action becomes meaningful.

Later, Landgraf explicitly links improvisation to emergence:

> I want to suggest that . . . we conceive of improvisation as an iterative and recursively operating process where dynamic structures emerge from the processing and reprocessing of elements. In neocybernetic discourses and in contemporary systems theory, the term "emergence" describes the arrival of something qualitatively new that was neither predictable nor planned. For dynamic systems, such "arrivals" do not come from some outside, but rather are the result of the recursive process itself, where errors, interferences, disruptions, and so on lead to alterations which may (or may not) achieve a certain degree of stability (closure) which can form the basis for further operations (or not).[77]

While Landgraf here offers a strong description of the advent of the new through iterative and recursive processes, I want to complicate his claim that newness does not come from the "outside." Undoubtedly, "errors, interferences, [and] disruptions" can emerge from within the art practice – think of a misspelled word that suggests a new line, or a bent note in a jazz performance that leads to an innovative interpretation of the basic melody. However, disruptions are not only the result of a hermetically sealed system; they can also come from perturbations in the environment itself, the surprising inputs that we saw in the model of interactive emergence. The new element of the work, in the case of a poem engaging its historical moment, is not simply inserted from the outside but is the result of the poetic text engaging and processing the outside through its own internal form. Unexpected encounters may prompt the invention that occurs in the poem itself, as it creatively adapts itself to that environmental event. Thus, it is misleading to speak of such a poem as either "closed" or "open"; instead, the emergent text exists at the point where artistic closure interacts with an ongoing and open attention to a changing world.[78]

In this way, a fluctuating external reality becomes a constitutive factor for the emergent artwork's internal process of composition. This interactivity, as a culminating insight of systems theory and systems aesthetics, allows us to return to the fundamental question with which we began: how do texts like *Leaves of Grass*, *The Cantos*, and *Song of the Andoumboulou* adapt to changes in their environment? Drawing on the theoretical background that I have just sketched, I can now offer a complete articulation of the model of emergent poetics that I will be using in this book. Exemplification is critical for any theory, and thus I present the model through readings of individual texts, further analyzing *Tape for the Turn of the Year* and then turning to a brief reading of Lyn Hejinian's *My Life*. In each poem, we can see a range of emergent strategies, forms, and effects; when examined alongside each other, Ammons and Hejinian illustrate the possibilities of reading for emergence as a critical practice.

Ammons's *Tape for the Turn of the Year* demonstrates both simple and interactive forms of emergence, developing a poetic text simultaneously closed and open to its environment. Ammons's initial act of *provisional closure* is a set of local operations: feed a roll of receipt tape into a type-writer, and then write a "long thin poem" every day until the tape is full. The receipt tape materializes Spencer Brown's "distinction"; in Ammons's case, the distinction is drawn both by the tape as a physical space for writing but also in the poetic operations that the tape makes possible – that is, the space created by the tape is the condition for imaginative creation. This creation is in turn limited to certain moves, akin to Conte's procedure: write every day, write in short or heavily enjambed lines (a requirement of the physical page space), and write until the receipt is full. From this originating simplicity, the poem will necessarily be emergent in the simple sense, generating unpredictable form from its original operations.

However, *Tape for the Turn of the Year* is continually perturbed by its environment, producing *interactive emergence* by way of a *feedback loop*. The requirement to write every day prompts Ammons to attend to simple details, from his diet and body to his daily routines. Weather in particular becomes a significant pattern. On the phenomenological level, Ammons reports the environment changes outside his window, marking the experience of time as the fluctuation of rain, sunshine, clouds, or snow. Larger seasonal expectations also become relevant, however, as the unusual temperature prompts "warm weather and windy / rain" (TTY 13), a source of surprise:

9:35 pm: lightning! what,
in December? just flashed
blue-bright and
thunder, moving slowly
and rumbling hard into
deep bursting depressions,
went all the way out over
the Atlantic: (TTY 15)

The wonder registered by the poem is eventually transformed to somber reflections in response to real-time historical events. Ammons begins the next section of the poem, "9 Dec.," with the following:

sunny again:

last night a plane
over Delaware struck the
storm
& 80 lives descended in
flames: It's

the nature of flame to
rise, celebrant, spirit

to whirl upward:
80

IIIIIIIIIIIIIIIIIIIIIII
IIIIIIIIIIIIIIIIIIIIIII
IIIIIIIIIIIIIIIIIIIIIII
IIIIIIIIIII   (TTY 16)

The plane crash is clearly an unanticipated environmental event, and yet it emerges as a meaningful moment in the poem's own systemic operations. "80" turning to 80 single digits becomes a new formal strategy, an attempt to correct the abstraction of number by visibly representing the lives lost, using the possibilities of the text as space to link to the now traumatic meaning of the storm. The poem, the weather, and its effects are functioning within a feedback loop: as the poem investigates the weather, changes within the weather transform the meaning and direction of the investigation, just as the poem makes the weather newly visible. Simple emergence and provisional closure (writing a long, thin poem) create the possibility for interactive emergence. The poem's later meditations on pattern, environment, experience, and form can be read as inspired by the initial trauma and wonder at lightning in December giving way to the horror of eighty dead. The poem registers both moments, focusing, shaping, and extending attention.

While *Tape for the Turn of the Year* clearly illustrates the dynamics of emergent poetics, Ammons works within a relatively constrained framework, writing the history of a single month and limiting himself formally by the materiality of the receipt tape. Lyn Hejinian's *My Life*, a more ambitious example of the mode, deploys emergent form to account for a longer timeline and to establish, as Hejinian puts it in another work, writing as "an aid to memory."[79] A work of autobiography written in the style of the "new sentence" of Language writing,[80] *My Life* is divided into individual sections of prose poetry, each with a sentence fragment as its title. These sections correspond to individual years in Hejinian's life, allowing the work to adapt to her age: first published in 1980, when Hejinian was thirty-seven years old, the text consisted of thirty-seven sections. Later editions increased to forty-five sections, while a second text, *My Life in the Nineties*, extended the original project. Deliberately evoking Lawrence Sterne's *Tristram Shandy*, which dramatized the conflicting timeframes of a human life and the activity of writing, Hejinian's speaker self-reflectively addresses the reader: "Please note that in my attempt to increase the accuracy of these sentences and the persistence and velocity with which they proceed, I'm pursuing change while trying to outrun the change that's pursuing me."[81] Days and years do not neatly correspond to pages. Hejinian's poem is caught up in a systemic process of change analogous to, yet not identical with, the change of her biological and phenomenological existence. The poem is structurally coupled to her life; it could not exist without her process of aging, and yet the poem becomes a distinct textual system producing memory in the face of time.

This pursuit and pursuing change becomes emergent through the combination of *iterative* and *recursive* formal components within the text. Each section, as a formal space dedicated to the linguistic exploration of autobiographical time (one year), gives the text an iterative shape, akin to temporal units like an hour or day. One of Hejinian's figures for this iteration is to imagine the day as a recurring singularity: "there has always only been one day, this one, departing with the dark and returning with the light, eternally collecting experience" (ML 116). Similarly, the prose units of the text repeat, like the calendar year, as an iterative space of possibility to be filled with language, in turn collecting and collating the experiences of the writer. This collection of "experience" occurs by way of a recursive formal element, the sentence fragments that initially appear as a title for an individual section and then, from that moment on, recur unexpectedly throughout the text. These recursive phrases create emergent lines of meaning throughout Hejinian's life, as the sense of each phrase is slightly modified and expanded each time it appears. Through this reappearance and recontextualization, the recursive lines allow the poem to reflect on its own experience, to represent its own representations. The resulting effect is a linguistic equivalent to the accretional process of aging, with each "poem year" contributing to the sense of the subsequent years that they make possible. In other words, the sentence fragment and the prose poem form create spaces of possibility to be discovered and explored through the historical, environmental events of a given year. Change pursues and is pursued.

To take but one example, the first section of the poem is titled "A pause, a rose, something on paper," an echo of the titles Gertrude Stein affixed to her *Tender Buttons*. Apart from the title, this phrase does not appear in part one itself. It does, however, recur in the third section of the poem, within a longer clause: "A pause, a rose, something on paper, in a nature scrapbook" (ML 8). Within the context of the section, the scrapbook is biographically significant, one item from Hejinian's memory of childhood forays among "snapdragons," "small stones, dried mud," a literal exploration of an environment (ML 8). But just as an individual's sense of the environment changes over time, so too does the meaning of the recursive phrase. Later sections incorporate trauma into the architecture of repetition, as when the speaker says that she "was more terrified of the FBI agents than of the unspecified man who had kidnapped, murdered, and buried the girl in the other fifth grade, in the hill behind school. A pause, a rose, something on paper" (ML 28).

Beyond memory, or at the intersection of memory and writing, the recursion of phrases throughout *My Life* emergently expands the fragment's capacity to signify: "A pause, a rose, something on paper – an example of parascription" (ML 52). The prefix "para-," as the OED tells us, forms a word "analogous or parallel to, but separate from or going beyond, what is denoted by the root word."[82] The phrase "A pause, a rose, something on paper," through its recursion and iteration, similarly produces a script beyond singular signification or meaning – it becomes a functional unit in a larger, unpredictable, and adaptive system. In other words, iteration and recursion as formal units interact to create a second, higher-order emergent form within the text as a whole. This emergence is not simply closed but is structurally coupled with the phenomenological, cognitive, and embodied components of Hejinian's own life, relying on her agency to generate

its own. Her interest in openness and closure, memory and language –
what she refers to as "rope and drift, loop and tug" – is thus made possible through the emergent properties of her own writing practice. As she
writes, "Let there be sentences – circular sentences; sentences incorporating pauses, roses. Life will add thickness ('the thickness of time')" (ML 119).
My Life uses writing to measure and produce this "thickness" as an effect
of emergent unpredictability within an expanding network of iterative and
recursive operations.

Hejinian's text allows us to return to the problem of form within literary
studies. By reading for the poem's generative structures, its systemic relationships, and its emergent effects, we can perceive form as the concrete
processes of interaction between the text and its social, cultural, historical, and autobiographical environment, an interaction that the text makes
possible, orienting and shaping Hejinian's attention. "Form" in *My Life*
exists on several interconnected systemic levels, moving from the first-
order forms of the iterative prose poem block and the recursive sentence
fragments to second-order structures. Formal processes enacted over time
become the condition for emergent formal effects. The critical practice of
reading for emergence attends to these multiple systemic functions simultaneously, as the poem enacts its form through structural coupling to concrete and yet unexpected historical events. Or, in other words, the form of
the emergent poem is itself a critical hermeneutic, an attempt to interpret
history as it happens.[83]

IV   Plan and Scope

Each of the following chapters investigates emergence, identifying the ways
in which a poem generates unpredictable effects through formal decisions
and imaginative projections while simultaneously responding to – and thus
interpreting – developments in the environment. By reading for emergence, the cultural and aesthetic work of these long poems becomes much
more visible. The poems appear as dynamic hermeneutic systems capable
of generating meaning in an immanent fashion, embedded firmly within
the environment *that they cause to appear*. This last point is a crucial difference between my approach and traditional models of historicist or contextual reading; within the conceptual framework that I have developed
in this introduction, the poem as a complex system plays a fundamental
role in establishing its own environment, using its own processes to transform the "chaotic complexity" of the world to that which is "manageably

complex."[84] Just as the world of the ant differs from the world of the blue jay due to their different systematic operations, so too the world of a given poem is, in many respects, constituted by its evolving form and processes. Some chapters, such as my reading of DuPlessis's *Drafts*, give more attention to the poem's capacities for internal emergence, while others, such as my analysis of Charles Olson's *Maximus*, focus more heavily on the poem's engagement with its environment. Such shifts in focus are the necessary consequence of closely attending to each poem on its own terms – my effort has been to respect the nuance and dynamism of emergence in all of its varied manifestations. As McHale puts it, "[formalist-style] literary historiography, with its zigzagging progress, its leaps and recoils, yields an untidy picture of literary phenomena" (ODW xi), and a literary history of emergent forms would be more, not less, untidy.

The chapters are arranged chronologically as a matter of convenience. My project is not a study of literary influence, but of individual complex poetic systems. The singularity of each chapter is counterbalanced by the overall picture of emergent poetics offered by the book as a whole. Inevitably, the chapter structure overlaps with existing models of literary history where influence is placed front and center; in particular, I take up several poets of the "Pound tradition," a term used to indicate the line of influence that stretches from *The Cantos* into postmodern poetry, including the midcentury "New American poets" like Olson and Robert Duncan and contemporary experimentalists like DuPlessis and Mackey. This overlap is inescapable, as the texts affiliated with the Pound tradition are some of the more ambitious nonnarrative long poems of the twentieth and twenty-first centuries. At the same time, my goal is to offer a capacious critical model for reading with applications well beyond the Pound tradition. To that end, I place each of my primary texts in conversation with other varieties of the long poem, from Wordsworth and Stevens to Lowell and Walcott. We should not ignore the texts of the Pound tradition simply because they have been placed within that framework; instead, as I hope to do here, we can develop new models for reading networks of literary-historical relationship. Each of the following chapters is intended to show how a poem develops emergence on its own terms while comparing and contrasting that development with a variety of contemporaneous poems and contributing to a larger, transperiod discourse of emergent poetics. By taking this approach – reading the local alongside the global, noting aesthetic affiliations as well as departures – I hope to at least reflect, although certainly not contain, the multitude that is the long poem.

With that context in mind, Chapter 2, "Emergent America: Walt Whitman's Enactive Democracy," reinterprets Whitman's relationship to nineteenth-century discourses of aesthetic organicism as theorized by Kant and Coleridge. *Leaves of Grass* offers an alternative organicism that bridges the political and the formal, attempting to uncover democratic poetics by offering a compelling literary example of transformation within continuity. I argue for three central emergent elements in Whitman's text. First, like an enactive organism, the overarching structure of *Leaves of Grass* incorporates unexpected environmental stimuli into its form, a process I illustrate through a reading of the iterative publications of *Leaves*. Second, in lieu of the common reading that Whitman is interested in the "one" and the "many," I suggest that Whitmanian practices, particularly parataxis, reflect the dynamic categories of "particular" and "all." A particular is always unique yet relational, situated within a larger network that, far from unified, is constantly transforming. I compare Whitman's use of an emergent poetic form with Wordsworth's *Prelude*, a work that has limited capacities for emergence due to its adherence to the formal structures of the traditional epic. Finally, I offer a reading of Whitman's response to language's own iterative properties (the same qualities that would later interest Noam Chomsky) through which poems can cross time, addressing an unknown future. Combined, these strategies of emergent composition generate an aesthetic correlative to Whitmanian democracy, a politics and poetics always to come.

Chapter 3, "Emergent Vocabulary: Ezra Pound's *Cantos* as Translation Machine," turns from the organism to the machine. Translation can serve as a mechanism for both simple and interactive emergence, using language to make a (complex) machine made out of words. Despite Pound's rather infamous claims for clarity, precision, and control, *The Cantos* can be read as a series of linked, unexpected translations, whereby the language of one canto becomes the "poetic vocabulary," in Barrett Watten's phrase,[85] through which another translation, text, or historical event can be encountered. Thus, Pound generates a textual system whose terms constantly forge new patterns, adapting to the real-time events of his environment. Pound's poem thus contrasts with T. S. Eliot's *The Waste Land*, to which it is often compared. Even though Eliot's text went through the iterative process of revision, *The Waste Land* does not create the conditions for ongoing environmental engagement. In contrast, *The Cantos* deliberately open their provisional closure to external events, such as Pound's incarceration at the end of World War II, which has been read as a radical shift in the poem's aesthetics. Far from being a break in the poem, this turn at Pisa is a moment of methodological self-consciousness, wherein the text's core practices become acutely visible. In this way, Pound's emergent form is a surprising response to Wallace Stevens's dictum that the supreme fiction "must change," offering us an alternative account of the modernist long poem's aesthetic aspirations.

Chapter 4, "Emergent History: Charles Olson's Housekeeping," shifts the emphasis from formal techniques of emergence to one poem's attempt to reflect a dynamic, adaptive ontology. Olson's relationship to process philosophies like those of Alfred North Whitehead led him to create a work that self-consciously arises from changing economic, political, and ecological systems. Olson approaches these historical systems as emergent phenomena; as a result, poetry discovers its own cultural power through its ability to observe, transform, and extend these dynamic processes. One of Olson's figures for this process is "housekeeping," a concept he derived from the Greek roots of the word "economy." Olson's housekeeping aligns with other Cold War poetry, which, as Edward Brunner has argued, was characterized by a turn to the domestic.[86] Robert Lowell's *Life Studies*, for instance, is another book-length work of domestic exploration that places primary emphasis on the familial and the psychological, in keeping with the aesthetics of confessional poetry. In contrast to Lowell's privatized domesticity, Olson's housekeeping is dynamic, responsive to an equally adaptive environment. As an illustration of this historical entanglement, I explore Olson's use of John Smith, one of the key cultural figures in *The Maximus Poems* who has been read, somewhat misleadingly, as a hero of the poem. In contrast to this interpretation, I suggest that Smith becomes an ambivalent force in the historical record, in need of poetic housekeeping that reveals new, emergent possibilities latent in the past.

In my fifth chapter, "Emergent Midrash: Rachel Blau DuPlessis Glosses Modernism," I argue that DuPlessis's work is born of the interaction of multiple literary systems, bridging the modernist tradition of the long poem with an ancient literary practice, the Jewish tradition of midrash or Talmudic commentary. In DuPlessis's hands, midrash enables an internal emergence while also providing the grounds for engagement with complex real-time events. This emergent midrash thus distinguishes DuPlessis's practice from other contemporary long poetry, including the Language writers with whom she is often affiliated, a point I illustrate through a brief examination of Ron Silliman's *Ketjak*. Like DuPlessis, Silliman deploys structures of iteration and expansion, relying on mathematical procedures to determine the evolution of *Ketjak*. While such an approach produces some emergent effects, Silliman's text deliberately resists the development of structural feedback loops that would transform the poem into an interpretive system. To show DuPlessis's own powerful yet self-consciously humble emergent hermeneutic, I conclude the chapter by analyzing her staged "conversation with Adorno," where *Drafts* uses emergent writing to generate a critical, post-Holocaust consciousness.

The emphasis on history, late modernity, and cultural trauma continues in Chapter 6, "Emergent Sounds: Nathanial Mackey's 'Post-Expectant Futurity.'" Drawing on the aesthetics of "Black music," Mackey's long texts *"mu," Song of the Andoumboulou*, and *From a Broken Bottle Traces of Perfume Still Emanate* present an intriguing example of Spencer Brown's "distinction." Each element of the work creates a new distinction or space of possibility, visible on the level of the line, the page, or the book. At the same time, these distinctions are structurally coupled to one another, with each text engaged in its own process of ongoing, improvisatory writing. These formal practices have profound cultural consequences, as Mackey turns the resources of emergent poetics to the unfolding consequences of postcolonial history. Mackey's work offers a model of "post-expectant futurity" as a humble hermeneutic in the tradition of Walter Benjamin, an alternative to Frederic Jameson's influential claims about modernist utopianism and postmodern "flat time." The chapter concludes by connecting that post-expectant hermeneutic to images of sea travel, situating Mackey's work within the long poetry of the haunted Atlantic. Comparing his ocean voyagers to the ghostly fragments of M. NourbeSe Philip's *Zong!* and the crafted mastery of Derek Walcott's *Omeros*, I argue that Mackey's emergent strategies develop feedback loops between postcolonial history and new environments, such as Hurricane Katrina, generating a thick, adaptive cultural memory.

In my conclusion, "Emergent Poetics and the Digital," I offer emergence as a potential resource for reimagining contemporary digital culture and its poetic interlocutors. In many respects, our present digital writing ecology brings into clearer focus the emergent poetries of the past. We can move in the opposite direction as well, drawing on these poems to better comprehend the present. To sketch this double-mediation, I consider some of the ways in which contemporary poetry has engaged the digital, paying particular attention to the work of Kenneth Goldsmith. In contrast to Goldsmith's "uncreative writing," emergent models retain a space for creativity and system memory in the midst of digital information flows.

Juliana Spahr's *This Connection of Everyone with Lungs* supports this claim. A post-9/11 text, Spahr's poem explores the intersection of mediation, textuality, global information networks, and poetic writing. By engaging the flow of digital news media through an iterative and recursive form, Spahr produces a poetic "connection" that transforms the connectivity of the digital, and, indeed, combines elements of the long poem with those of the lyric. Unlike the procedures of conceptualism, Spahr's work can be considered an update of Ammons's constrained emergence in *Tape for the Turn of the Year*: replacing the typewriter and receipt tape with a laptop and the digital news feed, Spahr writes through time in such a way that the space of the text becomes an adaptive investigation, encountering a surprising and often terrifying world.

These chapters, taken as a whole, demonstrate the broad flexibility of systems thinking for analyzing poetry. The prospects for extending this approach to other textual practices are intriguing. We might think of emergent properties in earlier long poems, for instance, such as *The Canterbury Tales* or in oral traditions. Alternatively, we might look for iteration, recursion, and feedback loops within the lyrical sequence, from Emily Dickinson's fascicles to the early modern sonnet cycle. Beyond poetry, we also see structural coupling and environmental interaction in the eighteenth-century serial novel, or, even earlier and more explicitly, within the self-referentiality of *Don Quixote*'s second volume.[87] In other words, complex adaptive textual systems have a much longer history than a single study can address; I can only point to these tantalizing possibilities for further analysis.

While I hope the concept of emergence has traction in other fields of literary criticism, this book, at its core, is an attempt to respect the dynamism, creativity, and continued timeliness of the long poem. The rapid expansion of digital technology has been one moment in the long series of unexpected events we call human history. Emerging communications media have flooded our lives with new relationships, surprising affects, and unforeseen consequences. Like Whitman in the Civil War or Mackey after Katrina, we are constantly asked to refocus our attention and reinterpret our past. Accompanying this social and cultural change, new scientific projects, from neuroscience to genetics, have suggested that the contingent and the emergent may be woven into the fabric of reality itself, characteristic of our most intimate and valued experiences, including our sense of self, our capacity for development, and our ability to adapt to, even to recognize, the new. For these reasons, I hope that an exploration of emergence as a poetic practice offers us some purchase on these new models of understanding and experiencing reality. It may be that these long poems, with their adventurous, adaptive, and surprising aesthetic energy, can be an imaginative resource for us as we seek to live in an emergent world. In doing so, they may show us that emergence, after all, is nothing new.

CHAPTER 2

Emergent America
Walt Whitman's Enactive Democracy

What kind of organisms are leaves of grass? To begin exploring Whitman's emergent poetics, I want to take a fresh look at the title of his book and consider its mode of life within the garden of nineteenth-century aesthetics, particularly in relation to the concept of organic form. As I will demonstrate, Whitman's titular leaves suggest an adaptive model of the organic, parting ways with models of static organicism that rely on notions of aesthetic unity or internal law. Exhibiting porous borders and unforeseen growth, Whitman's organisms respond enactively to their environment, as Varela would put it, establishing their formal identity by engaging with a world that they are causing to appear. This temporally adaptive variant of organic form parallels Whitman's conception of American democracy as a process of growing, interactive transformation. His emergent poetics simultaneously develop a textual praxis and offer an ontological claim about the nature of reality, presenting a worldview in which grass exceeds the stability of floral symmetry or lyric verses, those standard icons of nineteenth-century organic form. Reading Whitman through systems theory thus allows us to reinterpret his organicism as both a reflection of his historical moment and also a critical swerve within romanticism.

Leaves of Grass originated at a time of explicit philosophical and aesthetic organicism. Ralph Waldo Emerson argued that the poet is capable of transforming experience into speech in such a way that the expression grows from an internal unity. Such an utterance will produce a form according to its own intrinsic laws, comparable to the self-governing phenomena of the natural world. "For it is not metres," Emerson claims in "The Poet," "but a metre-making argument, that makes a poem, – a thought so passionate and alive, that, like the spirit of a plant or an animal, it has an architecture of its own, and adorns nature with a new thing."[1] The poem becomes a material representation of its own unique spirit, like an organism growing according to self-determining laws. Emerson's "thought so passionate and alive" recalls Samuel Taylor Coleridge's contrast between

39

"mechanical form" – the rote application of literary rules – and "organic form," which "is innate." Organic form, as Coleridge argued, "shapes as it develops itself from within, and the fullness of its development is one and the same with the perfection of its outward form. Such is the life, such is the form. Nature, the prime genial artist, inexhaustible in diverse powers, is equally inexhaustible in forms; each exterior is the physiognomy of the being within, its true image reflected and thrown out from the concave mirror."[2] It is in these terms of internal, organic law that Coleridge can defend the genius of Shakespeare, whose art grew innately out of his own visionary force. Shakespeare's work develops from its own "life," and thus must be understood on its sui generis terms, not according to the received conventions of theatrical taste. In either case, by approaching form as the materialization of an internal law, both authors suggest that natural or literary form springs from the life that is its pattern. Form follows life; it does not produce life.

We can trace Emerson and Coleridge's versions of organic form back to Immanuel Kant, where the model receives its most rigorous philosophical development. In *The Critique of Judgment*, one of Kant's primary concerns is the perception of "purposiveness" within nature. Kant suggests that the aesthetic allows us to experience a kind of internal purposiveness that parallels our experience with natural objects, objects that cannot be accounted for through an a priori concept of the understanding. Kant's analysis of imagination, pleasure, and the judgment of beauty ultimately leads him to a theory of the art object that mimics the purposive forms of natural objects. The true artwork grows "free from all constraint of arbitrary rules as if it were a product of mere nature."[3] The parallels between art and the organic result in a bidirectional analogy: "Nature is beautiful because it looks like Art; and Art can only be called beautiful if we are conscious of it as Art while yet it looks like Nature."[4]

In this transnational nineteenth-century discourse of organic form, a number of terms exist in complex relationship to one another. Internal laws, whether of natural objects or artistic works, stand in sharp contrast to external and "arbitrary" mechanical processes. The visible, external shape of the organic work becomes the image of that internal law or force. The form is the "life," as Coleridge puts it, so that the exterior becomes the "physiognomy" of the being within. Similarly, the passionate and living thought of Emerson's "metre-making argument" shapes the poem: the poem as such does not produce the thought. Theorists of organic form, somewhat paradoxically, sought to unite internal laws and external form by distinguishing between them.

Do these influential models of the organic sufficiently account for "leaves of grass"? Within the world of nineteenth-century aesthetics, Whitman's title seems, at first appearances, to be at home. If we read the poems as "leaves," with the pun on book "leaves" as well as the individual blades of grass, Whitman presents his text as simultaneously a textual, poetic entity and a natural phenomenon. Additionally, the two parts of the title appear to name both internal force and exterior form. "Grass" may be the internal law, manifesting itself in the form of each individual leaf. But "grass" could just as easily be the exterior form, the swarming fields that come readily to mind when we hear the word. Ordinary language tells us that "grass" is inherently multiple and expansive. Indeed, we might reverse the hierarchy, arguing that the leaves themselves are "internal" to the "exterior" form of a meadow or lawn. In other words, the causal relationship between form and law, spirit and shape becomes indeterminate in Whitman's title, troubling the models of unity with a difference articulated by his philosophical contemporaries. "Leaves of grass" suggests not an internal law manifesting an external form but a network of interacting levels of form, mutually supporting, generating, and modifying each other.

To put it another way: is grass a leaf or a field? Whitman's title suggests both, and in subtly indicating the shifting relationship between singularity and multiplicity, "leaves of grass" offers an apt image of Whitman's emergent poetics. In many respects, Whitman's approach to poetic form anticipates models of the organic pursued by later philosophers interested in emergence and cybernetics. Twentieth-century systems theorists transform nineteenth-century organicism in several significant ways. First, by bridging the mechanical and the living, exploring the way information is exchanged and processed in machines, humans, and organisms, mechanical and organic form are viewed as continuous, not contrasting, as Coleridge sees it. Equally important, systems theorists like Varela and Luhmann include in their conceptualization of the organic a fundamental role for time and the environment, with the form of the system unfolding in surprising ways, not as a static representation of an inner law. This emergent model of the organic clarifies Whitman's celebration of transformational forces that are both mechanical and organic, rote and inspired. By taking an enactive model of the organic as our framework, Whitman's poetry becomes newly legible as a complex variation on the organicism of his time. His poetry does not follow an "inner law" as much as it enacts form through environmentally entangled processes, a swarming poetic that makes possible dramatic and unexpected changes in the total architecture of the poem. Through these techniques, Whitman generates a poetics of futurity, where the text's form is adaptable and continuous, constituted by both leaves and grass. This aesthetic reflects his understanding of democracy itself as an autopoietic political, social, and cultural process replicating its own structures while transforming itself to fit unknown future worlds. Enactive organicism thus sheds new light on the entanglement Whitman always asserted between his poetics and his politics.

In what follows, I focus on three key, interacting examples of Whitman's emergent organicism. I begin with an analysis of the text's environment, taking the Civil War as an obviously disruptive event perturbing the system of the poem. By paying close attention to the poem's emergent form on the level of tone and the evolution of its volumes, we can see how Whitman's text meaningfully couples with his environment. Through these adaptations, *Leaves of Grass* shines new light on the Civil War, formally manifesting its cultural and social complexities. From there, I take up the ontological and political vision enacted by the poem, suggesting that the received critical accounts of the "one and the many" in Whitmanian democracy do not go far enough in explaining the poem's politics. An emergent ontology is evident in many of Whitman's common iterative and recursive poetic devices, such as the catalogue, and in the projective temporality of his language. I compare Whitman's interplay between ontological and formal dynamism with one of his contemporaries in the long poem, William Wordsworth, whose *Prelude* figures nature and the imagination as a dynamic inner law yet represents that law through more stable and inherited poetic form. Form, for Wordsworth, is capable of *representing* adaptive processes, like the development of consciousness, but does not robustly *generate* that adaptation. Whitman's text, in contrast, moves beyond representation: it actively produces adaptation and emergence through its form. This dynamic process is reflected in Whitman's metaphors of travel, which I explore in the final section of this chapter as instances of an emergent self-consciousness, moments in the poem where Whitman's textual existence within time and space becomes articulate. As these self-reflective poems suggest, we do not need to unearth Whitman's emergent textuality, extracting his signature organicism by way of a hermeneutic code. Like leaves of grass, his poem grows right on the surface.

By attending to Whitman's text as a single poetic enterprise, whose emergent organic aesthetics reinforced many of his explicit political aspirations, I also seek to offer a new framework for recent scholarship on Whitman. These studies not only reassess Whitman's immediate historical context but also reflect current intellectual developments in the analysis of sexuality, race, class, transnationalism, ecology, and textual studies, the latter projects receiving some impetus from the crucial work of digitizing Whitman's archive.[5] Approaching Whitman's entire project on the level of poetics may seem to run contrary to the spirit of these focused interpretations. However, by tracing the intersection of poetic practice, cultural materials, and environmental pressures, reading *Leaves of Grass* as an emergent text supports the many versions of Whitman uncovered by contemporary scholarship. Writing in real time complemented, indeed, made possible, Whitman's capacity for multiple selves and his engagement with diverse audiences, the same multiplicity that grounds much Whitman scholarship today. My focus on poetics is thus not proposing a formalist reading at the exclusion of historicizing or theorizing interpretations. Instead, an emergent model of form shows history, form, and theory as themselves networked, structurally coupled, and mutually illuminating. Understanding Whitman's textual practice as an adaptive system will only enhance our interpretations of his complex, conflicted, and profoundly influential cultural work.

I   The Enactions of America

While the concepts of autopoiesis and enaction originated in the twentieth century with Maturana and Varela, they owe an intellectual debt to nineteenth-century philosophers of organic form. As Varela and Andreas Weber have argued, autopoiesis allows us to reclaim Kant's notion of purposiveness for modern biology. Purposiveness is closely linked to teleology, a concept that has been highly contested in philosophy of science, as teleology is often taken to imply an ultimate purpose or guiding hand in processes like evolution. Reclaiming purposiveness as a useful category at the level of the individual organism, Weber and Varela suggest that "*organisms are subjects having purposes according to values encountered in the making of their living,*" so that "value and subjectivity [are] indispensable organic phenomena."[6] Organisms generate interpretive frameworks that both dictate and emerge from their interactions with the environment. Embeddedness implies a certain degree of purposiveness, an orientation in the world that reclaims a teleological or interpretive edge. "There cannot be an individuality which is isolated and folded into itself," Weber and Varela claim, but only "an individuality that copes, relates and couples with the surroundings, and inescapably provides its own world of sense."[7] By "world of sense," Weber and Varela distinguish the environment in its infinite complexity from the specific elements that an organism singles out for its survival. The organism as autopoietic machine actively produces

its environment, crafting a world out of its own drive for continued existence. Thus, the organism is individualized and self-perpetuating precisely
because it is embedded purposefully within a world outside itself. This
organicism is a far cry from an idea or force determining an outward form;
instead, it is a constantly self-transforming, world-making network of
processes. Form does not arise from the inner law but is enacted through
the real-time process of the organism's existence.

The evolution of Whitman's text offers a poetic example of this enactive emergence, at the intersection of purposiveness and perturbation,
poetic practice and environmental change. Whitman's conceptualization
of American democracy further complicates this process because the object
of his attention is a moving target; from the beginning, Whitman describes
America in language that recalls an emerging organism. "America," Whitman begins in the preface of the 1855 edition, "does not repel the past or
what it has produced under its forms or amid other politics or the idea of
castes or the old religions"[8] but instead embraces and integrates this past
into its own fluid processes of self-formation. Whitman represents America's acceptance of the past as a "stalwart and wellshaped heir," one who
reflects in his being the physiology of his ancestors (PP 5). The passage's
emphasis on transmission suggests that the heir is not simply an idealized
biological representative but is instead a moment in an ongoing process of
regeneration. The heir will be replaced by another to come, who in turn
will both replicate and depart from that inheritance. Political identity is
inseparable from recursive, reproductive processes.

This model of American life as a process of regeneration and transformation places demands on poetry, which must be "transcendent and new":

> It is to be indirect and not direct or descriptive or epic. Its quality goes
> through these to much more. Let the age and wars of other nations be
> chanted and their eras and characters be illustrated and that finish the verse.
> Not so the great psalm of the republic. Here the theme is creative and has
> vista. Here comes one among the wellbeloved stonecutters and plans with
> decision and science and sees the solid and beautiful forms of the future
> where there are now no solid forms. (PP 8)

While nineteenth-century American writers regularly called for a distinct
national literary voice, Whitman's stance is unique in that he does not propose a singular, fixed American form. Instead, he argues that American
verse will depart from epic narratives and "finished" histories by creating
a permeable aesthetic that creates and recreates America. The American
poet will always be new, occupying that generative space where forms take

shape. Just as the nation emerges, so too shall the truly American poet, constantly adapting the work in such a way that the transformation of and in time will be visible. The poet must be opened to "eternity" as the force that "makes the present spot the passage from what was to what shall be" (PP 23).

Thus, "America" is a sociopolitical name for the initial act of provisional closure that Whitman's poem establishes, a world of sense whose character he depicts as itself emergent, caught in time, redeploying past forms as the ground for as yet unidentifiable structures and ways of life. Such a vista directs Whitman's artistic attention within the environment, prompting him to identify developments in time that are meaningful for the process of democratic articulation that the poem has created. At the same time, by establishing this framework, Whitman is also able to register thwarted exceptions and unpredictable disruptions, that series of perturbations we retrospectively call "history." His provisional closure is torn open, at times violently, forcing the framework to reestablish its initial terms.

No environmental disruption had a more significant influence on *Leaves of Grass* than the Civil War. The War's effects on Whitman's text clearly illustrate the feedback loop of the poem, its embedded processes of historical interpretation. While the outbreak of war undoubtedly influenced Whitman's work, the war was also a much more intimate affair. On December 16, 1862, the *New York Tribune* reported that "First Lieutenant G. W. Whitmore [sic], Company D" had been wounded in the Battle of Fredericksburg.[9] "G. W. Whitmore" was George Whitman, the poet's brother. With this notice, the war called to Whitman personally, no longer simply a cause he could celebrate, and the poet quickly set off to find his injured sibling. Although George wasn't seriously injured, Walt stayed at his brother's military encampment, and eventually ended up caring for wounded soldiers. Unsurprisingly, the war and its aftermath gave Whitman a range of new material, some devastating. The wounded soldiers became a significant presence, while Abraham Lincoln's assassination prompted Whitman to write two of the most important elegies in American poetry. Beyond subject matter, the war also prompted an adaptation and expansion of Whitman's poetic tone. As Roy Morris points out, even early in the conflict Whitman "had already begun to grasp that his old enthusiastic style of writing was sadly unsuited for capturing the grim realities of [the soldiers'] war."[10]

One indication of this adaptation on the level of tone is Whitman's move from the loquacious, expansive articulations evident in the early poetry to a writing of gaps, fissures, and descriptions of the unspoken. In "Vigil

Strange I Kept on the Field One Night," for instance, the solemnity of the battlefield takes the paradoxical form of a spoken silence maintained while burying a fallen comrade: "Then on the earth partially reclining sat by your side leaning my chin in my hands, / Passing sweet hours, immortal and mystic hours with you dearest comrade – not a tear, not a word, / Vigil of silence, love and death, vigil for you my son and my soldier" (PP 439). Acknowledging a limit to his language, the poem marks death by speaking around the act of mourning, which itself is characterized by silence, "not a word." The subdued voice cannot directly convey that quiet vigil and must only trace its contours.

The tonal change is not only toward the silent, however, as Whitman's initial framework of meaning – American democracy – causes him to adapt broader, more disturbing, visions of war and its social work. The mournful, humble tone of "Vigil Strange" can be contrasted with other moments in *Drum Taps*, such as "Rise O Days from Your Fathomless Deeps," in which the war is figured as a mighty force surpassing even nature at her most sublime:

> Thunder on! stride on, Democracy! strike with vengeful stroke!
> And do you rise higher than ever yet O days, O cities!
> Crash heavier, heavier yet, O storms! you have done me good,
> . . .
> But now I no longer wait, I am fully satisfied, I am glutted,
> I have witness'd the true lighting, I have witness'd my cities electric,
> I have lived to behold man burst forth and warlike America rise,
> Hence I will seek no more the food of the northern solitary wilds,
> No more the mountains roam or sail the stormy sea.   (PP 428–9)

In war, Whitman's ecstatic imagination does not require the forces of nature to be animated; indeed, the natural phenomenon of lightning becomes a mere representation of the "true" flashing light, the spectacle of "warlike America" on the rise. The force of Whitman's language here is as powerful in celebration of war as his vigil of silence delicately conveys loss.

Transformations in a poet's tone and sensibility in response to historical events do not alone constitute an emergent form. However, the striking effect of Whitman's practice is to include these adaptations alongside the earlier moments of composition, thus revealing the recursive structure of the entire work. By accruing moments of shifting poetic voice, the text generates a second order of form, the emergence of dynamic and adaptive *relationships* between each unit of the poetic network. Such tonal shifts and subsequent formal developments are particularly significant when mapped onto the structural changes of *Leaves of Grass* over its six editions,[11] revealing the emergent architecture of the text. These expansions and additions demonstrate how the text enacted itself within its world of sense, not by simply responding to environmental change but also giving interpretive poetic shape to those events through its own processes. Far from inaugurating a new poem, Whitman's war writing reveals that the initial task of *Leaves* persisted – to provide America with a poetry equal to its own capacity for transformation. The text incorporates the conflict into its architecture, an interruption that Whitman certainly could not have anticipated when he began to write. Whitman's enactive organism thus shapes itself to historical trauma, attempting to read that event through the literary process he had already begun. In this manner, *Leaves* is neither a collection of lyrics nor an epic of the nation. Instead, it is an interpretation of history through a practice of emergent poetic thinking.[12]

These adaptations are particularly visible in the text's publication history and the pagination, titling, and binding of the different volumes. The first edition, appearing in 1855, was a mere ninety-five pages long, including the preface. The volume was composed of six poems, each of which bore the title "Leaves of Grass," an example of iterative form with recursive implications.[13] The iteration of "Leaves of Grass" produces a flat continuity, like the field of grass viewed from a distance, while the individual contents of the sections generate recursive links and networks. The singularity of each poetic unit, its individual work of language, thickens the iterative field. The 1855 *Leaves* thus puts into play a formal, structural, and thematic organicism of repetition and change, generating initial conditions that make possible later emergent transformations.

These transformations appeared as early as the 1856 edition, which increased in size significantly, to 384 pages. Along with the poems, the volume included an appendix titled "Leaves-Droppings," a heterogeneous collection of written responses to the book, such as an "anonymous" review (most likely Whitman's famous self-promotion) that includes such oddities as a footnote summarizing *"Phrenological Notes on W. Whitman*, by L. N. FOWLER, *July*, 1849."[14] Such encyclopedism brings fragments of disparate texts into the bound volume, allowing such material to coexist with the poetry, anticipating the collagist practices of Pound, Olson, and DuPlessis. Even the flippant title of this appendix is revealing, as it suggests that Whitman's *Leaves* are continuing to reproduce, to generate more writing. That systemic process of generation would lead to the 1860 version, with its 456 pages. Notably, however, each of these editions retains its singular identity as a work; there is no suggestion that the 1855 edition is somehow incomplete or unfinished. We might conceive of each volume as individual moments in the life of the organism that is *Leaves of Grass*. At each point, the network is complete and functional, even as processes are added, transformed, or adjusted in subsequent moments in response to new environmental pressures.

With the first three editions of *Leaves of Grass*, the trajectory of addition and revision clearly indicates a single, self-transforming work. However, with the 1867 publication, a momentary but significant break in the textual expansion occurs. *Leaves of Grass*, now 338 pages, has appended to it two separately paginated works, *Drum Taps* and *Songs Before Parting*. Appearing in 1865, *Drum Taps* was "the first book of poetry Whitman had published after 1855 that was not titled *Leaves of Grass*," Cristanne Miller notes, "suggesting that he may have seen these poems as markedly different from his earlier poems."[15] Whitman, it would seem, had decided to write two new books of poems, one of which explicitly speaks back to the war. By binding them together with *Leaves* in the 1867 publication, Whitman gives some indication that the texts are related, albeit distantly. Had Whitman stopped with this volume, the reasonable critical response would be to consider him the author of three major books of poems, and, in turn, to read the works as one reads any other series of texts attributed to a single author. But *Leaves of Grass* did not cease in 1867, and when the 1871–2 edition came out, its 384 pages now included revised versions of both *Drum Taps* and *Songs before Parting* as components of *Leaves* proper, with two new, separately paginated "annexes," including *Passage to India*.[16] Undoubtedly, the revisions of *Drum Taps* are significant, reflecting the changing political context of postwar reconstruction, so that Miller is right to argue that "the 1865 book of fifty-three poems (not including sequel) became a vastly different sequence of thirty-two poems in 1871."[17] But those revisions only demonstrate the point that *Leaves* integrated *Drum Taps* as a new function within its system, metabolizing that which had previously been peripheral or adjacent. The text would perform this act again in the 1881 edition, which was 382 pages long and included the prior annexes as part of the whole. Finally, the "deathbed" edition of 1891, 438 pages long, included two new annexes and a prose essay. The final essay suggests that Whitman could not actually "finish" *Leaves of Grass*; instead, he had to turn to prose as a parting gesture.

What can we learn from this involved textual history? Undoubtedly, there is an expansive logic to *Leaves of Grass*, a hermeneutic urge that enacts itself, to recall Varela, in relationship to the history that disrupts it. Texts and poems that seemed to have an independent identity, like *Drum Taps*, were ultimately incorporated into the work, written into the whole as a discrete function or process. As such, Whitman's war writing becomes contextualized by his earlier poetic processes, allowing a formal memory to emerge that would not have existed had *Drum Taps* remained independent of *Leaves of Grass*. The war suddenly becomes of a piece with the proclamations of "Song of Myself," the catalogues of American labor, and the eroticism of the "Calamus" poems. Each version of *Leaves* appears as complete as the next, even as the poem remains open to the future; the perturbations of history make possible the enactive organism's ongoing development. For these reasons, any notion of a predictable or narrative whole must be abandoned, even as the work retains its singular identity. There is no way *Drum Taps* could have been predicted by Whitman at the outset of the work, and yet, at the same time, the provisional closure and feedback processes constituted by the earlier moments of the poem establish an interpretive context for the text's later adaptations.

In the environment that is America, the Civil War was one of its most significant "perturbations," stretching the term to its widest meaning. The war was an "event" in Alain Badiou's sense,[18] arising from a set of material conditions and yet not entirely predictable. There is no doubt that the war influenced every writer working in its time, whether elliptically or directly. What is of interest is how that response was registered. In Whitman's case, the enactive organism of *Leaves of Grass* generated a world of meaning from which he could present an interpretive stance, creating his literary capacity to respond to that event and connect it to a broader vision of America. We cannot adequately account for *Leaves of Grass* without attending to this interaction between composition and comprehension; poetic form, in this case, emerges from the text's self-transforming operations, provisional closure, and feedback relationships with its environment. At the same time, the more fundamental questions of democracy, which troubled Whitman throughout his life, are not entirely evident in his changes in tone or adaptations in structure. In these matters, emergence as a model for collectivity, as well as the emergent potential of language itself, became essential tools for Whitman's figurations of democratic life.

II Democratic Ontology

"America" was one framework of meaning that motivated Whitman's emergent project, but it was in tension with another key political term – namely "democracy." For Whitman, democracy permeated the societies where it prospered, influencing spheres of life as diverse as education, religion, and the biopolitical regulation of physiology and desire. The extent of democracy's potential reach is explicitly articulated in *Democratic Vistas*: "Did you, too, O friend, suppose democracy was only for elections, for politics, and for a party name? I say democracy is only of use there that it may pass on and come to its flower and fruits in manners, in the highest forms of interaction between men, and their beliefs – in religion, literature, colleges and schools – democracy in all public and private life, and in the army and navy" (PP 980). However, this hope for a full "flowering" is tempered by a more pessimistic assessment of his contemporary moment. Whitman claims that "as a paramount scheme," democracy "has yet few or no full realizers and believers" (PP 980). Democracy had not flourished in America, and a compelling rhetorical drive behind his work was to define and to promote democracy in the America of his time.

For these reasons, democracy is presented by Whitman as essentially a problem, the inescapable paradox of cultivating individual identity in all of its potential variety while respecting collective being in all of its mutable arrangements. To complicate things further, Whitman saw each individual, in turn, as made up of multiplicities: "Do I contradict myself? / Very well then I contradict myself, (I am large, I contain multitudes.)" (PP 246). As George Kateb argues, for Whitman "all of us are always indefinitely more than we actually are,"[19] an understanding of personality that suggests virtual possibilities and emerging, unanticipated potentiality within the individual. This singular multiplicity characterizes nations as well. In the 1855 preface to *Leaves*, Whitman refers to the "United States themselves" (as opposed to the "United States itself"), a testimony to this political plurality: the "United States" *are* a multiplicity, yet brought together linguistically under a single name (PP 5). As an individual work, Whitman goes on to say, these states are the greatest poem. This double-edged relationship among the states reflects the tension between individual persons and the collective will of the country as a whole, another version of "containing multitudes."

In light of this movement between singularity and multiplicity, the democracy Whitman embraced has been read as a struggle between the many and the one. This conceptual approach has historical justification because the problem of the one and the many existed elsewhere within the national discourse. As Allen Grossman has argued, Whitman's concern for democratic union on the level of the poetic paralleled Lincoln's attempts to address union within difference on the level of policy. Whitman was the "literary master of union . . . for whom also the one justifiable order of the world was the order of the discourse by which he invented himself, his song"; his achievement was to "[devise] a 'song' that would reconcile variety and order, equality and constitution, one and many without compromising either term."[20]

This tension is central to Whitman's concerns, and thus critics are quick to turn to the categories of the one and the many when analyzing his poetics. For James Perrin Warren, *Democratic Vistas* was the "culmination of the poet's lifelong meditation upon language as the mediator between the many and the one," while for W. C. Harris, the problem of the one and the many was Whitman's "fundamental task."[21] There are limitations, however, to this approach. Most notably, one and many are ultimately static categories, similar to "original" and "representation," "set" and "member," or, to return to the discourse of organicism, "form" and "inner law." To approach democracy as the one and the many is to risk falling into an abstraction that often ignores the very material and concrete differences that concerned Whitman. Furthermore, "one" and "many" lend themselves to a synchronic imaginary, representing a state of affairs as a moment in time, and Whitman's concern was fundamentally diachronic, even prophetic, looking for a future possibility whose form and meaning had not yet arrived.

For these reasons, we can read *Leaves of Grass* more subtly by rethinking the "one and the many" through the framework of complex adaptive systems. One alternative is to substitute the terms "particular" and "all" for "one" and "many," applying those terms both to individuals, whether humans or things, and poems, whether as devices, sections, clusters, or bound volumes. A particular is any historical, material, and concrete entity, specific and unique in itself, unlike all other particulars yet constituted through its relationships to other particulars. I use "all," in turn, not to identify an essential unity, a category, or a representative term. Instead, "all" is closer to an aggregate, a network that brings together particulars, situating them in various relationships one to another without combining them into a fixed unity. The advantage of "all" is that it is never complete or necessary, even as it may be identifiable in a given moment – instead, "all" is like a momentary state in a network that is constantly transforming. For these reasons, the notion of particular/all, as opposed to one/many, escapes the static closure accompanying notions like the symbolic and the categorical. Instead, particular/all requires perpetual recombination, adaptive structural coupling, multiple acts of provisional closure, and the capacity for new additions and expansions.

The logic of particular/all is evident in many of Whitman's ontological statements, where he articulates a vision of the physical world underlying his textual project. For instance, in "Starting from Paumanok" we read:

> I will not make poems with reference to parts,
> But I will make poems, songs, thoughts, with reference to ensemble,
> And I will not sing with reference to a day, but with reference to all days,
> And I will not make a poem nor the least part of a poem but has
>   reference to the soul,
> Because having look'd at the objects of the universe, I find there is no
>   one nor any particle of one but has reference to the soul.   (PP 183)

While the language of this passage may appear at first as a declaration of metaphysical unity, there is a fundamental logic of emergent particularity at work here. Whitman's initial refusal to refer to "parts" may suggest a typological, symbolic, or generic approach to things, a denial of particulars as such, as if parts were too insignificant to warrant poetic attention. Yet the second line contains the rich Whitmanian term "ensemble," a word that shares a family resemblance to "network." The ensemble, for Whitman, acknowledges each part as an individual, in which no part can be substituted by or for another. "Parts" in the previous line, which Whitman refuses to sing, can then be understood as *representative* parts, metonymic replacements by which one element stands in for everything else. The third line of the stanza denies such replacements: Whitman does not claim that he will sing the essence or being of "day," some transcendent singularity underlying the identity of each individual day, but declares that he will sing "all days," the "all" a collection of unique, individual days. There is no universal day, but specific days, each prompting its discrete poetic treatment. The last two lines of the stanza, with their reference to the "soul," appear to be strongly metaphysical, and yet, when considered in terms of particular and all, are remarkably resistant to a hierarchy of being. For each apparently "least" part of a poem refers to the soul, as does each "particle" of the universe – both the particularities of language as well as the particularities of all other things contain unique value. By evoking that value, Whitman is effectively eliminating ideal order from both the universe and the poem. To be sure, the use of the definite article to describe "*the* soul" suggests essential oneness, and there is much to be found elsewhere in Whitman's own writings professing belief in this unity. Nevertheless, the language of particular/all used in this passage affords a powerful counterpoint to the language of metaphysical wholeness. If each particle contains the soul, then transcendence beyond particulars, or a transcendental signifier naming that unity, loses its significance. Similarly, as new particulars – new selves, bodies, souls, and days – appear in time, so too must the song of recognition continue as it transforms. Particularity in time necessarily leads to an emergent, adaptive, and networked all.

The concluding lines of the previous stanza in the poem are radical in their celebration of the particular all: "all the things of the universe are perfect miracles, each as profound as any" (PP 183). The poem premised on a universe of individual "miracles" is a far cry a mimetic metaphysics of original and copy, just as such a work resists any democracy that would find its political justification simply in the will of a majority. Furthermore, when each particular of the all can be called a "miracle," then miracles cease to be metaphysical exceptions. Instead, they constitute the very fabric of the universe that the speaker experiences: "As to me," Whitman writes elsewhere, "I know nothing else but miracles" (PP 513). Whitman thus uses the vocabulary of spirituality and transcendence to naturalize, as it were, the theological. A "mouse," he writes, "is miracle enough to stagger sextillions of infidels" – hyperbole, yes, but also a clear example of his commitment to particular things (PP 217).

Material particularity and an emergent all are not simply properties of objects, the world of mice and persons. *Leaves of Grass* was, as Whitman famously described it, "only a language experiment,"[22] and some of his most profound democratic poetic experiments stem from his recognition that language was a unique "mediator," as Warren puts it, for naming both the particular and the all simultaneously, acknowledging the multitude that Whitman saw in each entity.[23] Language in Whitman is both a specific utterance and a mode of repetition, an endlessly adaptable medium for relationships. This capacity for recursion and iteration is uniquely manifested in Whitman's use of personal pronouns. As Charles Altieri argues, the "I" in "Song of Myself" (and, by extension, in *Leaves* as a whole) "is not anchored in specific representations or bound to particular structures of power. Specific references to any one person seem far less important than the range of functions and investments that emerge simply by observing how the pronoun gets situated within aspects of the world. Instead of promoting a particular figure of social power, this purely functional 'I' floats freely so that its working can be attached to the self-reflexive activity of both author and readers."[24] This potential for self-reflection generates a provisional network, whereby a minimal "all," even a momentary democracy, emerges out of the multiple potential relationships possible at any given moment of writing or reading. The personal pronoun, in this sense, does not become a kind of Althusserian interpellation, arresting and creating the subject[25]; instead, the pronoun's capacity for iteration generates a malleable system of relationships between multiple potential individuals. The mode of address offered by a pronoun thus becomes a formal process infinitely transferable and yet uniquely particular.

This transferable relationality through language is particularly evident in "To You." In the poem's second stanza, we read: "Whoever you are, now I place my hand upon you, that you be my poem / I whisper with my lips close to your ear, / I have loved many women and men, but I love none better than you" (PP 375). At first, the poem's claims to a present connection between a speaker and a reader may appears as nothing more than fantastical wish-fulfillment, an example of Whitman's deliberate confusion between present, living bodies and supplementary, signifying words. As Mitchell Breitwieser argues, many of Whitman's "yous" rely upon the "ruse of shared colloquial presence," for "the 'you' whom Whitman addresses *reads* this feigning of *speaking*."[26] In the case of "To You," however, the ruse bares its mechanism of illusion by beginning with the phrase "Whoever you are," making anonymous and multiple the addressees. "Whoever you are" is a grammatical construction that speaks to every potential, and as yet unknown, "you," a sign with infinite possible referents, a capacity for unpredictable moments of structural coupling. The poem opens itself to those future, unknown selves, and thus each possible "you" can receive the song of praise. Nevertheless, the celebration remains singular, as the poem goes on to declare that "I should have blabb'd nothing but you, I should have chanted nothing but you" (PP 375). The particular focus, eliminating everything else, chanting you at the cost of all others, appears to counteract the apparent anonymity of "whoever you are." How can one reconcile "I should have chanted nothing but you," a gesture of uniqueness implicitly hierarchical, with "whoever you are," a grammatical form potentially available to all particulars, each one? How can the poem be chanting nothing but you if it is addressed to everyone? A later stanza provides the necessary reconciliation:

> Painters have painted their swarming groups and the centre-figure of all,
> From the head of the centre-figure spreading a nimbus of gold-color'd light,
> But I paint myriads of heads, but paint no head without its nimbus of
>   gold-color'd light,
> From my hand from the brain of every man and woman it streams,
>   effulgently flowing forever.   (PP 376)

Each head is sacred, deserving its own discrete marker of brilliance. Analogous to a world of nothing but miracles, Whitman here proposes a population of nothing but saints, yet one in which each saint is *peculiarly* holy. When Whitman states earlier in the poem that "I only am he who place over you no master, owner, better, God, beyond what waits intrinsically in yourself," he is declaring that each anonymous you contains an incomparable sanctity. Whitman's claim that he should have sung nothing but you is to admit this particular glory: your greatness, utterly individual, simply cannot be compared to any other greatness, and thus, on its own terms, it calls for its own song, a chant that abandons all else. Each particular iteration of "you" resists comparison to any other particular "you," even as the poem, using the anonymous address available in language, is written to all "you," connecting these particulars to one another in an emerging network.

"Whoever you are," as a syntactic form and grammatical structure, thus allows Whitman to speak *simultaneously* of the particular and the all, to create a linguistic act which, in its anonymity, is able to be infinitely replicated and extended. The poem becomes an emergent speech act, establishing a relationship with invisible, projective others. "To You," we might say, has not yet fully realized its object of address, remaining structurally open within Whitman's poem. As such, the poem offers an instance of "translation," a term Grossman identifies as Whitman's substitute for Coleridge's "imagination": "[instead] of a 'poetic language' . . . Whitman has devised a universal 'conjunctive principle' whose manifest structure is the sequence of end-stopped, nonequivalent, but equipollent lines."[27] This "conjunctive principle" appears not only on the level of the line but also on the level of iterative words like "you," deployed by the poem to project new networks of relationship into unforeseeable futures.

The particular and all, both in the world and in language, manifests a democratic ontology, where being is both iteratively particular, as a repetition of "you," as well as increasingly complex, embedded within a recursive structure of networked relationships. Whitman thus attempts to create a poetry of formal multiplicity as an emergent response to the multiplicity he detects in the world. Grossman has attributed Whitman's formal experiments in part to the hypothesis that the world is "composed of a 'limitless' series of brilliant finite events,"[28] and this limitlessness is a natural result of miraculous particularity. In a sense, "limitlessness" becomes even more complex as the all transforms in time: if each individual thing is a miracle, then each new particular emerging within history becomes significant. The celebration of this expanding particular/all becomes a central force propelling *Leaves of Grass*: "And limitless are leaves stiff or drooping in the fields, / And brown ants in the little wells beneath them, / And mossy scabs of the worm fence, heap'd stones, elder, mullein and poke-weed" (PP 192). No symbol, no narrative, and no static philosophical system can adequately address or account for these expanding miracles. If each thing, event, and person contains this miraculous particularity, than no entity surpasses another in a chain of reality, an order of being, or a distribution of political rights. "Mullein" can only be understood alongside, not above or below, "brown ants," which in turn exist in equality alongside the Whitmanian "I."

We can situate Whitman's poetics of process and multiplicity within a broader philosophical and literary context, a transformation that critics have noticed in Whitman's British predecessors Wordsworth and Coleridge. As Frank McConnell argues, Wordsworth and Coleridge were instrumental in "a crucial, epoch-making transformation of the sense of the word *philosophical*," although they may not have realized it themselves, a change which would move one from "the discursive structures of Hume, Berkeley, or Hartley" to writers like "Wittgenstein, Heidegger, [and] Sartre," a change in both "form [and] in the inevitable pressure of form upon thought."[29] Kenneth R. Johnston, writing about the poetic activities leading up to Wordsworth's *The Recluse*, provides a further definition of that transformation:

> It is an oversimplification, but a useful one, to say that Wordsworth and Coleridge were in the process of writing a new kind of poetry while still in thrall to an older conception of philosophy. They were pioneers in that 'breaking the crust of conventions' which John Dewey later set forth as philosophy's necessary new agenda, seeking to become what Richard Rorty has recently defined as *edifying* philosophers, for whom knowledge is a field of force (in W. V. Quine's metaphor), even though their functional model was still that of the great *systematic* philosophers, for whom it is an architectonic structure.[30]

The philosophical system, constructing a total and universally applicable intellectual architecture, as it were, parallels tendencies in traditional epic poetics. Homer, Dante, and Milton all attempt to offer a unified ordering of the world, an underlying stability of reference that gives their texts validity, coherence, and meaning. Whitman, like Wordsworth and Coleridge, undertakes a philosophical poetry that emphasizes poetics as an edifying practice, the ongoing "pressure of form upon thought."

As suggestive as Johnston's argument may be, this moment in the history of poetic thought, where force or process is revalued over a totalizing structure, does not result in a singular poetic practice. Indeed, Wordsworth's celebration of the imagination in *The Prelude* provides a useful comparison to Whitman's enactive poetics. Although Wordsworth figures the poetic imagination as an evolving, adaptive organism, growing through fructifying "spots of time," that imagination is manifested through comparatively stable poetic forms, most notably the blank verse and multibook epic narrative that Wordsworth inherited from Milton, whom he considered his immediate predecessor and rival.[31] Wordsworth thus uses a writing practice that resists emergence to represent an evolving, proto-emergent vision of the poetic imagination. Whitman, on the other hand, actively generates emergent properties through the writing practices of *Leaves of Grass*, establishing a network of relationships between imagination, poetic practices, and the poem's world of sense. Calling attention to this difference – between the use of a regulating form to represent an emergent ontology and a poetic practice that constitutes an emergent system in its form – helps clarify the relationship between Whitman and Wordsworth and situates their historical significance within the modern long poem. Wordsworth undoubtedly transforms the epic, shifting it from political, national, theological, and historical narratives to the evolution of the individual poetic imagination, but this shift did not accompany an attendant development in form.

As a narrative of poetic autobiography, *The Prelude* presents the imagination with many complex, adaptive characteristics. Wordsworth narrates his life as a series of recursive events, each of which contributes, unknowingly, to the dynamic imagination of the mature poet. M. H. Abrams points out that *The Prelude* is organized so that "the design inherent in [Wordsworth's life], which has become apparent only to his mature awareness, may stand revealed as a principle which was invisibly operative from the beginning."[32] Anne K. Mellor expands on this, arguing that the poem represents "three developmental stages of consciousness": "the unself-consciousness of the child who experiences the external world and his own being as one . . . , progressing through the growing self-consciousness of the schoolboy . . . , and arriving finally at the realization of the power of consciousness as such, at the achievement of that 'philosophic mind' which is the 'counterpart' of Nature's own creative power."[33] The epic form serves an important role in this process, narrating, describing, and connecting these moments in the poet's biography. Akin to Whitman's emergent ontology, Wordsworth's intellectual faculty is treated as an artwork developing within time:

> The mind of man is framed even like the breath
> And harmony of music. There is a dark
> Invisible worksmanship that reconciles
> Discordant elements, and makes them move
> In one society.[34]

As a musical piece builds up harmony out of distinct, even "discordant" notes, so too Wordsworth's mind is animated by an "invisible" force that reconciles, unifies, and expands the poetic subject. The music of the "prelude" is thus the emerging song of the poetic consciousness. We can see a similar emergence in Wordsworth's famous "spots of time," which have a "renovating virtue" (P XI.257–9), building up the mind over the course of one's life as a recurrent structure or invisible thread whose full meaning is manifest in the mature imagination. "Such moments," Wordsworth writes, "Are scattered everywhere, taking their date / From our first childhood" (P XI.273–5). The structure of relationships generated by these moments constitutes the poetic subject. Consequently, the epic narrative's task is to represent, and thus unite, these disparate notes or forces, depicting a complex and dynamic consciousness.

Like Whitman, Wordsworth ultimately correlates this imaginative subject with an image of an emergent natural world. At the climax of the epic narrative, the speaker discovers poetic creativity in nature itself, a reflection of the organicism we saw in Kant and Coleridge. The famous climb atop Mount Snowdon at the poem's end brings together the poetic and the natural into a single image. From the moonlit mountaintop, Wordsworth sees "a huge sea of mist" stretching out before him, an imitation of the "real sea" in the distance (P XIII.43, 49). The result is the following "perfect image of a mighty mind" (P XIII.68):

> Meanwhile, the moon looked down upon this shew
> In single glory, and we stood, the mist
> Touching our very feet; and from the shore
> At distance not the third part of a mile
> Was a blue chasm, a fracture in the vapour,
> A deep and gloomy breathing-place, through which
> Mounted the roar of waters, torrents, streams
> Innumerable, roaring with one voice.
> The universal spectacle throughout
> Was shaped for admiration and delight,
> Grand in itself alone, but in that breach
> Through which the homeless voice of waters rose,
> That dark thoroughfare, had Nature lodged
> The soul, the imagination of the whole.
>
> (P XIII.52–65)

The sound coming from the "blue chasm" in the "universal spectacle" serves two important functions. As a visual phenomenon, Wordsworth asserts that the sea of mist is powerful in its own right, capable of provoking delight and wonder. But it is the sound emanating from the breach, the "fracture in the vapour," that gives the scene its ultimate force, presumably as an aural replication of the sound of the ocean. The sound, echoing from the chasm, is described as "the soul" and "imagination of the whole" because it generates a natural symbol, joining the imitation (the mist) with its counterpart (the real ocean). More than simply a property of the scene, the chasm's voice becomes the crucial link between the object and the representation, giving the vision its power.

The rapport between nature and the poetic imagination is reinforced when the "fracture" is described as a "deep and gloomy breathing-place," a "voice," suggesting a linguistic faculty. The relationship between language and water runs deeply throughout *The Prelude*, initially when the murmurings of the river Derwent blend with the nurse's song and continuing in other passages (P I.271–6, II.215, IX.3, XIII.175–88). The sound of waters becomes a metaphorical manifestation of an endlessly vocalized imaginative movement within nature itself, that power pressing on things so that she "moulds them, and endues, abstracts, combines" them, the "brother of the glorious faculty / Which higher minds bear with them as their own," a combinatory power that allows them to "exalt" both the "enduring and the transient" (P XIII.79, 89–90, 97–8).

We can thus find in Wordsworth's poetic ontology a connection between creativity and adaptation, an organic system capable of endlessly "abstracting" and "combining" that operates in both the poet and in nature. The poem's project of self-comprehension does not eventuate in closure, a moment of final realization or arrival, but in movement, an "endless occupation for the soul" (P XIII.112). This insight, however, does not produce an equally endless, adaptive writing process; instead, writing makes visible this internal force common to both the poet and the natural world. Wordsworth's organic imagination functions as an asserted ground for the poetic text, not a result of its form. Remaining within the framework of the conventional epic, *The Prelude* narrates and figures its own internal laws. Time and process, while asserted as aesthetic and imaginative values, do not become constitutive of poetic form as such.

We can thus read for emergence in both Wordsworth and Whitman, revealing a shared philosophical commitment to dynamic, adaptive processes, and yet in each writer the emergent force differs in its relationship to poetic form. *The Prelude* presents this dynamism, in both nature and the poet, as its narrative object, while *Leaves of Grass* enacts emergence in its poetic architecture, using multiple levels of form to generate unpredictable effects as it is structurally coupled to an equally unpredictable environment. Wordsworth's intellectual and imaginative dynamism is represented as a cause for form in *The Prelude*, while Whitman's dynamism is generated through form as an iterative, recursive feedback loop. We see this difference in the dominant figures organizing each poem. Wordsworth's nature is the sound of the river, an endless flow ultimately blending into a single song. Whitman's nature is like an endlessly differential field of grass, where poke-weed, mullein, field mice, language, and the poet himself coexist, interact, and actively reshape themselves.

III   Time Travel

Thus far, Whitman's emergent poetics have been demonstrated through his recursive language use, his democratic ontology of particular/all, and the formal, enactive evolution of *Leaves of Grass*. These characteristics are self-reflectively figured in the text through the many images of travel, journey, or voyage, a trope that we will see recurring in other emergent texts. A striking number of Whitman's individual poems, including some of his most famous, derive their titles from journeys or evoke scenes of travel, suggesting that poetry and voyage are comparable activities. "Starting from Paumanok," "In Paths Untrodden," "Song of the Open Road," and "Crossing Brooklyn Ferry" are only a few examples, as is the entire cluster titled "By the Roadside." As a device of both spatial and temporal transformation, travel echoes his emergent model of organic growth, a link made explicit in the autobiographical poems: "Starting from fish-shaped Paumanok where I was born, / Well-begotten and rais'd by a perfect mother, / After roaming many lands, lover of populous pavements" (PP 176). The poem tracks Whitman's development and his preparation for his poetic task through the enactive experiences of moving within a changing environment, blending literal travel with psychological, physical, and linguistic growth. Scenes of travel offer an occasion for the projected effects found in "To You," as when, crossing Brooklyn Ferry, Whitman addresses "you that shall cross from shore to shore years hence" (PP 308). Traversing space becomes a proxy for crossing time. Far from collapsing or escaping time, however, Whitman views time as a medium through which connections between other selves can be forged and dissolved in a network of relationships.

The democratic potential of the road's spatiality and temporality is presented most clearly in "Song of the Open Road," where "the profound lesson of reception, nor preference nor denial" can be learned (PP 298). As a meeting ground open to participants regardless of race, class, gender, physical ability, education, and moral standing, Whitman's road becomes a structural precondition for equality: "The black with his woolly head, the felon, the diseas'd, the illiterate person, are not denied; / The birth, the hasting after the physician, the beggar's tramp, the drunkard's stagger, the laughing party of the mechanics" – all of these "pass, I also pass, any thing passes, none can be interdicted, / None but are accepted, none but shall be dear to me" (PP 298). The road in this poem thus becomes a site of liberated potentiality, occupied through time by anyone. In this way, it serves a similar function to Whitman's own poetic project, a parallel he acknowledges when, later in the text, he claims that the road "[expresses] me better than I can express myself / you shall be more to me than my poem" (PP 299). Whitman's text aspires to the condition of the road as an emergent space for travel, encounter, and difference. Just as the road makes possible "translations" through space and time, so too Whitman seeks to write a pathway between unforeseen possibilities and persons.

Whitman's poetics of voyage is thus simultaneously road, journey, and traveler, combining travelogue, map, and vehicle. The desire to fulfill these many functions could only be actualized, however, by specific literary devices, ones that enable the poem to achieve the aspiration of the road (a space of difference) as well as propel the traveler through time (a vehicle for journey). The poem needs to be both mechanism of change and register of change. This complex task was accomplished, in part, by Whitman's paratactic catalogues. Parataxis, as Barbara Herrnstein Smith argues in her classic study of poetic closure, is uniquely characterized by multiplicity and variability, or, to return to the language of complex systems, the twinned mechanisms of iteration and recursion. For Herrnstein Smith, in a nonparatactic structure, that is, a sequence developed through logical or necessary connections, "the dislocation or omission of any element will tend to make the sequence as a whole incomprehensible, or radically change its effect."[35] In paratactic texts, however, "thematic units can be omitted, added, or exchanged without destroying the coherence or effect of the poem's thematic structure."[36] Such catalogues create a virtual space of potential, generating the "unmade map" evoked in *Democratic Vistas* while simultaneously acknowledging and adapting to each particular traveler who enters into its course.

Parataxis as travel functions on several levels in Whitman's work. His self-described "omnivorous lines" are decidedly paratactic, often constructed as bursts of lists, only exceeded by the multitude of the world – they may attempt to contain all, but their very act of containment reveals the impossibility of that goal (PP 236). In this sense, a paratactic line shifts the emphasis from recording a stable world to something anticipating Pound's "periplum," following the linguistic encounter with particulars to its furthest, and yet unknown, destination.[37] The poetry of the 1855 edition begins with the famous declaration that "every atom belonging to me as good belongs to you" (PP 27), suggesting that each atom, in turn, needs to be included within the poem. The subsequent paratactic urges recur in the opening pages as if to make good on that promise. These urges manifest themselves in various forms, whether as a recursive expansion of the poet's own body and bodily sensations:

> The smoke of my own breath,
> Echos, ripples, and buzzed whispers . . . loveroot, silkthread, crotch
>   and vine,
> My respiration and inspiration . . . the beating of my heart . . . the
>   passing of blood and air through my lungs,   (PP 27)

as an iterative string of commands:

> You shall possess the good of the earth and sun . . . there are millions
>   of suns left,
> You shall no longer take things at second or third hand, . . . nor look
>   through the eyes of the dead . . . nor feed on the specters in books,
> You shall not look through my eyes either, nor take things from me,
> You shall listen to all sides and filter them from yourself.   (PP 28)

or as an inventory of social interactions:

> Trippers and askers surround me,
> People I meet . . . the effect upon me of my early life . . . of the ward
>   and city I live in . . . of the nation,
> The latest news . . . discoveries, inventions, societies . . . authors old
>   and new,
> My dinner, dress, associates, looks, business, compliments, dues[.]
>   (PP 29)

Indeed, the fabric of Whitman's poetry is a texture of paratactic threads, one list giving way to, or at times arrested by, another. In almost every instance, the list breaks off not as something complete but as a network temporarily abandoned, left for another movement of thought, another series of additions. Interminability, as Herrnstein Smith argues, is a formal consequence of parataxis, for "a generating principle that produces a paratactic structure cannot in itself determine a concluding point."[38] Herrnstein Smith points out that other structural principles can be used to bring about a conclusion, such as the employment of a thematic ending or a dramatic frame. In Whitman, however, those devices for conclusion are often missing, deliberately rejected, or replaced by the intersection of lists as multiple (and multiplying) textual systems. Parataxis is not simply a rhetorical or poetic device; in Whitman's hands, it becomes a formal condition for producing emergent networks of increasing complexity.

The centrality of parataxis in *Leaves of Grass*, as a mode of time travel attending to particulars while accumulating an ensemble, becomes dramatically clear in the first major catalogue of the 1855, one that remained in the subsequently entitled "Song of Myself." In the 1891–2 edition, this encyclopedia makes up almost the entirety of the fifteenth section of the poem. While it is largely a list of persons, those out of whom "one and all I weave the song of myself," there are several important points in the catalogue that show it should not be read as simply a metonymic description of "types" or "representative people." Instead, there are indications throughout to suggest that each element is irreducible to categories or stock figures, despite the obvious fact that there are many individuals who can participate in the activities delineated: "The pure contralto sings in the organ loft, / The carpenter dresses his plank, the tongue of his foreplane whistles its wild ascending lisp, / The married and unmarried children ride home to their Thanksgiving dinner" (PP 200). There are undoubtedly many contraltos, organ lofts, and Thanksgiving dinners in the America of 1855, and the poem could be accused here of engaging in an act of kitschy national symbolism. But idealized representation, let alone a national imaginary, ceases to apply when the list encounters "The lunatic" who "is carried at last to the asylum a confirm'd case, / (He will never sleep any more as he did in the cot in his mother's bed-room)" (PP 200). The parenthetical aside tears the lunatic from the category of "all madmen," and transforms the term into a moment of particularity: *this* lunatic. For not all lunatics sleep in cots in their mother's bedroom, and that detail, suggesting a complex family drama, refines the paratactic focus, shifting the poem from the representative to the deictic, creating a pointing gesture, not an idealization. Such deictic precision can then be extended to all the other elements in the catalogue: the poet is writing of *this* spinning-girl, *this* "jour printer with gray head and gaunt jaws," *this* "young sister [who] holds out the skein while the elder sister winds it off in a ball" (PP 200–2). The poem uses categorical names to indicate particulars designated by that name, the same way "To You" is written to all the persons hailed by "Whoever you are." The result is necessarily incomplete, shot through with virtual potential; by the catalogue's own logic it could extend indefinitely, as no two carpenters or lunatics is identical, each deserving his own "endless announcements!" (PP 184).

In the case of section 15 of "Song of Myself," Whitman generates his catalogue with the definite article "the" as an iterative mechanism, and the visual effect of this repetition on the printed page is dramatic:

The pilot seizes the king-pin, he heaves down with a strong arm,
The mate stands braced in the whale-boat, lance and harpoon are ready,
The duck-shooter walks by silent and cautious stretches,
The deacons are ordain'd with cross'd hands at the alter,
The spinning-girl retreats and advances to the hum of the big wheel.

(PP 200)

The eye is arrested by the column of "The," an element of the poetics only accessible in writing. In other lists, Whitman uses nouns ("Land of coal and iron! land of gold! land of cotton sugar rice!"), imperative verbs ("See, steamers steaming through my poems, / See, in my poems immigrants continually coming and landing"), and prepositions ("Over the growing sugar, over the yellow-flower'd cotton plant, over the rice in its low moist field") (PP 184, 187, 220). The catalogues of *Leaves of Grass* are thus fundamentally grammatical and writerly in their generation. The properties of language produce these lists as a mode of internal emergence, giving body to Whitman's call for "a word to clear one's path ahead endlessly!" (PP 188). The poem turns on the structurally coupled relationship between the iterative potential of language and the multiplicity of the world as such, an expanding reality requiring further textual expansion. Consequently, using Herrnstein Smith's terms, both thematic and structural components generate Whitmanian parataxis. Thematically, Whitman's insistence that each particular is a miracle forces a preoccupation with individuals, while structurally Whitman uses the repetition of individual words to provide a link in the paratactic chain. Syntax becomes a mechanism for navigating a universe of miraculous particulars, a flexible literary device that allows the poem to enact an emergent map or "tally." James E. Miller calls the latter word "a Whitman favorite for describing the poetic function, and it comes closer in meaning to *embodying* or *comprehending* than to merely *listing* or *enumerating*."[39] From the perspective of emergent systems, embodying and comprehending can occur *by* listing and enumerating, as the iterative and recursive processes generate a form that makes visible the world in its own complex unfolding.

Or, to use Robert Duncan's terms, the difference is between the "reflective" and the "adventurous": "I have chosen to address myself to the 'adventure' of Whitman's line with the sense of the difference between the poem of introspection or reflection and the adventuring poem, between the recollection of consciousness, for instance, brought forward in the poetry of Wordsworth, and the advance of consciousness beyond itself."[40] Duncan sidesteps the common reading of Whitman's verse as an "epic of the self," a *record* of the journey of the soul whose coherence relies upon the life of the individual poet, as in the case of Wordsworth's *Prelude*. Instead, the paratactical, adventurous writing found in *Leaves of Grass* exceeds the self, becomes a linguistic mechanism for endless inquiry structurally coupled to the self. Situated on the edge of transformation, the time traveler's map remains unfinished.

That incomplete map is acknowledged explicitly in the late poems. The late "Now Precedent Songs, Farewell," offers a retrospective hymn to the hymns that continues the theme of travel through change. In the poem, *Leaves* as a whole is figured as something of a pioneer adventure: "Now precedent songs, farewell – by every name farewell, / (Trains of a staggering line in many a strange procession, waggons, / From ups and downs – with intervals – from elder years, mid-age, or youth)" (PP 634). The "staggering line" of wagon trains may elicit overly nostalgic recollections of American expansion, but the image clearly implies that the "precedent songs" constitute a loose but continuous alignment, made up of independently existing yet collected parts. More wagons can be added to the line, can make up different "strange processions," and the train can be reordered in various ways. Even more telling, the unity that is the train navigates, travels through time and space, without any conclusive gesture or destination. It is a collective effort of journey, a mechanism for wandering when one lacks a permanent domicile. Elsewhere, to be sure, Whitman speaks of the text in more absolute and completed terms, describing the book, for instance, in "A Backward Glance o'er Travel'd Roads" as "now finish'd to the end of its opportunities and powers," his "definitive *carte visite* to the coming generations of the New World" (PP 656). Nevertheless, it is clear that, at least in "Now Precedent Songs, Farewell," Whitman presents his own book as a self-transforming unity for voyage.

These figures of the road, travel, and journey challenge a stable framework for Whitman's America and democracy, let alone his celebration of life, the organicism of his leaves. Images of the open road suggest that travel is an adaptive process whose transformation within time is inevitably emergent as it engages with the changing environment to which it is structurally coupled. Moreover, a staggering line of wagons is a far cry from the form/life relationship articulated by Coleridge and perpetuated by Emerson. Such a prospect of endless continuity through change seems incredible (or terrifying, depending on one's disposition), and Whitman's speaker admits as much when, in the late "By Broad Potomac's Shore," he writes, "again old tongue, / (Still uttering, still ejaculating, canst never cease this babble?)" (PP 591). The incredulity of the speaker points to the fact that, in many respects, *he* is not speaking. Instead, the poem as an enactive organism is the "old tongue," carrying him forward in its own logic, performing the ongoing processes in language it has set out for itself. To write the particular all, to rupture the plenitude of the symbol and the logic of narrative, to chart the map, is to embark on an interminable quest. In many respects, the risk of emergent poetics is indeed that of babble. Attempting to bring form and meaning to a multiplying world may, in the end, merely result in being carried away by the mass of language itself. And yet that risk does not preclude the undertaking because the poem is already dangerous business, a fact Whitman saw from the beginning: "I launch all men and women forward with me into the Unknown" (PP 238). The poet cannot say where the iterations and recursions of the emergent catalogue will end, just as an organism cannot anticipate the perturbations of its environment.

By reading *Leaves of Grass* as an emergent text, I have attempted to complicate and clarify our understanding of Whitman's variant of romantic organicism, as well as his use of terms such as "America" and "democracy." The discourse of emergence thus allows us to resituate Whitman within his own literary and historical context. But this approach also helps us connect *Leaves of Grass* with later moments in American poetics, simultaneously distinguishing and structurally coupling long poems of romanticism and modernism to establish new networks of affiliation across literary history. In the next chapter, I extend my account of emergent poetics by turning to Pound's *Cantos*, redeploying the key terms that have informed this chapter – iteration, recursion, environmental coupling, and provisional closure – while also elaborating other concepts, like the feedback loop. Where Whitman develops emergent strategies under the sign of the organic, Pound's emergence comes into being through the modernist ideals of the poet as craftsperson or technician. At the same time, reading *Leaves* through the framework of autopoietic enaction reveals the underlying mechanisms of Whitman's organicism, ultimately troubling the organic/inorganic distinction. This approach suggests a connection between Whitman's practice and the explicit embrace of the machine found in modernist aesthetics. Indeed, Pound's project shares a key word with Whitman's own poetics, namely translation, another term that crossed the mechanic and the organic by establishing an intimacy between form and process, text and environment. By reading for emergence, we see that Whitman's leaves of grass have more in common with Pound's translation machines than we might initially suppose.

CHAPTER 3

Emergent Vocabulary
Ezra Pound's Translation Machine

Modernism trafficked in machines: dynamos and music machines, reading machines and writing machines, driving machines and flying machines.[1] The dynamism, power, objectivity, and efficiency of mechanical devices served as an ideal figure for many modernist projects. In a famous example, F. T. Marinetti's Futurist manifesto praises "the beauty of speed" in the automobile and celebrates violent "shipyards . . . , greedy railway stations . . . , [and] factories hung on clouds by the crooked lines of their smoke."[2] In contrast to Marinetti's aggressive machines, William Carlos Williams admired mechanical efficiency. "[There's] nothing sentimental about a machine," he claimed, and a "poem is a small (or large) machine made of words."[3] The absence of sentimentality means that the poem as machine can possess "no part . . . that is redundant."[4] Williams's efficient machine anticipates, somewhat surprisingly, the literary values of New Criticism. W. K. Wimsatt and Monroe C. Beardsley argued that a poem succeeds when "what is irrelevant has been excluded, like lumps from pudding and 'bugs' from machinery."[5] Alongside this explicit discourse of machine aesthetics within modernism, scholarly responses *to* modernism have called attention to the way new technologies, whether the movie projector or the automobile, transformed affective experience and artistic values. An origin point for this tradition would be Walter Benjamin's famous argument regarding technical reproduction, while more recent work in media studies focuses on the way technologies of transmission influenced modernist authors.[6]

Systems theory, with its emphasis on adaptive, emergent, and environmentally coupled mechanisms, offers a fresh approach to this modernist tradition of machine poetics. Within a few decades of Williams and Benjamin, cybernetic thinkers were pursuing increasingly dynamic, complex versions of machines, characterized less by efficiency and more by responsive environmental engagement.[7] By taking these alternative models of the machine as a starting point, modernist celebrations of the machine might appear in a new light; that is, we can reconceptualize modernism as an historically specific aesthetic. Such an approach allows us to create transhistorical links as well. Since emergence bridges the machine and the organic, the concept suggests continuities between nineteenth-century organic poets, such as Whitman, and twentieth-century machine practitioners, including, as I shall argue, Ezra Pound. As this chapter demonstrates, instead of privileging efficiency and sentimentality, as does Williams, Pound's text is a modernist machine capable of producing adaptability, surprise, and experimental excess. *The Cantos* prompt us to ask a new question: what characterizes an *emergent* machine made out of words?

Pound's work reflects the many permutations of the modernist machine. When Pound endorsed the Vorticist manifestos published in the pages of *Blast* 1 (1914), he opposed certain versions of modernist machine aesthetics, most notably Futurism. Pound and Wyndham Lewis express disdain for Marinetti's technofetishism, what they refer to as "AUTOMO-BILISM . . . a hullo-bulloo about motor cars."[8] However, in their calls for a uniquely English art, one that grows as "a northern flower," technology plays a critical metaphorical role: "[our] industries, and the Will that determined, face to face with its needs, the direction of the modern world, has reared up steel trees where the green ones were lacking; has exploded in useful growths, and found wilder intricacies than those of Nature."[9] The English industrial revolution exceeds organic complexity, generating a supplement that actually supplants. Later, they write that "[machinery] is the greatest Earth-medium," and through this "mechanical inventiveness" the English have created the conditions for "new possibilities of expression in present life."[10] Art extends the machine's creative potential, inspiring the Vorticist without prompting the worship of the Futurist.

Pound's aesthetic and personal development beyond the Vorticist movement is well-documented, and the claims of the Vorticists cannot be taken as an *ars poetica* of *The Cantos*.[11] Still, these early texts clearly indicate that Pound's art deliberately engaged the modernist machine. Keeping this background in mind, in what follows I read *The Cantos* as an emergent example of what Brian McHale has called a "bachelor machine," one of the crucial, although at times neglected, genealogies of modernist machine aesthetics.[12] "Bachelor machines," as McHale argues, are "machines of reproduction and simulation: writing-machines, imaging-machines, duplicating-machines."[13] These machines sit on "the margins of mainstream modernism" while anticipating certain aspects of postmodern art.[14] McHale makes a passing reference to *The Cantos* as a bachelor machine, a version of "writing through" wherein a source text is transformed into another poem.[15] Picking up McHale's suggestion, my reading of Pound's bachelor machine demonstrates that the form of the poem is inseparable from the enactive process of generating a new language that, in turn, will become both the material and model of later texts. In Pound's work, each Canto recursively adapts the vocabulary from the previous Cantos, using this text as a machine for processing new material. *The Cantos* develop their form by taking an initial text, like *The Odyssey*, and translating it into a new language. This new language, in turn, is used to translate a text like Robert Browning's *Sordello*, with Homer and Browning together producing a vocabulary for reading Ovid's *Metamorphosis*. The resulting poetic form is an emergent poetic vocabulary, establishing a framework for interpreting new events and texts while generating a dynamically evolving and networked archive.

I borrow the notion of "poetic vocabulary" from Barrett Watten, who uses the concept to extend Williams's "machine made out of words."[16] As a substitute for the concept of poetic diction (language deemed "appropriate" for poetic expression), poetic vocabulary is "the notion that a poem can be *made* of a predetermined, objectified 'language,'" a "constructivist use."[17] Poetic vocabulary shifts the origin of poetic meaning from the poet's "expressive use" into "an autonomous existence whose horizons of meaning will be engaged but not determined by the poet."[18] Watten argues that Louis Zukofsky's "*A-9*" is the "inaugural moment of the creation of 'new meaning' by the use of a predetermined poetic vocabulary in American literature."[19] Watten's description of Zukofsky's text both illustrates the deployment of a poetic vocabulary and serves as a point of comparison to Pound's own methods:

> In the first half of the poem . . . , Zukofsky translates Guido Cavalcanti's canzone "Donna mi prega" (used as a touchstone for value in Pound's *Cantos*) into a vocabulary taken from the Everyman edition of Karl Marx's *Kapital*. In the second half of the poem, Zukofsky rewrites his original Marxist commitments by retranslating the same canzone into a vocabulary taken from Benedict Spinoza's writings.[20]

Watten's argument is that "Zukofsky's use of translation . . . is not to simplify a complex and unstable original but to reorient its claim to value and meaning," a transformation that occurs when "the *source text* (Cavalcanti) is rewritten by means of a 'poetic vocabulary' toward a *target form*; the value of the resulting poem is a synthesis of its prior languages."[21]

Zukofsky's use of poetic vocabulary parallels Pound's own textual methods – and it is striking that Watten's "inaugural moment" should deploy a common source text with Pound.[22] Questions of direct influence aside, Pound's translation machine "processes" outside texts through myriad strategies to generate the poetic vocabulary for subsequent additions to the poem. Pound's practice, less restricted than Zukofsky's, thus develops an *emergent* poetic vocabulary wherein the distinction between source and target is productively blurred. Each Canto directs attention, leading Pound to new textual materials for processing, while also becoming a repository of formal strategies that recursively shape the construction of the later Cantos. In other words, each moment in *The Cantos* becomes both source and target, generating an unanticipated poetic vocabulary through a constructivist feedback loop. The poetic output becomes a new input.

Approaching Pound's *Cantos* as a machine that generates an adaptive poetic vocabulary also allows us to reinterpret Franco Moretti's theory of mechanical construction. As explored in the previous chapters, many of our traditional models of organic form treat the work as a unitary whole, while for mechanical form the work presents itself in discrete, fabricated, and somewhat arbitrary pieces. According to Moretti, works like Goethe's *Faust* and Pound's *Cantos* present a "form that may be cut at will [and] . . . be *added* to at will."[23] The logic of addition suggests the assembly line, an accumulation of discrete elements. However, Moretti argues that this artistic practice ultimately prompted a need to "relearn how to 'conceive the whole,'" and he turns to Edgar Morin's language of emergence to conceptualize this transformation: the organized whole possesses "emerging qualities . . . [that] are empirically observable, but . . . not logically deducible. Such emerging qualities retroact upon the parts, and may stimulate the latter to express their potentialities."[24] Moretti's turn to emergence implies a conclusion that he does not fully articulate. Complex mechanical form is not only transformed by an arbitrary "will"; rather, the textual system can self-organize through the interaction between its internal procedures and external environmental. Additions and exclusions are the result of the poem's own iterative, recursive, and emergent processes, which, in turn, make visible the changing historical context in which the poem exists. In the case of *The Cantos*, we can see this responsiveness to environmental change most clearly when the poem allows Pound to "see" and interpret traumatic, unexpected events, like his incarceration in Pisa. These environmental disruptions, in turn, reconfigure the vocabulary of the translation machine.

Finally, reading *The Cantos* as translation machine allows us to reexamine the intractability of Pound's work, explaining why readers struggle with it and why it is important. *The Cantos* may be one of the major texts of twentieth-century Anglo-American poetry, but it is also one of the most unreadable. The poem troubles and repels us, in part because it does not conform to our commonplace models of textuality. The work seems to promise modern epic adaptations but, like a malformed repetition, scatters and disperses into endless reformations. At times the poem captivates us with its lyrical control, but then it devolves into blocks of prosaic text or dirty jokes. Even more troubling, *The Cantos* unsettle us because it is undeniably a work shot through with political violence, the anger of an avowed fascist and anti-Semite who cannot hide his contempt for certain developments within modernity. As this chapter attempts to make sense of *The Cantos* on the level of its emergent structure, Pound's politics cannot be ignored.[25] As I suggest in the conclusion, however, Pound's practice – of reinterpretation and rewriting – models a critical response to his political commitments, a procedure that would be taken up by later poets seeking to correct his fascist politics through new practices of writing in real time. Reading Pound for emergence thus allows us to clarify his position within modernist machine aesthetics, situate his practice within the tradition of the long poem, and, finally, better understand the complex relationship between his textual practice and cultural values.

I Translation, Performance, Improvisation

The poetics of the translation machine are evident from the opening lines of Pound's work. Consider the beginning, simultaneously an input and output, a poem structurally coupled to an external text:

> And then went down to the ship,
> Set keel to breakers, forth on the godly sea, and
> We set up mast and sail on that swart ship,
> Bore sheep aboard her, and our bodies also
> Heavy with weeping, and winds from sternward
> Bore us out onward with bellying canvas,
> Circe's this craft, the trim-coiffed goddess.[26]

These opening lines are appealing on a first read. They seem to cohere in their own right, and we find ourselves in the relatively recognizable world of narrative and heroic verse. At the same time, the opening lines instigate an unstable *process* of writing, disrupting the poem's apparent conventionality and calling attention to the activity of poem-as-translation. Like the traditional epic, Pound's text begins *in media res*, with the narrative already in progress. But epics typically demonstrate this convention on the level of narrative action: the battle is already underway when the poet begins his tale. In contrast, Pound's opening lines begin so abruptly that there is a clear grammatical precondition to the poem, with other sentences and verses evoked virtually with that initiating "And." In other words, grammatical incompleteness at the outset shows that *The Cantos*, unlike earlier epics, does not begin in the middle of ongoing action but is a linguistic phenomenon, an act of transmission and transformation in textual history. The ontology of this opening line is not the storyworld of fiction, nor the past events of history, but the virtual, literary space of writing. By translating another text, disrupting its prior existence and incorporating it into a new textual system, Pound effectively draws a distinction between source and target, input and output, opening up the possibility for new acts of composition.

The appearance of Circe in line 7 identifies that literary space as Homer's *Odyssey*, but, as Hugh Kenner and other scholars have pointed out, there is more than one text operating within this translation machine. The sound of the poem recalls the Anglo-Saxon metrics of Pound's earlier rendition of "The Seafarer," and so "the earliest English ('Seafarer' rhythms and diction)" carves "the earliest Greek" into the shape of modern English, "the beginnings of the 20th-century Vortex."[27] In other words, Canto I establishes a network of translations, where more than one text is at work constituting the new poem. When these intersecting sources are taken into account, the aesthetic work of the poem cannot be located merely, or even primarily, in the speaker's actions but in the self-conscious linguistic construction that deliberately unites and transforms these disparate textual histories. The form of *The Cantos* becomes the emerging processes of this interactive multitextual network.

As a result, the text of Canto I is replete with movement, ghosting cross-cultural and intertextual transmission behind the apparent and immediate narrative action of ships and sails. Those processes become more evident as the canto continues: "And then Anticlea came. / Lie quiet Divus. I mean, that is, Andreas Divus, / In officina Wecheli, 1538, out of Homer" (C 5). Pound relies on Divus, a Renaissance translator who rendered Homer into Latin, to construct his own translation. Calling explicit attention to the vocabulary of that source text, even if only to subdue it, adds a fourth layer to the translating act. That Pound uses Divus is less remarkable than his act of integrating, into the poem, the traces of that use in the form of direct references to names and publication dates. In doing so, he brings into focus not only the preconditions of his own poetic discourse but also the generative processes by which that discourse comes into existence. Translation, after all, is a form of literary iteration and recursion, establishing and extending a network of textuality. Pound's poem contains history because it structurally couples itself to the earlier translations that have made it possible, integrating these past moments into its form. In this way, *The Cantos* become emergent: the form of the poem is the unexpected, second-order structure generated by the processes of translation, a continuously expanding textual network unpredictably arising from the initial conditions of the source material.

Consequently, Pound's translation machine cannot be measured by rigorous philological methods; instead, the machine is closer to a creative performance. Kenner has called this performance "mimetic homage," wherein each translation retains a "stubborn reminder that transposition, not recreation, is going on, that the mind remains anchored in these times, not those."[28] Such stubborn reminders of the present performance creep up everywhere in *The Cantos*, from Seafarer rhythms, to Divus's rebuke, to American slang placed in the mouth of Italian Renaissance nobles, to the Greek "*krēdemnon*," a disputed word for some sort of shawl that becomes, in Pound's rendition, the flagrantly anachronistic "bikini."[29] Reading *The Cantos* as a complex adaptive system complicates Kenner's account, however, as Pound's performance is not merely to show his own ingenuity or "modernize" the past. Instead, the poem reconfigures the texts of the past by perpetually linking these texts to other moments of writing. We might be tempted to think of a palimpsest here, but Kenner's performance is more telling: "We are to stay aware [when reading *The Cantos*], in short, of a performance by a man in a particular place and time, in the presence of particular ancient models" and translation, "once this principle is understood, becomes merely a special case of the act of writing."[30] *The Cantos* are thus an active poetic practice that generates a form inseparable from the contours of the history it transforms. The mimetic homage recreates both the old text and the new performance, establishing "*krēdemnon*" and "bikini" within a second-order, emergent network.

Exceeding Kenner's notions of performance and translation, Pound's use of the literary past is a constructivist mode of *improvisation*, a writing in real time that emphasizes unpredictable outcomes through the engagement with preexisting material (earlier moments in the system) and new inputs (external texts being integrated into the translation machine). As Edgar Landgraf argues, improvisation relies on an interaction with earlier conditions of meaning, including prior texts and iterations of the artistic system. For Landgraf, "the known and predictable define the conceptual horizon that limits and simultaneously enables the recognition of inventiveness in improvisation" and "[it] is in this sense that an improvised performance is always already mediated by the (cultural) knowledge that limits the space of its possibility."[31] In Pound's case, the textual history of *The Odyssey* becomes a space of possibility for further operations, in turn generating the "new space" of Canto I, out of which other improvisatory translations can emerge. Through these iterative spaces of possibility, what has come before does not fully determine the next addition to the poem but creates the context, the "conceptual horizon," within which the new writing occurs. This adaptive translation machine thus includes inputs, outputs, feedback loops, and unpredictable, even risky, results. As Landgraf notes, "the incalculable in improvisation (and art) is the result of 'calculation' in the broader sense, that is, not of the implementation of plans or rules, but of processes and strategies that, calculating incalculability, are able to construct unpredictable outcomes."[32] Such a space directs attention, giving Pound, in this case, a hermeneutic orientation, helping him establish patterns of meaning within a changing environment.

By integrating Kenner's early insights regarding performance into this emergent model of improvisatory translation machines, the fundamental generative form of *The Cantos* comes into clearer focus. As Pound translates past linguistic artifacts into new poems, his work actively revises these texts. This process, as the example of Canto I demonstrates, generates new vocabularies that in turn are used to process other texts, allowing both the vocabulary and form of *The Cantos* to emerge across forty years of open composition. Consequently, the work as a whole retains an unmistakable provisional quality (the first major volume of collected *Cantos* was titled, after all, *Drafts of XXX Cantos*) even as it produces a dynamic formal identity over time. In principle, any text or document can be integrated into this endlessly generative machine; in practice, however, the accidents of history and library shelves – those environmental perturbations – fundamentally influenced the evolution of Pound's work. For this reason, *The Cantos* dramatically self-modify as they go forward, even as the accumulative whole produces a formal identity.

Reading the form of Pound's work as an emergent translation machine allows us to rearticulate some of the central critical debates surrounding the poem's structure, debates that raise fundamental questions about the nature of language. Although it is difficult to make any generalization about the tenor of Pound criticism, given its vast scope, two modes of reading the poem's structure dominate the field. These two approaches often result in mutually exclusive conceptions of the text's aesthetics, and yet both find supporting evidence in Pound's personal, political, and aesthetic archive. As an added difficulty, both approaches, when applied with sufficient rigor, can offer coherent accounts of *The Cantos*, despite their contradictory emphases. For the sake of simplicity, I call these two critical orientations "referential" and "textualist."

A referential approach to the poem seeks to identify a unifying architecture holding together Pound's multiple textual outputs, a master code that provides a coherent ground for his work. The sources for such a master code are varied. In autobiographical readings, that textual center is Pound himself. Ronald Bush glosses Eliot's description of *The Cantos* as "reticent biography" to mean a "dramatization of a sensibility in the process of understanding itself," an approach that places the unity of the poem in Pound's self-reflexive mind.[33] Other referential readings of the text rely heavily on Pound's interest in "right words," good economics, and sound government, or in Pound's avowed fascism, often interpreting *The Cantos* as a rhetorical treatise advocating these principles. Michael André Bernstein describes the poem as an "explicit series of specific recommendations to both ruler and ruled."[34] In a related approach, some critics identify a single trope by which the poem develops. Stephen Sicari, although conceding that the text reflects a certain elasticity, centers the poem on the figure of "the epic wanderer whose journey strains toward order amidst the seeming anarchy of Western history," a unifying device derived from Dante.[35] Finally, many have claimed that *The Cantos* are an aesthetic failure by measuring it according to a generic code, demonstrating that it does not adequately adhere to its formal models. Several of Pound's earliest critics, working out of a strict mythic or narrative conception of epic poetry, made such an assessment, attempting to use the traditional epic form as the aesthetic standard against which the poem was declared to be unsuccessful.[36]

In contrast to these referential approaches, a textualist reading emphasizes the fragmentary, clashing, and unstable surface of the page with its many signsystems. Marjorie Perloff's analysis in *Poetics of Indeterminacy* is the canonical example of such an approach. Perloff argues that "the basic strategy in the *Cantos* is to create a flat surface, as in a cubist or early Dada collage, upon which verbal elements . . . are brought into collision."[37] In such a text, the referent sought by other readers of the poem, while not entirely "cut off," is "subordinated" to the surface of the signifier.[38] Thus, for instance, a section like the Malatesta Cantos does not "recreate history"; instead, the poem "decompose[s] and fragment[s] historical time and action so as to draw the 'events' recorded into the world of the text."[39] This textual world becomes the only world with which *The Cantos* are concerned, according to Perloff, one that does not fundamentally derive its meaning from some historical or referential order. Text, language, and the sign *qua* sign trump the grounding desires of a signified. The textualist Canto holds our interest as an appearance, not as a representation.

As basic coordinates in the critical field, these two approaches have numerous variations. The binary between text and referent can be formulated in a number of ways, and most critical maneuvers around *The Cantos* privilege one side over the other. This disagreement over Pound's work conceals a more complex problem, one burdened with substantial philosophical weight, and for this reason the alternating approaches to the poem are significant not simply in what they do individually but in their dialectical relationship. For understanding the poem's structure leads one to reconsider fundamental debates about the status of the sign in Western thought and poetic writing, the fraught relationship between meaning and transmission. Systems thinking can provide some clarity on this point, as these two approaches differ primarily on the level of structural coupling. For textualists, the referential world to which language refers becomes inconsequential, while for referentialists, the text itself tends to be subordinated to some other dominant system within the external world, whether the system of author, ideology, or historical context. Translation as emergent performance and cultural revision offers a way to reimagine this relationship, drawing together the two critical orientations. For translation is something of a scandal, particularly when it presents itself as an original work and as a translation *at the same time*. Such a text violates both the logic of the referent and the materiality of the sign, for although the text is no longer entirely faithful to its origins, neither is it merely an autonomous entity, a surface lacking external signification. A poem that functions as an emergent translation machine opens up a space for thought and poetry *between* texts and the complexity of a material world that resists closure and autonomy: every work of value, according to Pound, deserves to be rewritten. In Pound's case, this rewriting connects text to text, producing an emergent network of writing that disrupts the singularity of both the textualist and referentialist traditions. Neither stable reference nor text as sign fully account for this dynamism.

Several decades ago, Joseph Riddel used the language of deconstruction to describe this metamorphic element of the text. According to Riddel, Pound's interest in the "luminous detail" (a clear concern for the referentialists) does not require a metaphysical source of meaning outside language. Instead, the luminous detail was "metaphor itself," which "maintains relations by multiplying analogies, therefore resisting any reduction of analogy to a unified field theory."[40] There cannot be a single "underlying order" to these performances, only a revelation of "the disturbing metamorphic work (form-making and form-destroying) of language."[41] Riddel's risk, however, is to remove language from history and reference altogether, ignoring how language is constantly interacting with a world outside of itself. Reading the text as a complex adaptive system accounts for this structural coupling with the environment, returning us to Pound's own acute attention to history. There are too many material and historical remnants marking *The Cantos*, too many transmissional remainders revealing that language, for all of its constructive and destructive metaphorical power, functions in a complex world constituted by other systems – human bodies, economic orders, physical objects, and the traditions of art. As an emergent translation machine, Pound's text makes visible both the worldly work of textual production and the many environments in which those texts are embedded, where they are appropriated, transformed, recast, and shaped. From this perspective, *The Cantos* demonstrate a radical affirmation of the activity of poetic thinking as poetic writing, offering an aesthetics of real time that often runs contrary to Pound's own ideological and philosophical commitments.

II Ways of Making It New

The specific processes of the translation machine vary throughout Pound's text. Although not all passages have the concentrated multitextual blending of Canto I, each of *The Cantos* enacts translation, retransmission, or revision in some way.[42] As the poem progresses, the density and scope of the poetic vocabulary increases, as the elements of earlier revisions become the tools by which new texts are read. A reading of *The Cantos* as emergent machine thus becomes a reading of these processes of textual transformation, the ways in which Pound manufactures his own idiosyncratic modernism. Tracing the adaptations and evolutions in Pound's procedures also helps us explain the multigeneric properties of the work, its participation in epic, lyric, confessional, historiographic, and philological discourses, among many others.

One of Pound's common translating tactics produced some important lyrical moments in *The Cantos*, namely the imagistic revisions of source texts. Pound was a consummate lyricist, and on the level of free verse sound and imagery – what he called "melopoeia" and "phanopoeia"[43] – his skills were understandably praised. This form of translational performance allowed him to generate early tropes and images that were then deployed, often for very different and surprising ends, in later Cantos. Such an instance is Canto II, which recreates a tale from Ovid's *Metamorphosis*.[44] The poem begins with an evocation of Browning's *Sordello* (Pound's most immediate predecessor in long poetics), moving through Pound's own invented Asian deities, Aeschylus's *Agamemnon*, some cribs from *The Iliad*, and the tale of Tyro, encountered in *The Odyssey*.[45] *The Metamorphosis* haunts much of *The Cantos*, not only as a source of mythological figures but also as a figure for translation itself. In the particular tale retold in Canto II, would-be slave traders unknowingly capture Dionysius as a young boy; as punishment, they are turned into porpoises, and the ship is overrun with grape vines and wild cats, traditional symbols for the wine god. The ancient tale is remade through twentieth-century imagist technique:

> The sky overshot, dry, with no tempest,
> Sniff and pad-foot of beasts,
>   fur brushing my knee-skin,
> Rustle of airy sheaths,
>   dry forms in the *aether*.
> And the ship like a keel in ship-yard,
>   slung like an ox in smith's sling,
> Ribs stuck fast in the ways,
>   grape-cluster over pin-rack,
>   void air taking pelt.   (C 8)

The spondaic repetitions reinforce the semantic compression of compound phrases, both techniques that characterized Pound's lyrical poetry: "pad-foot," "knee-skin," "grape-cluster." The syntactic leaps of these lines, essentially a collection of grammatical fragments hung together through the imagined scene and narrative, mediate the outbursts of energy described in the scene to produce the imagistic effect of both movement and stasis. The metamorphic and metric qualities of a line like "void air taking pelt" can be read as a distant sonic cousin to Pound's "Petals on a wet, black bough," albeit in a very different metaphysical register.[46]

Despite these similarities in technique, a critical textual relationship in Canto II is absent from "In a Station of the Metro." For the former imagistic composition effectively *reads* Ovid, while the latter poem requires no immediate text other than itself for justification, a metaphor drawn from the natural world to describe a decidedly unmythic moment of human perception. Pound's pelts are acting in the world of language and textual transmission in a way that his petals are not. It is here that the referential elements of the poem become significant. Were one to read *The Cantos* through Pound's own ideological commitments, one could note, following Lawrence Rainey, that Pound wanted to bring about a new paganism to follow the Christian era that he saw ending with Joyce's *Ulysses*, and the Dionysian ethos was a central value in that revised religion.[47] Such a reading would point out that an imagistic retelling of the myth seeks to convey that theology aesthetically, the poetry of a new dispensation attempting to show twentieth-century readers the gods who "float in the [present] azure air" as well as the gods as they are represented in the Ovidian text (C 11). For this reason, the translation machine's revision of an old text and an old world through modern poetic technique is vitally necessary for the didactic inauguration of a new one, demonstrating that an emergent textuality becomes the condition for a complex, transhistorical referentiality. Text and referent are structurally coupled, entangled in a mutually transforming process.

If in one Canto imagistic translation marries mythic paganism with modernity, in other Cantos translation is used to engage the mundane processes of political life. One of Pound's major aesthetic developments is the collage, most easily demonstrated in the famous mailbag of Canto IX. The technique represented in this Canto has been called "one of the decisive turning points in modern poetics,"[48] a poem often cited by readers like Perloff who are interested in the poetic equivalent of Cubist edges made visible through the juxtaposition of texts on a page. In collagist poetics we see Pound's transmissional focus most clearly, for, as Guy Davenport notes, "Pound, unlike Eliot or Coleridge, rarely appropriates a quoted line, but borrows it, frames it, and is careful to keep its identity [as a quotation], for its identity is its reason for being in the poem at all."[49] In *The Waste Land*, for instance, Eliot's quotations from Charles Baudelaire, Richard Wagner, and the Upanishads are transformed by the symbolic and mythic structure of the work, its momentary unification of the disparate fragments ostensibly justifying the repose of "Shantih shantih shantih."[50] Such an example of what Joseph Frank has called modernist "spatial form" arrests time, allowing *The Waste Land* to arrange its fragments into a semi-autonomous whole and ultimately transform them into a single aesthetic identity.[51] Pound, despite all of his rhetoric of wholeness, constantly disrupts any efforts at idealistic unification by highlighting the act of transmission in the work, making visible the source text and his creative revisions.

The post-bag of Canto IX reveals its historical journeys through a formal arrangement inspired by actual events drawn from the life of Sigismundo of Malatesta, one of the major hero-figures in the work. Among the numerous mishaps surrounding Malatesta's life was the theft of his mail while he was in the process of building his Tempio, the latter being for Pound an ideal architectural representation of the Italian Renaissance. The theft of the mailbag inspires Pound's crucial poetic innovation. "And this is what they found in the post-bag":[52]

> *Ex Arimino die xxii Decembris*
> *"Magnifice ac potens domine, mi singularissime*
> "I advise yr. Lordship how
> "I have been with master Alwidge who
> "has shown me the design of the nave that goes in the middle,
> "of the church and the design for the roof and . . . "
> "JHesus,
> *"Magnifico exso.* Signor Mio
> "Sence to-day I am recommanded that I have to tel you my
> "father's opinium that he has shode to Mr. Genare about the
> "valts of the cherch . . . etc . . .
> "Giovane of Master always P. S. I think it advisabl that
> "I shud go to rome to talk to mister Albert so as I can no
> "what he thinks about it rite.   (C 37–8)

Letters are a valuable asset for a "poem containing history," particularly those that include interactions between the patron, the designer, and the craftsman, all building an epic edifice like the Tempio. A monument of such expanse is not constructed without tremendous effort by many hands, a process of technique uniting Renaissance masters like Alberti, the "mister Albert" above who designed the Tempio, with nameless workers who, though far less literate, possess skills absolutely necessary for the work to be accomplished. Furthermore, a letter requesting additional instructions for specific operations, as does the second letter in the quoted passage, makes history present in a unique way, for the letter must be understood as part of the craft itself, an instrument used in the construction of the edifice. Language, here, is *in action*, the letter a textual tool employed to create art. Furthermore, letters also function like a system by iteratively and recursively producing spaces of difference and continuity. Letters thus serve as a figure for form within *The Cantos*, textual artifacts acquiring historical traces as they generate a network of language that is acting in the world.

Nevertheless, the actions of Sigismundo's letter are not fully present in the poem itself. For the letters are self-consciously changed through the workings of Pound's machine: we are not reading the physical manuscripts pasted onto the page nor even their facsimile reproduction, as we would in a Cubist collage where real Metro tickets are affixed to the canvas. Instead, the source material is transformed in a number of ways. First, the prose letters in this passage are turned into free verse lines, although elsewhere Pound reproduces entire passages of unlineated prose. Second, and more significantly, the letter is only partially translated. The greeting and mailing address in the first letter remain in Latin, the italicization marking them as foreign script. The Italian greeting "Signor mio," however, is left in roman type, as if it were English, or, more to the point, as if the writing were moving from an English to an Italian text. The most notable traces of the translation machine are found in the re-creation of the craftsman's letter, with its deliberate misspellings and homonymic renditions. Pound relies on such license elsewhere in the text, rendering the language of Italian nobles into American slang or Chinese history into Jazz Age vernacular. Each instance conveys some sense of Kenner's "mimetic homage," not a faithful translation of an original text but an improvised, performative response to the texture of the language in which that source poem is made.

This foregrounding of printing processes, poetic technique, and the material layout of the page makes the poem an instance of what N. Katherine Hayles calls a "technotext," when "a literary works interrogates the inscription technology that produces it" and thus "mobilizes reflexive loops between its imaginative world and the material apparatus [or, we might add, conditions of material reception and transmission] embodying that creation as a physical presence."[53] Jerome McGann detects a similar feedback loop in Pound's work: "[any] page of the *Cantos* immediately strikes one with its material weight and physique. . . . Letters, words, and phrasal units are treated as material things, so that we encounter the page both as configuration and as discourse."[54] Pound's page calls attention to itself as writing and language, as the physical facts of manuscripts, dialects, and misplaced letters as well as the cultural meanings attached to those utterances. Nearly every sentence in the post-bag section of the Canto is presented as an actual historical referent, proof that Sigismundo "lived and ruled" (C 41), and yet, to argue against a primarily referential approach to the text, each referent fails to be as central to the poem as the *act of referencing* itself, the writing-as-translation of the poetic process. But neither does Pound's work "subordinate" that referent, as Perloff tends to emphasize, turning *The Cantos* into a pure linguistic construction. For the textual fragments Pound translates were profoundly engaged with the world of living and ruling. Pound turns to language that was itself being used to recreate and transform the world – laying brick and constructing buildings. The adaptations of the translation machine thus offer an account of writing embedded within a material and aesthetic history.

Pound's work is not the only long poem of modernism interested in historical processes, of course. We might think of Zukofsky's *A*, Muriel Rukeyser's *Book of the Dead*, H. D.'s *Helen in Egypt*, William Carlos Williams's *Paterson*, Melvin Tolson's *Harlem Gallery*, or Eliot's *Waste Land*, each of which enacts a discrete poetics of history. How does Pound's emergent treatment of history compare to these different iterations of the modernist long poem on the level of form? While this question can only be answered on a case-by-case basis, reading *The Waste Land* and *The Cantos* together offers a useful illustration of the continuum of poetic emergence. These texts share more than a family resemblance. Pound had a significant influence on the development of Eliot's text from its initial conception as "He Do the Police in Different Voices." Indeed, the substantial revisions of Eliot's poem, as with most revisions, emerged through an iterative process, with repetitions and new drafts leading to the final version of the work. Similarly, Eliot's use of fragmentation, quotation, juxtaposition, and multilingualism was directly influenced by Pound's techniques, often prompting critics to see *The Cantos* as an overgrown version of the aesthetics found in *The Waste Land*.[55]

Despite these similarities, the most important difference between the two poems is that *The Waste Land* does not include iterative and recursive processes *within its form*. Consequently, the poem's representation of history does not share the emergent relationship to time that we find in *The Cantos*. Instead, closed form replaces the iteration of composition, offering a finished text wherein the original materials achieve meaning through the poem's complete structure, not through their adaptive, evolving relationship to an environment. Eliot's poem constrains history into a mythic and brilliant synthesis; the legend of the Fisher King, for instance, is a regulating force that allows Eliot to categorize historical events, linking the Arthurian world and modern Europe. Thus, while *The Waste Land* undoubtedly emerged through a process of revision and iteration, Eliot's form is one of completion, what we might call the spatialization of time, following Joseph Frank. In contrast, Pound's translation machine incorporates iteration within its form, generating acts of provisional closure within history that are reopened, reactivating processes of transformation, metamorphosis, and repetition. Where Eliot uses form to articulate his own time and its relationship to the past, Pound's text uses form to generate a constantly evolving relationship with time.

At the intersection of form and history, then, Eliot's modernism shares many of Pound's techniques, and yet his work departs significantly from the dynamic, immanent hermeneutic of *The Cantos*. Pound's translation machine made product and process inseparable, blurring the line between source text and target form to produce an emergent vocabulary in time. Both texts, in turn, are simply points in the larger networks of modernism and the long poem, existing in dynamic and singular relationships to both their period and that other form of history we call literature. Comparing the two reveals the distinctiveness of Pound's emergent historiography while also suggesting that literary modernism itself is a complex system – entangled, enacted, constantly subject to adaptations from within and perturbations from without.

III Accidental History

Reading *The Cantos* as an emergent translation machine allows us to take literally Pound's paradoxical statement that "one cannot exclude something [from *The Cantos*] merely because it didn't fit."[56] Including that which "does not fit" suggests that form *is* the process of adaptation and recursive transformation: the new addition retrospectively changes the previous iterations of the poem that have made it visible, just as a new translation expands the poetic vocabulary. This approach to poetic form calls attention to the ways in which language is inseparable from arbitrary and accidental events of writing, accidents that in turn generate meanings one cannot predict or control. By attempting to contain secular history,[57] Pound's text registers those accidents, embraces them as the structural preconditions for its own procedures. That Pound's embrace was a radical one has troubled many of his readers, not least the textual scholars who are faced with the daunting task of determining when Pound's notoriously idiosyncratic (if not outright "bad") translations of texts were intentional, used for some poetic or rhetorical effect, or merely a mistake, made either in ignorance, haste, or forgetfulness.

Christine Froula has intelligently addressed translation in *The Cantos* as both an editorial and philosophical problem by showing that for Pound the poem's own textual history and its open form are inseparable. In her study *To Write Paradise: Style and Error in Pound's* Cantos, Froula argues that Pound's poem demonstrates a "commitment to the struggle of transforming the traditional model of epic authority, transcendent and absolute, into a human and historical one."[58] A "human and historical" account is full of mistakes and dumb luck, not only on the level of social and individual action but also in language itself, in writing, publishing and printing. Any translation machine, in other words, will have bugs, ghosts, unexpected feedback loops within its processes. According to Froula, "the relations between epic wandering, modern history, and error in Pound's poem suggest that the modern epic differs categorically from earlier epics in that the wandering that defines the genre is no longer closed by any such plotted 'redemption' as concludes [other epics]."[59] Although Froula does not use the model of an adaptive, emergent system, her language suggests the interplay among process, form, and environment that we have been exploring in this study, concluding that *The Cantos* seek "to conceive history apart from the certainty of story and the closure of form," which is precisely why Pound was content to leave his "errors" as they were, to allow the contingencies of printing and proofs to remain in the published work.[60] Errors and contingency characterize an aesthetic of structural coupling, where the material conditions of textual production are inseparable from its poetics. For the translation machine, anything worth writing is worth transforming, and to send a poem containing history out into the world meant allowing the world to change that poem.

Just like the circulation of his poem in a world of accidents, Pound's own reading and rewriting, the input and output of the translation machine, is not prospectively predictable; in "an age of experiment," Pound told Donald Hall, one "can't follow the Dantesquan cosmos."[61] The order behind Dante's progressive rise from Inferno to Paradise eludes the modern writer. One challenging example of "accidental reading" is Pound's use of textual sampling, the key translation procedure of the "John Adams" Cantos. The Adams Cantos emerged from Pound's reading of *The Works of John Adams*, a ten-volume compendium edited by Adams's grandson Charles Francis Adams.[62] The peculiarities of publication impinge heavily on Pound's rendition of Adams's work – binding and print consistently trump historical chronology. Pound composes these Cantos not to reflect the temporal order of Adams's life but according to the contours of the ten volumes, which itself has its own history. For instance, Canto LXII and the start of Canto LXIII rely on the first volume of the *Works*, "a biography of John Adams by Charles Francis Adams, who used as his opening chapters the completed portion of a projected biography by John Quincy Adams."[63] The textual layering, one autobiography on top of another, does not go unremarked by Pound: at one point he playfully refers to a comment by "Chawles Fwancis" (C 342). The second part of Canto LXIII moves into Adams's own diary, published as a later volume of the *Works*, which brings one back to his early education, experiences in law school, and travels. This autobiographical time travel marks the remainder of the Adams Cantos, a writing of reading in time, not a historical chronology. The poem wanders through history as that history was printed; Adams's story does not unfold in causal order.

Pound's revision of Adams's life presents difficulties for interpretation not only in its strange chronology but also in its extreme fragmentation. Phrases are pulled from disparate passages in the original *Works* and arranged on the page as a series of free verse lines, often in such a way that the original meaning is dramatically changed. After opening Canto LXII with a summary and compression of Charles Francis's own disclaimer in the preface to the first volume of the *Works*, Pound goes on to summarize the history of the Adams family in America, one as material and textual as it is genealogical and political. Declarations ("TO THE GOVERNOR AND THE COMPANIE") intersect with latitudes ("40° to 48°") upon which grants ("ten head 40 acres at 3/ (shillings) per acre") become the seeds for family businesses ("at decease left a malting establishment") (C 341). The birth of John Adams occurs 20 lines, and 106 years of chronological time, after the beginning of the Canto. Or not quite. For Charles Francis published the *Works* between 1850 and 1856, and the preface to the autobiography must have been written shortly before that time. So, in fact, the 20 lines move from 1850 to 1628 to 1735, with the slightest hint, in line 13, of Pound's reading/writing, the first original contribution to the poem besides the unique arrangement of source material: "(abbreviated)" (C 341). The parenthetical aside, here nearly a diacritical mark, calls attention to the cutting and revising of the reader/writer as a compositional process. In no traditional sense could such dramatic cutting and pasting be considered history. Instead, we are reading history layered through an emerging poetic vocabulary: Ezra Pound's translation machine cantoing atop and within Charles Francis's biography, which itself was a repetition and revision of John Quincy's intended work, derived from the family narrative of texts and events at the founding of the American colonies. The local processes of each individual text generate emergent, unexpected configurations within the global space of Pound's system.

Through this process of sampling, textual discoveries expand the emerging poetic vocabulary of *The Cantos*. For instance, Charles Francis's own allusion to Cadmus, the founder of Thebes who built the city according to the myth by sowing dragon's teeth, does not go unnoticed by Pound: "Gent standing in his doorway got 2 balls in the arm / and five deaders 'never Cadmus . . .' etc / was more pregnant" (C 342). The original text, commenting on the "Boston massacre" of 1770, claims that the "drops of blood then shed in Boston were like the dragon's teeth of ancient fable – the seeds, from which spring up the multitudes who would recognize no arbitration but the deadly one of the battle-field."[64] Cadmus recurs throughout *The Cantos*, mentioned in passing in Canto II (C 9), evoked explicitly in Canto IV ("Cadmus of Golden Prows!" [C 13]), and later retooled into a figure for the Russian Revolution in the mouth of a laborer: "Me Cadmus sowed in the earth" (C 132). Pound's choice to quote Charles Francis's use of the legend of Cadmus in reference to the American Revolution thus links Troy, Russia, and America, adding one more possible signified to the signifier and expanding the breadth of the sign in the process. There is no single or foundational referent behind "Cadmus," merely a multitude of environments in which the term can be deployed and through which it acquires meaning. From one perspective, Pound's discovery of the legend of Cadmus in the first volume of the *Works* is purely coincidental, and yet, at the same time, the previous iterations of the legend in the poem recursively shape his attention as he reads the text, identifying this "accident" as meaningful by fitting it within the hermeneutic space that the text has produced. Iteration and recursion as twinned functions in the translation machine produce an emergent meaning of "Cadmus," one capable of further transformation.[65]

Within this context of an adaptive, emergent poetic vocabulary, the shifts in tone and focus found in the Pisan Cantos are not the dramatic reconceptualization of the poetic project that they are often taken to be.[66] Instead, the texts produced after Pound was incarcerated by Allied forces at the end of World War II turn the poem's gaze upon itself, assessing its own unfolding conditions of literary existence. This is not to say that the particular self-consciousness of Pisa was peaceful; undoubtedly, the Pisan Cantos are a record of poetic and personal rupture. But that break can be understood as the point at which the poem more deliberately embraces the radical consequences of its own practice, the gamble that a work can be undertaken both about history and within it, that it could unfold indefinitely and unexpectedly as an activity of writing in real time. Each instance of metamorphosis, that Dionysian trait Pound revisits throughout the work, must be necessarily unique while still continuous. From the perspective of poetic genesis, there may be no metamorphosis so remarkable in the development of *The Cantos* than the end of Mussolini's reign and Pound's arrest, for no longer could the poet wander through the libraries and texts of the past freely. Instead, he was confined to a cage, with only the books and manuscripts he could carry or, happily, find. Faced with surprising and unexpected environmental pressures, the poem inevitably had to change yet again.

Pound-as-poet realized this problem of change and transformation acutely, and the question of continuity in the face of tragedy occupies the opening, mournful lines of Canto LXXIV:

> Thus Ben and la Clara *a Milano*
>> by the heels at Milano
> That maggots shd/ eat the dead bullock
> DIGONOS, Δίγονος, but the twice crucified
>>> where in history will you find it?
>>>> (C 445)

One must not blink when reading these lines: they are the lament of a fascist, not for an error, but for a defeat. The dream of an earthly fascist "paradise" had fallen to the Allied armies. Yet it is striking to note the translation machine persistently engaging both old texts and present realities. Significantly, his attempts at revision in Pisa fail more often then they succeed; we might think of this passage as a near short-circuit of the machine's processes. "Ben" Mussolini was hung upside down after his death, doubly killed, as Pound figures it. The poem wants to recall Dionysius through "Digonos," Greek for "twice born," as a way of reading this event, but the revision is too feeble.[67] The "twice crucified" is unprecedented, at least for Pound: "where in history will you find it?" The incommensurability between the old text and the new event means that translation, here, signifies a difference or an absence. "Digonos" cannot be an adequate term for comprehending the present events, alluded to as nothing more than an ironic inversion of a political dream destroyed. But those ironies do not make the translation useless. Instead, the poetic vocabulary already established by the text is necessary to show the gaps between events and meanings. Although these absences are tenuous, they will suffice to keep the poem moving forward.

For these reasons, the Pisan Cantos, by evolving new lyrical, autobiographical, and descriptive procedures, do not indicate a departure from the core poetics of Pound's project but, instead, are an extension of the process of emergent adaptation in the face of historical change. The clear shift in language and attention we find in the Pisan Cantos can be read as a moment of poetic self-reflectivity, where Pound becomes aware, in part, of the potential of his practice as an adaptive hermeneutic. Neither textualist nor referentialist approaches can adequately account for these dynamics, but a systems-theoretical reading makes the work's dynamism identifiable.

That emergent aesthetic also sheds light on Pound's personal and cultural commitments, and so, by way of conclusion, I want to offer a consideration of Pound's metaphysical and political beliefs, which become particularly visible in his use of paradisiacal language.

IV Paradise in Artifice

Despite the political and personal disaster that culminated in his imprisonment in Pisa, Pound's hopes for paradise were not entirely abandoned. Originally, paradise was presented as an actual political organization, something he saw in the Italian Renaissance and in ancient China and, he hoped, in fascist Italy. The end of World War II guaranteed that this dream would not be realized. Nevertheless, Canto XCII offers an image of an emergent, unpredictable paradisical discourse:

> Le Paradis n'est pas artificiel
> > but it is jagged,
> For a flash,
> > for an hour.
> Then agony,
> > then an hour,
> > > then agony,
> > [. . .] the Divine Mind is abundant
> > unceasing
> > *improvisatore*   (C 640)

The Divine Mind expresses itself not as a complete and contained being but as a restless improviser, a repetition-machine pulling jagged fragments into momentary (and unanticipated) formations of beauty. Meaning exists in pieces scattered throughout time, becoming visible through the network of relationships established through the "Divine Mind" and, by extension, the poet. The task of the poem containing either history or Paradise cannot be adequately established in static form, for it achieves itself only through improvisatory processes, responding to and establishing themselves within time. Mimetic homage thus shows itself to be more than simply a technique of translation; Pound's performances are now attempting the audacious status of divine insight.

What might be initially surprising, Pound's continued pursuit of the divine and mystical in the later Cantos corresponds to an increase in sign systems. *The Cantos* are multilingual from the very beginning, even visual, as when an image of a sign at an officers' club is reproduced in Canto XXII (C 103). But, beginning with Pisa, the later Cantos include signs as diverse as musical notation (two kinds) (C 470, 630), Arabic (C 494), an increased percentage of Chinese characters in *Section: Rock-Drill De Los Cantares* (C 561–667), a greater variety of font and letter sizes (C 585, 588), the four suits of a playing card deck (C 609), Egyptian hieroglyphs (C 643), and illustrations in the text itself (C 700).[68] This proliferation of signifying systems appears to be at odds with the thematic emphasis on the spiritual and divine found in the later sections of the work. Writing has always been a problem for the mystical and the ideal, and, as Derrida mentions in passing, Pound's return to the written poetics of the Chinese character via Ernest Fenollosa "decenters" speech as the privileged bearer of being and the good in Western metaphysics, a "first break in the most entrenched Western tradition."[69] Derrida's reading points to a fundamental tension in the later Cantos between the rhetoric of the divine and the poetics of the written, the mystical claims and the scripted practice. As Pound increasingly desires to attain an improvised Paradise, he must do the earthly work of incorporating more and more textual pieces, translating and revising disparate sign systems.

This interplay between the written and the metaphysical is strikingly visible in Canto XCV. After sampling and quoting from the Venerable Bede on God as the "spirit of the world" in Latin and Greek, akin to the techniques seen in the Adams Cantos, Pound goes on to cite Adams and Dante, finally interspersing Greek words with some French lines from Villon:

> πόλις, πολιτική
>
> reproducteur,
>
> contribuable. Paradis peint
>
> but πολεύω meaning to plough
>
> πολύγλωσσος   (C 663)

Many of *The Cantos* thematic concerns are reflected in these lines. The polis and the political orders rest on adequate reproduction and proper tax-paying,[70] themselves dependent on the abundance and good management of nature and agriculture ("to plough"). Paradise may or may not be painted, an ambivalent phrase suggesting both paradise through art or paradise as a kind of gilded artifice, only present as an illusion. Whatever this dream may turn out to be, it must be πολύγλωσσος or "many-tongued," like *The Cantos* themselves. We can read these lines on a formal level as an extension of the themes Pound explores throughout the poem. But when considered as material signs, the lines also illustrate a radical form of translation, a type of multireferential adaptation for which Pound has been critiqued by philologists and translators. Πόλις and πολιτική are forms of the same word – the political in both Greek and English emerges from the word for the city-state, the *polis*, and the etymological links between the two words is registered by the poem. But πολεύω, in its first sylla-ble, sounds and looks like πόλις, and this connection between signs Pound would likely have found highly significant, for throughout his writing he adamantly declared that the cultured productivity of the earth was the root of all good government and economics. The sonic and visual echo roots πολεύω in the heart of the πόλις, a happy correspondence. And just when this wordplay may begin to sound like interpretive license, Pound moves from Greek to English to Greek in a kind of double-transliteration, demon-strating that the passage is being constructed exactly according to this lan-guage game. Πολεύω translated by Pound means "to plough," carrying over the *pl* sound into a different sign system while retaining the semantic core, and yet "plough" suggests a different *pl* word, again in Greek, πολύγλωσ-σος, granted that the "l" and the "o" sounds are inverted. Finally, these metamorphoses return us home, as the first syllable of πολύγλωσσος recalls πόλις.

The many-tongues of πολύγλωσσος thus occur literally, figuratively, and dramatically, a wordplay as suspicious as it is witty. Πόλις equals "plough" equals πολύγλωσσος in an iterative and recursive logic. In an even more radical moment of proliferating signification, Pound writes later in the same Canto, "(vine-leaf? San Denys, / spelled Dionisio)" (C 667), which, according to Cookson, "puns Dionysius with Dionysius the Are-opagite, who was converted by St. Paul and is said to have been the first bishop of Athens where he was martyred."[71] The Greek Dionysius, read at least since Nietzsche as an anti-Christian figure, becomes a Christian martyr because of a name. Or the other way around. One cannot forget that this signifying double-speak occurs in the middle of a Canto dedi-cated to the divine and the mystical, the paradisiacal light Pound desired to find. To speak of God and eternity, as well as politics and ploughing, in five different language systems on a single page, implying as many different historical theologies and political orders, either points to the existence of God, paradise, and good government outside of language or it suggests that language itself is a kind of emergent translation machine, producing and reproducing in adaptive, responsive, and enactive ways. To return to Rid-del's terms, we are either in the presence of a non-linguistic Luminous Gist or in the throes of "metaphor itself." The fact that the two options are ulti-mately undecidable, that we cannot come down on the side of God outside of language or God as a symptom of language, abandons one to *writing*, to a constant replication of the languages that both suggest and refuse their metaphysical potential. Perhaps the God of *The Cantos* is language itself, that uncanny multitude of correspondences suggested not just by meaning and signification but also by the sight and sounds of signifiers. No final homecoming occurs in such a textual practice, despite what some critics and philosophers would want to suggest[72]; there are only endless transformations and emergent surprises, in which Dionysius revises Dionysius and "plough" carves out πόλις.

Pound's unique marriage of the linguistic and the paradisiacal recalls another canonical modernist long poem, Wallace Stevens's "Notes Toward a Supreme Fiction," and a brief detour through this text shows the broader implications of emergent poetics within the complex desires of modernism. Stevens's first dictum, that the supreme fiction "must be abstract," leads the poem to explore moments of origin or self-identity, either in the natural world, as in the "idea of the sun," or in human myths of origin, such as Phoebus, Adam and Eve in Eden, or the "giant" who becomes the "thinker of the first idea."[73] Although the religious paradise is no longer available for Stevens, the power of the "idea," in its capacity to abstract and unify, becomes a substitute for the myth of origin. Yet the idea alone is insufficient to account for the fundamental temporality of the world, where "inconstant objects of inconstant cause" inhabit "a universe of inconstancy" (SF 216). Hence, Stevens's second axiom, that the supreme fiction "must change," responding to "the new-come bee," a pun on "being" as both buzzing, moving, multiple, and returning each year (SF 217).

While the bee of being might suggest an iterative, recursive ontology, Stevens presents abstraction and change as existing within a vacillating dialectic, a source of tension between opposites that sparks desire and gives way to his third claim, that the supreme fiction must give pleasure:

> Two things of opposite natures seem to depend
> On one another, as a man depends
> On a woman, day on night, the imagined
> On the real. This is the origin of change.
>
> (SF 218)

Instead of the emergent adaptations of Pound's translation machine, Stevens presents change as a process of mutual interdependence between two opposites, where imagination and reality fluctuate. This dialectic activates language, as the "poem goes from the poet's gibberish to / The gibberish of the vulgate and back again" (SF 222). These cycles within language, moving back and forth between abstraction and change, become the ground for a sufficiently supreme fiction. The second part of the poem ends: "Of these beginnings, gay and green, propose / The suitable amours. Time will write them down" (SF 224). The "gay and green" "beginnings" recall the Edenic origins and ideas of "It Must Be Abstract," and yet these ideas are mediated by time figured as an act of writing. The supreme fiction embraces both abstraction and change by positing ideas that are only capable of articulation by writing in time.

In both "Notes Toward a Supreme Fiction" and *The Cantos*, language becomes the mediator of time, change, abstraction, and even pleasure. Stevens, with his valorization of the "first idea [as] an imagined thing" (SF 213), emphasizes the dialectics of imagination and reality, poem and world, using his text to represent these turnings, displacements, and substitutions. Pound's translation machine, in a departure from this cyclical model, can be read as an enactive, adapting version of the change that Stevens imagines. Instead of beginning with the idea and the abstraction, Pound's practice continually produces and transforms "the idea," the accumulation of iterative, recursive, and improvisatory functions within his text, so that paradise does not originate in the abstract idea but as an *effect* of linguistic repetition and difference. *The Cantos* thus present an alternative solution to the problem that Stevens poses, offering a complex textual system functioning as an interpretation of the world, attuned through its processes to those buzzing, inconstant transformations.

This chapter has argued that Pound's text presents us with a unique textualist variant of the modernist machine, creating a complex adaptive system that recasts the concerns with time, change, and form evident in other modernist long poems. But does emergence give us any purchase on the political commitments that informed Pound's textual practices? One cannot take leave of this work without noting that the generative movements of *The Cantos* produce not only an emergent textuality but also the fundamental aporia at the heart of Pound's work, the conflict between the metaphysics of fascism and the antimetaphysical (or multimetaphysical) textual practices of his poetic writing. Pound's poem embraces language in all of its materiality and history, not merely as a depository of ideas but as a collection of texts to be transmitted and reused. Those material qualities of language enable mimetic homage or translation-as-performance, and through these practices he crafted one of the most influential experimental texts of the twentieth century. At the same time, Pound the fascist and radio propagandist interspersed this emergent poetics with a clear desire for the noncontingent and the ahistorical, the hope for an actual earthly paradise that would effectively erase the differences and accidents of language and return one to solid, unshakeable ground, a tribe whose tale could be told with an adequate beginning, middle, and end. The temptation of an earthly paradise allowed Pound to see his ideal statesman in someone like Mussolini. The endless task of translation thus coexists, uncomfortably, with an explicit attachment to a violent, racist political program.

As on just about every other topic, Pound's critics are divided in their approaches to this conflict. A reader like Froula, emphasizing the willing embrace of error on Pound's part, claims that if "Pound did not find what he was seeking, the 'natural' language of the transparent metaphor posited in Fenollosa's poetics, still his commitment to the unendingly diverse actualities of the world he lived in kept him from imposing a linguistic and formal order he did not find."[74] Pound, according this reading, was at least honest, and although the desire to "make it cohere" is explicitly stated in "Canto CXVI," the poet refused to force an unearned finality (C 816). On the other hand, fascism, as an ideological frame and grounding metaphysics, could provide that necessary unity, and a reader like McGann unequivocally states that the "*Cantos* is a fascist epic in the precise historical sense."[75] As fascist epic, the contingent and transmissional properties of language are subordinated to the didactic and programmatic agendas of anti-Semitism and antiusury, or celebrating martyrdom for the nationstate (as Pound does in the Italian Cantos LXXII and LXXIII). Language is treated as transparent and instrumental when appropriated by such an agenda, and the binary between idealized meaning and material instantiation is reinforced.

The translation machine offers us partial clarity even in this, the most difficult and morally repugnant quality of Pound's work. Approaching *The Cantos* on the level of technique, as ongoing adaptive revision, allows us to account not only for their errors but also for their political evils, as actualizations of a dreadful potential always present when one wanders through language. Poetic writing cannot guarantee either its reception or its results. Pound's own reading, his interaction with other texts, clearly influenced, even if it did not fully determine, his fascism and anti-Semitism. Similarly, as his textual revisions were sent out into history, they can be used and will be received in any number of contexts, read and interpreted for both good and nefarious purposes. To follow Pound's model of poetry, to endlessly read and write, requires us to acknowledge its moral risks and failures. But it also allows one to acknowledge the fascism of *The Cantos* without rejecting the work tout court.

Thus, appropriately, the poem leaves us between metaphysics and materiality. To hazard a generalization, one could do worse than to claim that fascism confronts us as both the acme and rejection of much in Western thought: it appears in the form of a hyperorganized technological nation-state, dependent on all of the instrumental logics of scientific rationalism, and yet this modernity is contradicted by its rhetorical self-defensive appeals to the preindustrial identity of land and home, *volk* and *geist*. Pound, like Martin Heidegger, bears the self-inflicted scars of this ideological contradiction visibly in his powerful work. And yet, paradoxically, perhaps the best approach to that duplicitous textual and historical scene is precisely through the kind of reading and writing *The Cantos* perform, with the historical margin of the text present, pressing back through the layers of language and culture. Pound's emergent textual strategy, somewhat ironically, indicates one way to set out on just such an open, and perhaps ethical, historiography, a realization that would influence and prompt the work of later poets like Olson and DuPlessis. As McGann points out, Pound's fascist poem, despite itself, "is (still) being written in a kind of encrypted discourse, because it is still sending messages, making communications, which Pound, the maker of the scripts, cannot master."[76] There is an emergent excess in Pound's translation machine that rewrites his own willed intentions.

CHAPTER 4

Emergent History
Charles Olson's Housekeeping

Charles Olson's house served as both dwelling and text. In photographs of the house taken by Olson scholar George Butterick, we see a window frame covered in handwritten notes and rough drafts, where Olson worked through concepts that undoubtedly found their way into *The Maximus Poems*.[1] Writing on the house, of the house, and in the house was a recurring cultural activity that animated Olson's poetic practices. This house-writing, informal and ad hoc, recalls other home discourses, like gossip. The second verse in *The Maximus Poems: Volume Three* recounts one gossipy interaction between Olson and his neighbor, Mrs. Pauline Tarantino, the occupant of "the yellow house / on fort constructed / like a block-house house."[2] Mrs. Tarantino accuses Olson of excessive investigation: "You have a long nose, meaning / you stick it into every other person's / business, do you not?" (MP 378). The "long nose" of the busybody does not keep its proper place. Inquisitive and intrusive, Olson violates the codes of domestic and communitarian propriety, invading the many houses of the text. The poet concedes, "And I couldn't / say anything / but that I / do" (MP 378). Olson's poetic gossip is inseparable from his attention to the domestic structure of Gloucester, the community to which he dedicated his literary investigations.

Olson's houses are not unique. Houses were a preoccupation in midcentury American poetry, when there was a noticeable turn toward domestic and private themes. Edward Brunner argues that the domesticity of the late 1950s and early 1960s found in poets like Sylvia Plath, Anne Sexton, and Karl Shapiro was symptomatic of political anxiety, "a poetry that is, below its amiable surface, a discourse of alienation, disgust, and sorrow that insists, helplessly, on the primacy of the individual and the family over the state."[3] The inverted politics of home life was particularly well suited for the interiority of the confessional poetry movement. An exemplary instance of this domestic turn would be Robert Lowell's *Life Studies*, his 1959 volume that helped launch confessional poetry and a text that offers a useful contrast with *The Maximus Poems*. A multigeneric blending of prose and verse, *Life Studies* reflects many characteristics of the twentieth-century long poem. The volume is divided into four parts, with each section exploring moments in Lowell's life and the lives of others. Houses figure prominently throughout the entire work, most obviously in "91 Revere Street," the address of Lowell's childhood home in Boston and the title of an extended prose piece. The homes of *Life Studies* are familial, conflicted, and often Oedipal, reminiscent of Nathanial Hawthorne's own haunted hereditary Massachusetts. Early in the collection, the poem "The Banker's Daughter" tells us of Marie de Medici, who was "exiled by her son and lived in a house lent to her by Rubens," while the final sections of the text end with strained visits to Lowell's grandfather's house and the sale of Lowell's deceased father's cottage.[4] The narratives of "91 Revere Street" are particularly vexed, fractured by Lowell's mother's thwarted ambitions and his father's uninspiring career. The household is literally divided between two buildings, as Lowell's father, a naval officer, is required by his commander to maintain a house on the military base. The architectural division amplifies the tense familial relationships. In one telling passage, when his father is called back to duty on Christmas Eve, Lowell's mother runs to his bedroom: "She hugged me. She said, 'Oh, Bobby, it's such a comfort to have a man in the house.' 'I am not a man,' I said, 'I am a boy.'"[5]

Lowell's use of houses in *Life Studies* is striking for its emphasis on domestic closure, stable familial artifacts, arrested hereditary memory, and aesthetic completion.[6] Lowell's imagined 91 Revere Street becomes a repository of his family history, valued for its ability to capture and constrain the past. After offering a narrative sketch of Major Mordecai Myers, one of his maternal ancestors who fought in the war of 1812, Lowell returns to the present of private memory:

> [The Major's] portrait has been mislaid past finding, but out of my memories I often come on it in the setting of our Revere Street house, a setting now fixed in the mind, where it survives all the distortions of fantasy, all the blank befogging of forgetfulness. There, the vast number of remembered *things* remains rocklike. Each is in its place, each has its function, its history, its drama. There, all is preserved by that motherly care that one either ignored or resented in his youth. The things and their owners come back urgent with life and meaning – because finished, they are endurable and perfect.[7]

Lowell imagines the house as a "rocklike" arrangement of mental furniture. Unlike the real portrait of the Major, capable of being displaced and lost, Lowell's recollected furniture remains in place, serving as an index of ancestral lives that have meaning because they are "finished," "endurable and perfect." Home as memory is stable, complete, and associated with closure and privacy, albeit a private world made public through the literary display of poetic memory that constitutes "91 Revere Street."

In contrast to the domesticity of *Life Studies*, Olson presents the home not for stability but as a space of transformation, shot through with immanent political, economic, and ecological possibility. Olson's poetry is not a memorialization of the house but an emergent activity of *housekeeping*, an iterative, creative reconstruction of the inherited living spaces that projects a future world. Instead of stabilizing memory, houses in *The Maximus Poems* are continually reproduced sites of collective dwelling, establishing the larger polis with which they are entangled. This dynamic approach to housekeeping originates in Olson's philosophical commitment to a process-oriented ontology. Stable models of domestication are incompatible with a world of constant reproduction; indeed, a changing universe requires a new model of homemaking, where one continually recrafts the home in response to the world's own contingent, unpredictable processes. *The Maximus Poems* both represent and participate in this dynamism, creating a poetic home that behaves like a complex adaptive system, necessarily transforming its own terms while constraining itself to the bounds of a particular, material history.[8]

As a poet of the "open field" and projective verse, Olson's work can be read as a self-reflective moment in the history of emergent textuality. Although he does not use the language of complex adaptive systems, Olson owes a clear debt to process philosophy, most notably the work of Alfred North Whitehead. Whitehead's influence on Olson has been explored by a number of scholars, from recent work by Shahar Bram and Miriam Nichols to earlier studies by Don Byrd, Robert von Hallberg, and Robin Blaser.[9] Moving further back in the philosophical tradition, Stephen Fredman has traced a connection between Olson and Emerson, thus placing *The Maximus Poems* within an intellectual history that includes pragmatism, which also directly influenced Whitehead.[10] Without offering a full explication of Olson's rich engagement with this philosophical background, I want to highlight the philosophy of poetic composition that Olson developed from his dialogue with Whitehead. Such an overview will establish the philosophical foundation for the remainder of this chapter, which offers a close reading of Olson's emergent poetic housekeeping at work.

Olson's influential manifesto of composition by field, "Projective Verse," articulates an early process-oriented poetics. Olson's concern in this essay is as much time, and transmission through time, as it is space as a bounded field, declaring that in poetry "ONE PERCEPTION MUST IMMEDI-ATELY AND DIRECTLY LEAD TO A FURTHER PERCEPTION."[11] This process of perception requires an interaction between activity and receptivity, organism and environment. The indicative "must" demands an active role for the poet in linking perception, implying that the poet could do otherwise, could not attend to this chain of perceptions. At the same time, a perception is oriented toward a thing perceived, arising only through contact with an external environment. Indeed, this interplay between interiority and exteriority anticipates the "object" nature of the human that Olson explores later in the essay, a kind of cybernetic inter-face between poem, poet, and world that echoes the concerns of the Macy Conferences that were occurring at the time of Olson's writing. This evolv-ing relationship between objects and perception would later be embod-ied in the metaphysics of *The Maximus Poems*, what Joshua Hoeynck has described as a vision of a "grand and inexplicable system of relations gov-erning the cosmos" wherein "materials collide and synthesize with other materials to create new relations that cause one to feel this ordered yet indescribable pluriverse."[12]

Olson elaborates these principles in a sequel to the manifesto, "Pro-jective Verse II." While unpublished in Olson's lifetime, the essay draws much more directly on the work of Whitehead. The first two propositions of "Projective Verse II" articulate a transformational world of unexpected variety, both within poetry and "creation herself":

> 1. The poem's job is to be able to attend, and to get attention to, the variety of order in creation.
> 1.1 It does this for two reasons: that the requisites for experience be increased, both for whoever reads, and for creation itself, which awaits each novel advance men make as further evidence of herself.[13]

Poetry focuses and directs attention on natural "variety." This variety includes human creations, those "novel advances" that in their newness par-ticipate within that field of multiplicity. Poetry is an observer of nature and a participant within nature, extending and advancing its variety. Perception and creation are thus interdependent, as the poem becomes an instance of the same variety that it is charged to observe, establishing a feedback loop between the poem's creativity and that of nature. Nature's variety makes possible the perceptions that ground the poem, while the poem's newness extends the variety it is observing.

By attending to and producing variety, Olson's poem both registers and generates surprise. In this way, Olson suggests that poetry becomes an emergent activity of engagement with the external world as well as the manifestation of newness produced by that world. The new is never a pure advent out of nonexistence; instead, fully material and immanent, it arises out of existing conditions, just as the poem emerges from a rigorous attention to the environment with which it is coupled. As Olson writes in early notes for "Projective Verse II," "natura . . . does nothing but leap," and so "extensive relations do not make determinate *what* is transmitted; but they do determine conditions to which all transmission must conform. They represent the systematic scheme which is involved in the real potentiality from which every actual occasion (of which a poem is made up) *arises*."[14] The poem emerges from real material potentiality, shaped by the prior conditions of the environment (and, in the case of a long poem, its own internal systemic operations). Nevertheless, the actual event or creative act of attention cannot be fully predicted by those prior conditions.

Olson freely acknowledges his debt to Whitehead in developing this conceptual vocabulary of attention, interaction, and novelty, and the latter's own writings clarify Olson's agenda. In a series of lectures published as *Modes of Thought*, which anticipate his later opus *Process and Reality*, Whitehead claims that "importance (or interest) is embedded in the very being of animal experience," and it is through this interest that "a perspective is imposed upon the universe of things felt."[15] Interest as attention becomes a dynamic yet systematic activity, akin to one perception immediately following another – we might say that Whiteheadean "importance" links the chain of perceptions in "Projective Verse," directing and shaping attention. This importance, however, can never been crystalized into a stable, hierarchical order. As Whitehead argues, the "essence of life is to be found in the frustrations of established order. The Universe refuses the deadening influence of complete conformity. And yet in its refusal, it passes towards novel order as a primary requisite for important experience."[16] Order does not become entropic but instead erupts into unexpected structures of being and experience. Consequently, every historically existent object contains the seeds for unknown future forms:

> All actuality involves the realization of form derived from factual data. It is both a composition of qualities, and it is also a form of composition. The form of composition dictates how those forms as thus realized in the data enter into a finite process of composition, thus achieving new actuality with its own exemplifications and discards. There is a form of process dealing with a complex form of data and issuing into a novel completion of actuality. But no actuality is a static fact. The historic character of the universe belongs to its essence. The completed fact is only to be understood as taking its place among the active data forming the future.[17]

Ella Csikós understands this process of "realizing form" as an emergent component to Whitehead's metaphysics, wherein "every actual entity" in its becoming "[creates] a new unity from the multiplicity."[18] Actual historical existence and its metaphysical ground are both understood as emergent processes in Whitehead's cosmology, the "novel completion of actuality."

From this perspective, the home is another novel completion of actuality, an enactive system always in the process of transforming itself in response to changing conditions. Such a model of the home, deployed throughout *The Maximus Poems*, offers an alternative to other domestic poetries of the midcentury, like that of *Life Studies*, characterized by closure, privacy, and stasis. In a broader literary context, Olson takes his place in the history of emergent writing as a theorist of a changing universe, generating a philosophical poetics that affirms the intersection of form, subjectivity, creation, and the environment. Like the other poets examined in this study, Olson deploys iterative and recursive strategies to establish provisional closure and generate feedback loops with his environment, most evidently through the device of the letter, an ongoing correspondence with the city of Gloucester. But his project is less notable for its specific poetic techniques then for the way he treats cultural and historical material as *already* emergent, participating in adaptive, self-transforming processes occurring within nature. In what follows, I read the trope of housekeeping as a figure for this emergent orientation, tracing its network of associations within Olson's text. The many senses of housekeeping – social, ecological, economic, and personal – in turn provide a more precise understanding of Olson's creative historiography, including his use of colonial figures like Captain John Smith. As I show in the second part of this chapter, Smith set the stage for many possible "actual worlds," inaugurating the capitalist exploitation that Olson criticizes alongside the ecological and linguistic precision he praises. History in the form of Smith thus requires continual recreation and reinterpretation within the framework of the economies of the midcentury. Olson's emergent act of rewriting Smith is particularly visible in "Some Good News," a long section toward the end of the first volume of *The Maximus Poems*. As Olson's treatment of Smith illustrates, poetic housekeeping reestablishes its own processes and forms in response to an equally changing universe.

I   The Endless Work of Poetic Economy

Olson's understanding of the house as a material, historical, and political object is particularly evident in the story of Roger Conant, governor of the Dorchester Company's settlement, whose house was torn down by

Governor John Endecott and taken to Salem (MP 49).[19] This displacement of property by the powerful echoes the poem's larger concern with alienation from land and things, characterized by Olson as the abandonment of the local and particular for distorting abstractions. But the house is more than an image of displacement, as Olson sees Conant's mansion as a "sign," with its "handsome . . . old carpentry" in the "Tudor" style, that "Gloucester, your first house was as Elizabeth's / England" (MP 50). The house signifies Gloucester's history as a transnational colony, materializing the political change that the city has experienced. The "Tudor house" transforms into Gloucester and, ultimately, to Maximus/Olson as the inhabitant of this haunted space:

> Elizabeth dead,
> and Tudor went to James
> (as quick as Conant's house
> was snatched to Salem
>
> As you did not go,
> Gloucester: you tipped, you were our
> scales
>
> > (as I have been witness
> > in my time,
> > to all slide
> > national, international,
> > even learning slide   (MP 50)

World-historical transformation occurs through Gloucester, evidence that the local can afford a material perspective on the global, and, by extension, the endless variety of creation itself. In this way, the displacement of one house, an apparently minor event, becomes a reflection of England's own political fortunes. The larger house that is Gloucester allows Maximus to weigh and "witness" his own "national [and] international" sliding, the home becoming not a place of stability or nostalgia but a transforming field, exemplifying Rosemary George's claim that the home "is a way of establishing difference."[20] This difference constitutes Maximus himself, for Conant's Tudor architecture, as Olson writes, "sat / where my own house has been (where I am / founded" (MP 50). Olson's subject of history lives in a displaced home, abides in the remnants of his own foundations.

Michael André Bernstein observes that "[history], for Olson, is like a perpetually changing character in search of the author who can discern, latent within the flux, a lasting form and significance."[21] While Bernstein is correct to see history in *Maximus* as "perpetually changing," Olson's response to change is not to build a structure resistant to all decay, like Lowell's imagined Revere Street home. Instead, he attempts to develop an adaptive interaction with history's architecture, producing forms that adequately engage the transformative energy of both the universe and human history. The emphasis throughout the work is on iterative remaking, not on the monumentality of the final result. In *The Special View of History*, Olson calls this generative principle "the ontogenetic truth: what happens now, creates,"[22] implying that the ontological present, being as such, is manifest as fabrication. Since the new is always on the cusp of emergence, collectivities and individuals (themselves part of the manifold, since "a man is himself an object" [CP 247]) can attempt to grasp that potential, channeling and remaking the process into an inhabitable reality. What Olson calls the "human universe" is thus characterized neither by infinite chaos nor predictable order but by the laws of complex, emergent *poiesis*.[23]

Beyond the general sense of creating an inhabitable arrangement within history's flux, "housekeeping" has several etymological resonances that inform Olson's use of the phrase. Two passages in *The Maximus Poems* draw explicit attention to the origins of the word. In "A Maximus," a visual-poetic map of key figures and concepts, the right-hand side of the page includes the following cluster:

$$
\begin{array}{cc}
& \text{houses} \\
& \text{finance} \\
& \text{wood (ekonomikos} \\
\text{sculpture} & \overline{\text{(MP 193)}}
\end{array}
$$

As Butterick points out, Olson here adapts the Greek adjective *oikonomikos*, a compound word derived from the noun *oikos*, "house" and the verb *nemein*, "to manage."[24] The link to "finance" calls attention to a related Greek noun that is the source of the English word "economy," *oikonomia*. Along with "household management," Classical Greek usage of *oikonomia* included "husbandry" and "thrift," while Hellenistic Greek added the senses of "principles of government," and, intriguingly enough, the "arrangement of a literary work" – perhaps explaining the link in the poem to "sculpture."[25] Olson's use of the Greek calls attention to the etymology of "economics," revealing that it is a conceptual blend of domestic housekeeping, general forms of husbandry, governmental activities, and poetic composition. Like *The Maximus Poems*, "economy" is another instance of endless restructuring, and so the "economics & poetics" (MP 74) of any situation are the inherited processes that have brought the situation into being, establishing a self-reflexive feedback loop. For this reason, the economic is not merely an order of legal and financial codes or impersonal historical forces, but, instead, an imaginative, innovative practice. Olson evokes this projective and etymological sense of the economic in "Some Good News" when he speaks of we "who come from a housekeeping / which old mother [John] Smith / started" (MP 130), a call not merely to historical self-consciousness but also to new poetry demanded by that complex *oikonomia*.

I want to examine in more detail the specific ambiguities of "old mother Smith's" housekeeping, but first it is necessary to understand how economy, in the narrower sense of markets and exchange (though never forgetting its many complicated echoes) functions as an emergent historical force in *The Maximus Poems*. Economic theory was a particularly fraught enterprise for the composer of an American long poem in the wake of Pound's *Cantos*, with the latter's correlation of fascism, art, and economic order. Certain aspects of Olson's economics, such as his concern for the land and his emphasis on local productions, do resemble Pound's monetary and political values. But Olson's process-oriented economics was a marked departure from many of Pound's mystifications regarding credit, debt, and "unnatural" usury. Olson constantly returns to the generative potential present in the most physical as well as the most intellectual of labor, contrasting this human creativity with the bad husbandry that would suppress or distort it. As he writes in the essay "Human Universe," the "truth is that the management [another echo of *oikonomia*] of external nature so that none of its virtu [*sic*] is lost, in vegetables or in art, is as much a delicate juggling of her content as is the same juggling by any one of us of our own" (CP 159). Nature, art, and the human organism share in the same adaptive mode of being, and agency is not the result of escaping these processes but, instead, emerges from "juggling." "Management" in this context does not mean subjection to a predetermined or external ideal but rather designates an adaptive response to a situation. This improvisatory order is necessary, Olson goes on to argue, for "when men are not such jugglers, are not able to manage a means of expression the equal of their own or nature's intricacy, the flesh does choke" (CP 159). When this happens, as Olson claims that it had in mid-twentieth-century America, work as a creative activity is replaced with "spectatorism," where "bonuses and prizes are the rewards of labor contrived by the monopolies of business and government to protect themselves from the advancement in position of able men or that old assertion of an inventive man, his own shop" (CP 159–60). Alienation, in this situation, takes on the camouflage of cheap leisure incentives. Play becomes mere distraction, a weak substitute for the outlay of creative human force evident in the workshop and the writer's desk.

At the same time, the material practices of craft and human labor enabling capitalist and technocratic alienation can be an antidote against the choking of the flesh. Olson valued the aesthetic potential in work, seeking to reclaim human work as a poetic, dynamic, environmentally entangled activity. Several figures throughout the poem reflect this aesthetics of work, including the Gloucester carpenter, a "first Maximus" "who left Plymouth Plantation, / and came to Gloucester, / to build boats," anticipating the generations of fishing fleets that would follow in his wake (MP 34). Maximus characterizes this carpenter as "the first to make things, / not just live off nature," one who exercises his own force, like a projective poet, within his environment, thus demonstrating "necessities the practice of the self, / that matter, that wood" (MP 35). Wood, like other material facts in the environment with which we are entangled, provokes self-practicing. The self in this passage is not an essence but an activity structurally coupled to other physical objects and made manifest through those materials. As a result, this carpenter-Maximus refuses to separate himself from the rest of the world. Indeed, this early carpenter attends to his ecology: he "must have been the first to see the tansy / take root" (MP 34). The tansy, in "Letter 3," cures Gloucester of "the smell / of all owners," a polis-making growth that the poet offers to the citizens of his city (MP 13). Thus, for the carpenter to note the tansy emerging from the landscape suggests that he is not merely a precursor of the owners and capitalists but, instead, an early source for that other economy promoted by Olson throughout the poem. Watching tansies becomes an act both aesthetic and revolutionary, or, in this context, poetic.

The carpenter represents Olson's broader conception of a poetic economy, usefully sketched by Bariş Gümüşbaş:

> In Olson's project, economic activity revolves around three concerns. The first one is the physical reality of the organism, the body of the human subject and its "physiology" . . . . This is the internal economy of the body. Secondly, there is human activity to keep the house functioning. Such activity involves using the body in interaction with nature and with other members of the community. Thirdly, these two activities are possible only with care about the well-being of our environment.[26]

The economy of the body emerges in the carpenter's "practice of the self" among the wood and other materials, while the activity to "keep the house functioning" can be seen in the building of ships for the fish harvest.

Furthermore, the carpenter's attention to the tansy flowers can be read as a nascent care for the well-being of the environment, a recognition that the human organism exists in a world of other forces and materials.

However, as useful as this sketch of Olson's economics might be, Gümüşbaş draws a potentially misleading conclusion: "The ideal economy Olson has in mind is strictly 'subsistence-oriented.' The activity of fishing perfectly fits in the context of an economy as such, because fishing, by its nature, is not a mode of production but a harvesting of what [nature's] 'eros' yields."[27] A subsistence economy may have a certain romantic appeal, compatible with Olson's obvious concern for the body and human creativity, as well as his distaste for the processes of contemporary global capital. Nevertheless, a call for a return to the eros of nature as a desirable ideal misses the significance of social and human history in the *Maximus* poems, a history that is inescapably intertwined with the present. For if the carpenter exemplifies an aesthetic of work, it is equally clear that he represents larger and more abstract economies, coming to Gloucester in response to the religious-eschatological colonization of Plymouth Plantation only to be ousted again. The carpenter's creative attributes are thus inseparable from forces of potential extraction and exploitation, proving that Gloucester fishing (at least as practiced by the European colonizers) was never purely, or even primarily, a subsistence endeavor. It emerged, instead, at the nexus of transnational and geopolitical enterprises coming to shore. For these reasons, the present alienation that Olson decries cannot be simply overcome, for it has deep historical roots that must be confronted, indeed, with which one must learn to live. A new future must emerge out of that past, with all of its contradictions and complexities, a future that Olson seeks to make possible through his poetic practice.

This sense of creatively adapting the past to the promise of a future does not imply endorsing the present, for Olson is clearly at odds with the complex web of alienation produced by contemporary capitalism, the pressure of the economic environment in which the poem is being composed. "I, Maximus of Gloucester, to You" condemns the "mu-sick, mu-sick, mu-sick" that distracts the fishermen from their traditional pursuits, the "sick muses" heard in the line suggesting a relationship between poetics and economics (MP 7). Maximus later didactically calls on his fellow-citizens to "kill kill kill kill kill / those / who advertise [them] / out" (MP 8). Advertising and popular music thus reveal an alienation from language and, by extension, a destruction of poetry. This destruction of the word is tied to selves and bodies in "Letter 3," for "those who use words cheap" are also the

ones who "use us cheap" (MP 13). In one of the many seductive transformations of capital, the creation of surplus value in fact diminishes human
organisms and their collective expression.

The excessive extraction of wealth also leads to the impoverishment of
the environment. Companies like Gorton-Pew, the large fish processor and
distributor located in Gloucester, exemplify this exploitation of the land.
At one point in the poem, Olson ironically advocates putting images of
fish on "the covers of the TV dinners / to let children know that mack-
erel is a different / looking thing than herrings" (MP 208).[28] Unable to
directly experience or understand the origins of their food, children are
left to rely on marketing. Even more dramatically, capitalist exchange can
alienate a community from history, particularly the history of capitalism
itself. In "Letter 2," Maximus tries to reclaim that historical consciousness by reflecting on the continuities between the past and the present
of Gloucester's streets: "the light, there, at the corner (because of the big
elm / and the reflecting houses) winter or summer stays / as it was when
they lived there" (MP 9). The poem abruptly shifts from this apparently
idealized, domesticated light to the politically suppressed: "they hid, or
tried to hide, the fact the cargo their ships brought back / was black (the
Library, too, possibly so founded)" (MP 9).[29] The light of Gloucester's
houses can cover over, and thus cause us to forget, the conditions of international exchange and exploitation inextricably embedded in the town's
history, including Gloucester's historical slave cargo. Returning to the
light's intensity, Olson comments on the tension between white and black,
using the phenomenological moment to reveal the less-visible colors of
history:

> coming from the sea, up Middle, it is more white, very white
> as it passes the grey of the Unitarian church. But at Pleasant Street,
> it is abruptly
> black
>
> (hidden
> city   (MP 9)

The assessment one offers of the community depends on the light through
which it is perceived. The hidden city becomes a city that hides itself, deny-
ing the cargo of its ships and its dependence on a capitalism that violently
extracted surplus value from black bodies. The bright, white light abruptly
turning black along the streets of Gloucester, when viewed in the shadow
of the slave trade, produces a gothic return of the repressed, making visible
what has always been present but hidden. Olson's poem thus reveals the

multiple alienating effects of capitalism, its will-to-forgetting, in this one moment of imaginative historical reclamation.

II   John Smith's Complexities

Clearly, a sophisticated web of significations makes up Olson's use of "housekeeping," including a general sense of economy, the arrangements of the home, the creative juggling of the earth and the self's resources, and a critique of alienating forms of capitalism. Combined, housekeeping in Olson's work is the poetic, adaptive reconfiguration of intersecting networks, a necessarily emergent activity with unpredictable results. But what does poetic housekeeping look like in practice? To answer this question, I now turn to a more extensive instance of Olson's historiography, where the aesthetics and politics of housekeeping are most apparent. Olson's historiographic poems do not offer a record of inevitability or a nostalgic recollection of praiseworthy historical figures. Instead, historical individuals and events are presented as conflicted sites of potential, possessing both opportunity and liability for the present. A creative rewriting of history can actualize this potential, thus revealing the historical to be not a collection of finished facts but a complex network capable of generating new, emergent meanings.

One notable figure connected to Olson's notion of housekeeping is John Smith, the androgynous "old mother" whose legacy, as will be shown, is in need of renovation. Smith as a prior housekeeper initiated the economy with which Olson struggles, and yet Smith also offers an antidote against it. To claim that Olson must "rewrite" Smith may appear to run contrary to the poet's own admiration for the seventeenth-century explorer. Throughout his corpus Olson returns to this figure with explicit praise; he may have been only "Five Foot Four," but for Olson "Smith Was a Giant" (CP 322). Olson celebrates Smith for his spatial and linguistic "bite," an authentic alternative to the present abstractions of market capitalism and its deceptive languages. Smith "*knew* the country as not only not one other did (not even a West Country fisherman) but said it in prose like as no one has since" (CP 319). In epic language Olson continues: "Why I sing John Smith is this, that the *geographic*, the sudden *land* of the place, is in there, not described, not local, not represented – like all advertisement, all the shit now pours out, the American Road, the filthiness, of graphic words" (CP 319). Smith's writing does not merely mimetically reflect the newly explored landscape but actually conveys it through composition; in the language of "Projective Verse II," Smith's writing was both attending to nature and extending it.

Writing of place, writing *in* place, becomes the sign of Smith's greatness, an early example of human force acting within a field of forces that Olson advocates in "Projective Verse." Such writing is figured as antirhetorical, an instance of language used dearly, not cheaply, in opposition to the vacuous manipulations of the present which "advertise [Gloucester] / out" (MP 8). The appeal of Smith thus coincides with all of the broad public, political, and individual concerns of *The Maximus Poems*.

We see Smith's writing of America in "The Sea Marke," included in "Letter 15," the only outside poem, as Sherman Paul notes, "incorporated" into *The Maximus Poems*.[30] The second stanza gives some sense of that "geographic bite" Olson so praised:

> If in or outward you be bound,
>   do not forget to sound;
> Neglect of that was cause of this
>   to steere amisse:
> The Seas were calme, the wind was faire,
>   that made me so secure,
>   that now I must indure
> All weathers be they foule or faire
>   (MP 74)

The speaker, warning travelers, describes his failure to adequately measure the sea on which he sailed. The poem as a whole, however, demonstrates Smith's personal knowledge of navigation and his use of that experience to revise poetic tradition. Byrd points out that while the "sea as an image of chaos has been one of the most persistent in western poetry, . . . in 'The Sea Marke' Maximus finds an awareness of the 'undisclosed because not apparent' forms of the sea."[31] The sea's form is the intersection of its multiple forces (water, sand, wind), processes that the attentive writer/sailor will detect as well as use in his poetry; the poem's warning and figures are based not on inherited tropes or conventions but from experiential knowledge, a geographic "bite" responsive to the dynamism of a changing universe. Later in "Letter 15," Olson links Smith's "prose" to "Brer Fox," "Rapallo" (an allusion to Pound), and the "American epos," firmly grounding Smith as the precursor to American pragmatic, projectivist, and vernacular poetics (MP 75). Olson elsewhere claims that while Smith is criticized for not being "a great stylist," he is a precursor to Williams, Pound, and Hart Crane, writers in the American grain compromised in British eyes by "neologisms" and "barbarisms" (CP 319).

Following Olson, the critical tradition has largely viewed Smith as a hero of *The Maximus Poems*. Byrd suggests that Smith is one of several "rhymes" for Maximus himself, someone who embodied all of the political and poetic goals Olson attempts to enact.[32] Byrd claims that *Maximus* presents Smith as a turning point in the Western imagination: "For the first time since Dante it is possible to figure forth a hero who need not act 'solely in terms of man's capacity to overthrow or dominate external reality' . . . . Smith is capable of revealing the heroic dimension by no device other than his statement of 'quantity and precision.'"[33] Paul echoes Byrd's assessment of Smith's heroic attributes as ones of "quantity and precision." A "great exemplary figure," Smith is praised because his "virtue of discovering is one with writing," and, for this reason, he "is another model of the self with whom Maximus identifies . . . , a discoverer, namer, mapmaker, who has the distinction of so faithfully charting things we recognize them."[34]

Paul also contrasts Smith with a number of the villains in *The Maximus Poems*, most of whom represent the profit-driven colonization and exploitation that Olson critiques. The villainous figures, for Paul, include "John Hawkins" who "did not plant a civilization but the feral Roman present of American empire," Nathaniel Bowditch, "founder of insurance companies" and an inaugural figure in the development of finance capitalism, and Stephen Higginson, who "trafficked in arms and disparaged the fishermen of Gloucester."[35] Another commentator, Enikó Bollobás, views those individuals as "makers of pejorocracy, the 'merchandize men' making quick money" who are placed in contrast with Smith and other examples of "pre-industrial morality and integrity."[36] Bollobás presents that duality in stark terms: "In this drama of heroes and villains, explorers are opposed to colonizers, participants to profit makers, obedience to exploitation, need to gain, polis values to mercantile attitudes."[37]

Undoubtedly, Olson finds very little to praise in the mercenary values of a Miles Standish and much to celebrate in an explorer like Smith. However, does this dualism, with its heroes and villains, adequately represent the complex notion of historical process, and the subsequent need for an ongoing, emergent poetic historiography, that Olson develops throughout his work? When examined closely, Olson's writing reveals Smith to be a more complex and compromised figure than these critics suggest. Returning to "Letter 15," for instance, certain tensions in Smith become apparent. Olson first introduces him through a reference to his book "ADVERTISE-MENTS / for the unexperienced Planters / of New-England," retaining the capital letters both to mark the historical source text and also to call attention to the term (MP 73). When read next to Olson's prose declaration that Smith is in contrast to the "filthy" contemporary advertisers, this line becomes ambivalent, if not ironic. In a related irony, Olson acknowledges elsewhere that one cannot "use a country as stupid as this" if one is afraid to take on a cliché, which Crane did with Pocahontas and which Olson claims to do with Smith (CP 318). In other words, even in "Letter 15" and his other unapologetic essayistic celebrations of Smith, Olson appears to be aware that Smith was embedded within a larger historical moment, in which many economic and poetic arrangements were potentially in conflict. The Smith of "Letter 15" might have anticipated new American poetry, but he also may have "ADVERTISED" for a country of clichés in which "o / Tell-A-Vision, the best / is soap. The true troubadours / are CBS" (MP 75).

In fact, like every historical actor, Smith was "a complex of occasions" (MP 185), a combination of powerful forces that trouble his status as an uncompromised hero. One needs only go to his original writing, the texts Olson so praised for their "bite" and "geographic," to see contradictions in Smith that inaugurate the very social and economic conflicts *The Maximus Poems* attempt to domesticate. Smith was a figure caught in the transnational drama of colonialism and venture capitalism, two historical processes that would significantly influence Gloucester. Olson engages this network of historical forces through Smith, rewriting the latter's housekeeping by unearthing and transforming those past-and-present forces. If Smith can be reclaimed as a hero, it is precisely because the explorer's spatial language and geographic awareness can be creatively disentangled from his interest in extraction. Olson takes up Smith to recover the attentive poet against the advertising capitalist, making it possible for a renovated poetic economy to emerge from a marketplace of abstraction.

Poet and capitalist are both present in Smith's *General Historie of Virginia, New-England, and the Summer Isles*, a work published in 1624. The sixth book of this volume was primarily dedicated to the exploration and settlement of New England, a revision of two earlier books, *Description of New England* (1616) and *New Englands Trials* (1620).[38] In these texts, Smith clearly anticipates the fishing industry that would find its home in Gloucester, but he does not write to the prospective ship carpenters or sea captains, the practitioners of an attentive, Olsonian economy. Instead, he addresses venture capitalists and potential colonialists, entrepreneurs whom he believed were necessary for developing the resources of the new world. Smith's personal motivations for the advertisements were likely complex: the geo-poet whom Olson praises can also be detected in the *General Historie*. But as capitalist, colonialist, and adman, Smith reveals himself to be an agent of alienating historical forces, a perpetrator of that life of conquest that would mark the housekeeping (economic, cultural, and psychological) Olson claims to have inherited from this forefather.

Smith the capitalist is quite evident throughout the *General Historie*. The explorer first voyaged to New England in 1614, and his description of the trip is couched almost exclusively in terms of profit and loss. He and his companions intended "to take Whales . . . and also to make trialls of a Mine of gold and copper; if these failed Fish and Furs were then [their] refuge."[39] The whaling turns out to be harder than anticipated and the fishing unexpectedly seasonal; consequently, the catch was "not sufficient to defray so great a charge as [the] stay required" (CW 400). Trading "trifles" with the indigenous peoples for furs becomes Smith's personal task, which he accomplishes with some success. The trip ends with a slim return, but Smith carefully describes the price brought by the fish and other commodities, attempting to encourage more ventures by documenting actual profits.

To bolster those ventures, much of Smith's writing in Book Six is devoted to defending New England's most valuable resource, namely fish. In one passage, Smith points to Dutch fishermen as proof of the advantages of this seemingly "mean and . . . base Commoditie," his language blending the cultural value of work with the capitalist gains through trade:

> But who doth not know that the poore Hollanders chiefly by fishing at great charge and labour in all weathers in the open Sea, are made a people so hardy and industrious, and by the venting this poore Commoditie to the Easterlings for as meane, which is Wood, Flax, Pitch, Tarre, Rozen, Cordage, and such like; which they exchange againe to the French, Spaniards, Portugals, and English, etc. for what they want, are made so mighty, strong, and rich, as no state but Venice of twice their magnitude is so well furnished, with so many faire Cities, goodly Townes, strong Fortresses, and that abundance of shipping, and all sorts of Merchandize, as well of Gold, Silver, Pearles, Diamonds, pretious Stones, Silkes, Velvets, and Cloth of Gold; as Fish, Pitch, Wood, or such grosse Commodities? (CW 409)

The rigors of fishing will make a people, like the Hollanders, "hardy and industrious," but more significantly fish afford an entrance into a global market, both for the Dutch and, potentially, for the inhabitants of the new world. This commodity can be exchanged from one market to another, ultimately transformed from mere cod and haddock to gold, silver, and diamonds. While Smith acknowledges something like an aesthetic of work when he reflects on the physical and mental benefits of fishing, that creative activity is justified by a larger marketplace, in which all of the subtle transformations through abstraction, and abstraction's accompanying alienation, can and will occur. Smith's personal interest may well be a poetic activity, merely using economics to seduce his capitalist compatriots to New England. Even so, his rhetoric sets the stage for the commodity's triumph over creation, initiating a future wherein "billboards" will replace "that which matters, that which insists, that which will last" (MP 6).

Similar appeals to the benefits of global trade lead Smith to advocate more invasive forms of colonization through market expansion. He argues that once New England is settled, the "assistance of the Salvages . . . may easily be had . . . towards fishing, planting, and destroying woods," and the happy result of this development will be that his invested audience "may serve all Europe better and farre cheaper then can the Iland Fishers, or the Hollanders, Cape-blanke, or Newfound land, who must be at much more charge" (CW 415). Smith here further adopts a logic of globalization, in which a commodity's identity is determined by its exchange value, not its history or place of origin. Later, the case is made in even stronger terms because, compared with other fishing countries, "New England hath much advantage of the most of those parts, to serve Europe farre cheaper then they can, who at home have neither wood, salt, nor food, but at great rates, at Sea nothing but what they carry in their ships, an hundred or two hundred leagues from their habitation" (CW 439). Again, the several consequences of Smith's arguments potentially conflict. Fishing in New England has the promise to surpass the current fish-producing countries, as the commodity can be generated there at lower cost, thus providing an abundance of cheaper product to the European consumer and an increased return for the investors. Decreased production costs, coupled with exchange, generate surplus value. At the same time, New England's productivity stems from the local conditions, a home where the necessities for life and the provisions for voyage are readily available. Smith's New Englander already lives at sea, and this householding grants him an edge in a transnational market. Clearly, Smith's attunement to local resources enabled him to project a profitable future, albeit a future with profoundly unanticipated ecological consequences. The *General Historie* concludes with an advertisement for these fishy futures, again rhetorically transforming natural resources into extracted surplus value, making cod into gold: "Therefore honourable and worthy Country men, let not the meanesse of the word fish distaste you, for it will afford as good gold as the Mines of Guiana or Potassie, with lesse hazard and charge, and more certainty and facility" (CW 474).

III Housekeeping at Work: Maximus Tidies Up

In Smith, Olson recognizes the historical potential for multiple futures, a moment of contingency whose emergent effects were still shaping the political, social, and economic environment within which *The Maximus Poems* were being composed. Thus, a renovated housekeeping would need to account for past potential, incorporating and transforming the past in an unexpected poetic act. As his original writings demonstrate, "old mother" Smith's housekeeping inaugurated a major industry, setting the stage for the "advertising out" that Olson would critique, even as Smith's awareness of the land, his "bite," offers a dynamic and grounded measure of the human universe. Maximus, one of Smith's children, inherits this contradictory situation, in which fishing, as a practice responsive to the body and the earth, provides the conditions for the disembodied and groundless fishing *industry*. The leveling power of the latter reality, the house rule of global capitalism, threatens to displace the former, particularly by the time those market forces had developed into the world of 1950s America. Smith's *oikonomia* does not provide a model to be imitated but, instead, necessitates Olson's own housekeeping as an ongoing activity of cultural reformation. The explorer's vision of early America thus holds both a threat and promise for contemporary Gloucester.

Olson's efforts to rewrite Smith's inheritance into a new, emergent domesticity are apparent in "Some Good News," a sweeping meditation toward the end of the first volume of *Maximus* that blends material history, the political and colonial past, geography, myth, personal biography, and contemporary American life. Olson uses the environmental realities of his present to generate an immanent interpretive framework of the past that has brought that very present into being. History and the contemporary thus exist in a dynamic feedback loop made visible through the poetic work of *The Maximus Poems*, an example of Olson's insistence that all living processes are inextricably connected, continually producing unexpected effects. And, like *The Maximus Poems*, "Some Good News" is too complicated for a single summary account, its many semantic registers and cultural concerns blending and refracting one another. Thus, the interpretation offered here merely highlights some of the major movements of the piece to give a sense of how Olson's poetic use of history enacts new economies and unexpected cultural forms.

Through the attention generated by the poem, the establishment of a small fishing colony by fourteen Dorchester Company fishermen "setting down / on Cape Ann" is not merely "small news" but, in fact, marks a "permanent change," a new manifestation of earlier processes (MP 124). The relationship between Puritanism and fish at Gloucester's founding, a persistent focus throughout the early poems, immediately asserts itself in this permanent change, for the fishermen had landed on a place that was patented by England to be used by the Plymouth colony.[40] The "permanent change" thus anticipates conflict between the fishermen, generally praised by Olson, and the imperial colonialists, whom Olson largely criticizes. But instead of resolving that conflict, the poem moves to place-names, speculating on the origin of "St. George's" shoal ("who gave her their / patron saint – England? / Aragon? or Portyngales?" [MP 124]), only to then combine the imperial, the geographic, the material, and the mythic, so that "(the Westward motion) / comes here, / to land" (MP 125). In the context of the work as a whole, "Westward motion" sounds many resonances. In a broad political sense, the motion reflects the movement of empire that would turn the American continent into a site of European conquest and migration, a process Olson traces back to prehistoric eras. Olson also notes that fishermen "have / been showing" this fact for a long time, thus associating the "Westward motion" with an ecological awareness, a sense reinforced by the next section of the poem, which turns to the terror of the shoals, worse "than rock because / they do blow shift lie, / are changing as you sound," a passage which calls to mind "The Sea Marke" (MP 125). The dangerous shifting sands of the East coast are also the product of a Westward motion in the ocean, the waves shaping the geography that would ultimately give a place its character. Finally, Olson will later use the phrase in *"Maximus to Gloucester, Letter 27* [withheld]" to designate the excessive sources of the self, the "predecessions" and "precessions" of subjectivity, which come from "all that I no longer am, yet am, / the slow westward motion of / more than I am" (MP 184). This "westward motion" cannot be reduced to a Cartesian ego; the self, instead, is excessive, changing, and complex, a networked subjectivity born out of history. Similarly, what happened at Cape Ann "wasn't new," but this happening, this news, cannot be explained by some more abstract account, for "[it's] where, / and when it / did" that matters (MP 125).

"Some Good News" thus pays rigorous attention to the particularity of Gloucester's local identity even as the poem situates it within a larger transnational movement. As one agent in that process, Smith enters the verse as a "stater of / quantity and / precision" (MP 126). The precision takes both immanent and reflexive forms, attending to the present and the past. One drags the bottom, like a sailor, of a "shifty new / land" (new because it shifts) to keep from running aground, while, at the same time, historical meaning cannot always be recognized in its moment, just as Smith was

> too early yet
> to be understood
> to be the sign
> of present
>
> paternities
> (MP 126–7)

In other words, the emergent potential of Smith's actions were not fully visible in his own time, thus locating historical meaning not in the consciousness of those who experienced the past but in longer processes of evolution and transformation. In these lines the poem takes an explicit turn to the familial, the domestic, and the contemporary, bridging the public world of fishermen, land disputes, and geography with the "private" realities of home life, demonstrating that this ancestry is multiple. Smith, characterized as "Androgyne," becomes both mother and father, and thus stages the Oedipal drama in a single person. But far from retreating into Lowell's privatized familial triangle, the poem quickly returns to the political by suggesting a parallel between explorers like Smith and Caesar's dream "that he'd been intimate / with his mother," a vision interpreted to mean "that you shall conquer / the world" (MP 127). Through this comparison Olson's praise of Smith becomes ambivalent. This father figure of precision and measure, who "changed / everything" and whose virtues were misunderstood by his contemporaries (MP 128, 127), was also an avowed conqueror and colonialist. Thus, Smith/Caesar/Father/Mother embodies the Westward motion in all of its contradictions and potential, and the poem's rapid transformations bring these complex processes to light.

The poem continues by narrowing its focus, tracing a relationship between Smith and the development of American imperialism. Smith's conquering tendencies later manifest themselves in a more violent fashion in the Puritans' replacement for Smith, Miles Standish, who conducted "corporative / murder" by "drop[ping] / bombs" (MP 129). Smith is contrasted with Standish, but clearly predicts or sheds light upon him as well. Olson implicates one through the actions of the other: Standish lacks Smith's geographical acumen, but Smith anticipates Standish's bombs. The latter, of course, did not drop bombs in the modern sense, but Olson traces a line of continuity through America's many wars. The poem thus makes Smith and Caesar participants within the contemporary war machine, presenting a genealogy that includes Standish, the American Civil War, and the modern tactics used in the two World Wars. The poetry allows these proliferating references to accumulate:

> Yet Grant
>
> still is a name
> for butcher, for how
> he did finally hammer out
> a victory over
>
> Clotho Lee, the spinner
> the stocking frame
> undid: textile
> us, South
> and North – the world,
>
> tomorrow, and all
> without fate
> tomorrow,
> if we,
> who come from a housekeeping
>
> which old mother Smith
> started,
> don't find out the inert
> is as gleaming as,
> and as fat as,
>
> fish   (MP 129–30)

Grant's mercantile-funded victory over Lee leads to the present imperial potential of the United States. Tomorrow might be the conquest of the world, proof that the Westward motion is still in process, a motion that birthed and was perpetuated by Smith the explorer and discoverer. Nevertheless, the responsibility placed on "we" proves that those processes are by no means determined, not dictated by "fate." The poem suggests that although Smith's housekeeping gave rise to the dangers of contemporary market and political exploitation, history can also be a resource for rediscovery and cultural change. Agency emerges from the same real-time movements that appear to determine human action, when precise soundings of the shifty cultural landscape, through the kind of adaptive poetic historiography Olson attempts, may be the only way one can reclaim that agency. Melville's "Divine Inert" here is figured as "gleaming" and "fat" fish – nature's own productivity and its connection to human life, precisely and responsively measured, must be recognized if Smith's housekeeping is to be put back in order.⁴¹ The domestic economy thus bears all of the weight of a political, mythic, and personal unconscious that the poem has made visible, and, in doing so, imaginatively transformed.

The verse ends with a contemporary metaphor for the "hustings" from which Melville's Divine Inert springs. Olson connects hustings to the "'trash', / industrial fish" that are now caught in Gloucester, an indifferent extraction of "anything / nature puts in the sea," which is then taken to the "De-Hy / to be turned into catfood, / and fertilizer" (MP 131). The commercial and mechanized harvest recalls many of the poem's concerns: new industry, commodified exchange, indifference to nature, and alienation from "the subjective." The dehydrated fish are a far cry from the "fat" and "gleaming" inert, while the movement "inland" of this commodity is yet one more echo of the Westward motion, now determined not by political ends but by corporate exchange (although the poem has demonstrated that the two have not been separable from at least the time of the Dorchester fishermen). The carpenter's ability to see the tansy flower is long forgotten, and thus the De-Hy can be read as the logical result of ecological conquest by capital, separating human life from its necessary ground. In light of this contemporary reality, the poem ends with an ambivalent appeal:

> From then
> – from Smith – some good news
> better
> get after   (MP 131)

Although Smith has inaugurated the dangers of the contemporary economy, he offers the potential for new "good news." The language suggests hope and uncertainty, a command and a desire. Gloucester must actively "get" after good news by actively reinterpreting the past in the present, but Gloucester also *needs* good news to refashion contemporary domesticity.

As "Some Good News" illustrates, Smith, for all of his productive qualities, cannot be entirely separated from the many forces that exceeded his own intentions and designs, movements that continue to bear dark fruit in Gloucester. The "Westward motions" that occupied Smith are consistent with Olson's view of history as a process, an emerging multiplicity of often conflicting facts. For this reason, heroifying Smith may actually block the creation of a new polis by ignoring history's many possibilities, reducing the past to a single, complete narrative. At the same time, the poem illustrates how *The Maximus Poems* work on and through a figure like Smith to offer open, transformational poetics as a substitute for an idealized domestic program. The good news is in fact performed by the poem, through an emergent representation of the past so that history's suppressed possibilities, those alternative *oikonomikoi*, can come to light. As a form of psychic and cultural recreation, Olson's task of housekeeping thus resembles Cornelius Castoriadis's characterization of psychoanalysis as a "practicopoetic activity" whereby a new autonomy is brought into active being not by transcending the past but by artistically reinhabiting it.[42] *The Maximus Poems* endlessly offer the promise, if not the actualization, of "some good news."

This creative "practicopoetic" housekeeping, furthermore, expands the possibilities for personal experience, preparing human beings to live in these new, emergent homes. Just as figures like Smith are shown to be historically determined as well as potentially revolutionary, the poem demonstrates that individual perception and experience is structurally coupled to history. As Olson declares in *The Special View of History*, "history is the continuum which man is, and if a man does not live in the thought that he is a history, he is not capable of himself."[43] In a strange articulation of self-consciousness, it is only by recognizing that the individual is both *in* history and *a* history that his words and deeds become culturally significant. This definition of the self is illustrated in a representative untitled verse late in *Maximus*, in which the speaker shuttles back and forth between considerations of long-dead figures like Abraham Robinson and Elinor Hill to "now writing this spring day of 1966" to the sighting of "a fox" or some other "swift quiet animal" to wondering "why / the neck I am on was from 1642 called / Planters Neck" (MP 517–18). The willing movement from the archival to the phenomenological, the recorded to the ephemeral, can be explained by Olson's own acknowledgement that the "17th Century within my eyes & on my skin as / in my mind and, in fact and in fact belief I / write and map for you" (MP 518). The embodiment of the Puritan histories converts centuries-old American life into a scene of continual writing, a physical experience as well as a mental one. The phenomenological, through Olson's audacious poetic practice, becomes the historical, an addition through poetry to the archive which, in adding, transforms the inherited order and affords Olson, and an unnamed, Whitmanian "you," new occupancy within history's home.

Thus, poetry as housekeeping, an economy of the practicopoetic, through which the personal and the present dwell within the cusp of past and future, can only occur in and as active, emergent writing. Instead of Walter Benjamin's mourning angel, driven from the garden of paradise and forced to watch the wreckage of history accrue at its feet,[44] Olson attempts to create a stance through which history can be made livable, by constantly reconfiguring the forces born of the past. *The Maximus Poems* actualize Olson's claim that "history, like religion, myth, and poetry, share the common property that a thing done is not simply done but is re-done or pre-done. It is at once commemorative, magical, and prospective."[45] A poetic *oikonomikos* endlessly transforms the political economy that would keep it confined to the merely decorative or naively heroic, allowing Olson to define as he discovered, to think as he created.

"FORM," Olson famously insisted, "IS NEVER MORE THAN AN EXTENSION OF CONTENT" (CP 240). The focus of this book has been on emergent forms, and so a chapter on Olson that focuses primarily on his themes and "content" may appear as something of a departure from our formal concerns. However, Olson is significant in this study for the emergent perspective on history he articulates, creating a poetry that was an "extension" of the complex transformations that he saw in the broader universe. Olson's form, in other words, is a porous boundary, a provisional configuration of the network of complex, adaptive relationships in which his text is embedded: archival, geographic, spatial, literary, and embodied. The extension of nature's variety, to return to "Projective Verse II," was also an observation of that variety; Olson offers an emergent vision of poetry as the mechanism whereby nature autopoietically reflects on its own processes. Olson's work can thus be read as a pivot in the tradition of American long poetry, when emergence was expressly articulated as a poetic value. While not adhering to Olson's metaphysics or politics, many late twentieth-century practitioners of the long poem adopted a similar emergent perspective, imagining the present to exist on the cusp of an unforeseeable future and attempting to create a work sufficiently responsive to that change. In my final chapters, I examine two contemporary emergent projects that bring other traditions of adaptive, dynamic composition into the American long poem. The first of these poets, Rachel Blau DuPlessis, renovates modernism by rewriting it through the ancient textual practice of midrash, recursively transforming modernist ideology and secular Jewish practice. In doing so, DuPlessis's work integrates the unwritten into its formal structure, making space, as it were, for writing to come.

CHAPTER 5

Emergent Midrash
Rachel Blau DuPlessis Glosses Modernism

Thus far, reading for emergence has afforded a multidimensional perspective on the American long poem. Through concepts like iteration, recursion, provisional closure, feedback loops, autopoiesis, enaction, and structural coupling, the emergent properties of individual long poems have become newly legible. We have seen iterative and recursive feedback loops in Ammons and Hejinian, an expansive enaction in Whitman, the adaptive poetic vocabulary of Pound's translation machine, and the emergent view of history in Olson's projective verse. This approach has resituated these poems in their local context, showing how emergent poetic strategies transform dominant features of romanticist, modernist, and mid-twentieth-century aesthetics. Additionally, tracing emergent practices makes visible relationships across literary periods, allowing us to see how diverse projects like *Leaves of Grass*, *The Cantos*, and *My Life* share the common properties of complex adaptive systems.

As a conceptual framework, then, emergent poetics offers a dynamic picture of *intertextual* relationships. These relationships, in turn, suggest new methods for criticism. What happens when we think of literary history as a kind of system, adaptive and unpredictable? New critical questions arise if we look for iteration and recursion not only within individual texts but between them, imagining, for example, *My Life* iterating *Leaves of Grass*, in turn structurally coupled to *The Cantos* or "Howl" while engaged in a feedback loop with the long poems of its own time, like Ron Silliman's *Ketjak* or Rachel Blau DuPlessis's *Drafts*. Models of literary history as a dynamic, continually evolving intertextual network already exist, of course; in the twentieth century, we might look to the Russian Formalist Yuri Tynyanov's 1927 essay "On Literary Evolution" or Franco Moretti's later Marxist revision of Tynyanov's approach.[1] Similarly, as discussed in the introduction, Niklas Luhmann extensively analyzes art as an autopoietic system, provocatively claiming that the "[art] object is the system's memory."[2]

But approaching literature as an adaptive, environmentally embedded intertextual system is not a twentieth-century phenomenon. Precursors can be found in ancient textual practices, such as midrash, the Jewish tradition of Talmudic commentary, gloss, and reinterpretation. It is this tradition that DuPlessis deploys in *Drafts*, creating a unique model of poetic form that deliberately makes space for writing to come, establishing an emergent intertextuality *within* her poem. As an extension of that intertextual approach, DuPlessis structurally couples midrash with the modernism of the American long poem, entangling these two literary networks to generate a distinctive aesthetic capable of modernism's radical critique while also bearing witness to memory, trauma, and loss. In *Drafts*, we see midrash reading modernism, just as we observe modernism reading midrash. Consequently, DuPlessis's work is significant not only as a contemporary instance of an emergent text but also as a poem that offers a chance to reflect on the long poem tradition as a whole. To adapt Luhmann's language, we might say that *Drafts* is a revisionary memory of the long poem as literary system.

DuPlessis's modernist credentials are extensive. She was mentored by the Objectivist George Oppen, wrote her dissertation on William Carlos Williams's *Paterson* and Pound's *Pisan Cantos*, and, as Lynn Keller argues, has been profoundly influenced by Robert Duncan's developments in serial form.[3] *Drafts* owes its title, in part, to Pound's *A Draft of XXX Cantos*, but DuPlessis's relationship with Pound is complex. While she notes that her work was "involved with Pound from its inception," her intentions were to offer "a critical resistance to the impact of [his] work," to "make an alternative *Cantos*, a counter-*Cantos*."[4] This statement comes from an essay in which she criticizes Pound's politics and poetics as being fractured by "paradoxical, embittering contradictions": on the one hand, *The Cantos* develop an open poetic practice grounded upon "deferrals and displacements of meanings" yet, on the other, Pound personally held to a notion of "language without sociality, language as pure force beamed into the brains of others," a belief that had bearing upon his totalitarian and anti-Semitic politics.[5] As the genealogy of her poem's title reveals, DuPlessis engages with the modernist tradition by way of critical resistance, actively revising and extending modernist experimental practices while reinterpreting some of its accompanying ideologies, including its exclusions based on ethnicity or gender.

That revisionary stance is visible in "Draft 85: Hard Copy," in which DuPlessis deliberately speaks back to her mentor Oppen in a homage conversation with his long poem "Of Being Numerous." The twenty-ninth section of Oppen's poem is an address to his daughter, confessing that the speaker "cannot judge" the living, subjected as he is to "The baffling hierarchies / Of father and child."[6] Oppen's humility in the face of biological and social orders, including, by implication, patriarchy, is picked up by DuPlessis in "Draft 85: Hard Copy," where she draws on the Torah to generate an intertextual gloss on Oppen. She begins her own section 29 with an allusion to the Biblical story of Rachel's theft of her father's household idols, "rare black stones" which Rachel hides: "cover them with the ass of female claim, / settle in for the duration, and refuse / ('being in the way of women') / to rise."[7] In the context of *Drafts* as a whole (and "Draft 85: Hard Copy" as a poem), the biblical narrative is of interest for many reasons. It employs euphemism to demonstrate an anxiety over the menstruating female body; it evokes the aesthetic, the religious, and the domestic in the form of a household idol; it is a story of a woman engaging in theft and deception as a form of resistance to patriarchal order; and, in a pun DuPlessis employs elsewhere in the work, the story of another "Rachel" is extended into the poet's position as artist and woman.

In light of this history, DuPlessis can respond more deliberately to Oppen:

> Say you are neither disloyal nor pilferer.
> And sit tight on the icons and rocks of meaning
> gathered from the paternal household,
> the talismanic counterfoils, even
> the fewest and smallest
> from the fierce storehouses of articulation
> and defensiveness.
> You will remake these goods in your own blood.[8]

Rejecting the accusation that the female poet is merely derivative or one who denies her own inheritance, the poem calls for a deliberate exploitation of paternalistic art (that "fierce storehouse of articulation"), icons of the past that would include a work like "Of Being Numerous." Actively adopting that other Rachel's position, the poet calls for an iterative and recursive transformation of cultural history through a rewriting of what are already, although insufficiently, "goods," artistically adapting that otherwise silenced female body. Within the context of a poem that echoes Oppen's work, these lines perform precisely such a re-creation, articulating the blank spaces of Oppen's own poetry and making visible a new, emergent meaning that arises through the network of relationships between "Of Being Numerous," the Torah, and "Draft 85." By critically historicizing Oppen – and the modernist tradition he represents – through the book of Genesis, DuPlessis offers a poetic midrash, "remaking the [modernist] goods in [her] own blood" and generating a new vision of the long poem's social history.

This passage from "Draft 85: Hard Copy," with its reliance on the book of Genesis, illustrates the profound influence of Jewish textual traditions on *Drafts*. DuPlessis has argued that modernism remains an unfinished cultural project, having insufficiently challenged the ideological constrictions of gender identities.[9] In light of the fascism and anti-Semitism that marked many canonical writers, that incomplete revolution is also evident in modernist responses to Jewishness. At the same time, DuPlessis does not affirm an orthodox or uncritical Judaism as a rejoinder to modernism. As she argues in her essay "Midrashic Sensibilities," "there is no one-size-fits-all concept of Judaism," and the versions of Jewish culture that interest her are characterized by the ongoing work of writing: "How do I define my creolized Jewishness? Not the least in my skepticism, resistance, intuitive exilism, and quarrel with that curiosity called God. And in my deep commitment to the book and to textuality. 'Is there such a thing as Jewish destiny?' If it exists, [as Edmond Jabès has suggested] . . . it is in and of 'the book.'"[10] Skepticism, resistance, and exile as inherited sensibilities produce a culture of writing, one of "endless interpretation rather than Incarnation," a "fascinating and profound aspect of Judaism" (MS 214). In this endless interpretation as a response to a "Jewish destiny," DuPlessis offers a new cultural framework for emergent practice. History becomes articulate as a scene of ongoing writing, the process of discovering unexpected meaning in inherited texts while structurally coupling those texts to surprising environmental circumstances.

If DuPlessis's "creolized Jewishness" continues the tradition of exilic and resistant dialogue, that tradition is inseparable from midrash, which she acknowledges is "the key genre animating *Drafts*" (MS 219).[11] DuPlessis briefly defines the practice as "a continuous and generations-long commentary on sacred texts by those – males, in Orthodox tradition – invested with the spiritual authority to discuss them," and points out that "*Drafts* as a whole project alludes to – but secularizes – this genre of serious commentary and continuous gloss," a genre that reflects the need for "continual interpretation and reinterpretation, never completed, and never fulfilled" (MS 219). Among the specific devices that midrash offers *Drafts* is "a strategy of self-citation and recurrent reflection upon the poems' themes and images," an "endless unrolling of elaboration via gloss, self-reading, reconsideration, citation and debate . . . [which is] a way of living in textuality characteristic of a Jewish heritage" (MS 220). DuPlessis's characterization of midrash clearly reflects an emergent textual practice, where meaning is subject to a continual process of iteration and recursion, with local writing procedures producing unexpected, second-order patterns of meaning, in turn enabling new additions and trajectories within the text.

In this capacity to produce emergent forms in response to existing texts, midrash can be found, as David Stern has pointed out, "at the point" where "exegesis turns into literature."[12] As we have seen in the previous chapters, complex adaptive systems dwell at this intersection, developing a hermeneutic perspective through the recreation of their own processes. Consequently, DuPlessis's use of midrash is not simply a formal device; the practice also enables a distinctively poetic reflection on the changing historical conditions of late twentieth-century life. In particular, *Drafts* deploys midrash to develop an emergent commentary on the status of poetry "inside the grief of a century,"[13] offering a post-Holocaust investigation of loss, trauma, and silence. As Stern has argued, midrash is a sign of a Rabbinic humility born out of a self-acknowledged belatedness, a way of interpretation without mastery.[14] In the context of the American long poem, with the tradition of domineering hermeneutic rhetoric in writers like Whitman and Pound, midrash becomes a reinterpretation of interpretation, another model of literary form that embraces the contingencies of the poem as it moves through and responds to the world. To see these processes and forms at work, I now turn to a more detailed account of midrash's traditional modes and functions. I then demonstrate how midrash has profoundly shaped the emergent form, structure, and thematic preoccupations of *Drafts*, along the way drawing contrasts and parallels between DuPlessis's work and another late twentieth-century writer, Ron Silliman. Silliman's long poem *Ketjak*, a central text of Language poetry, approaches and resists the kind of emergent hermeneutic offered by DuPlessis, offering a useful illustration of the way emergence can exist in varying degrees in any given poem. *Drafts* and *Ketjak* are different points along a continuum of emergent possibilities, the former developing complex, second order emergent patterns that the latter deliberately resists. The chapter ends with a specific case study of a midrashic dialogue, where DuPlessis uses emergent strategies to rewrite and critique Theodor Adorno's infamous claims about poetry after Auschwitz.

I Midrash in History

Like the practice itself, the scholarly interpretations of midrash vary widely. According to Jacob Neusner, in its most basic sense "midrash" refers to the practice of scriptural exegesis as well as to the textual compilations of those written commentaries, a definition that suggests a feedback loop between midrash-as-text and midrash-as-writing. These commentaries and compilations were composed "by diverse groups of Jews from the time of ancient Israel to nearly the present day."[15] Midrash emerges from the belief that there is a complex relationship between divine revelation and human interpretation, the process by which that revelation is understood, although, as Ithamar Gruenwald points out, that distinction is in fact hard to maintain (WM 7). A fundamental assumption of midrashic interpretation is that multiple meanings can be continually uncovered in a given passage of revelation, all of which are relevant and significant in understanding God, the text, and the historical situation of the interpreter.

Those meanings are brought to light through a variety of compositional strategies, yet each form of midrash relies heavily on the generative potential of language, a power that is put to use in the service of a specific rhetorical or interpretive task. Neusner divides midrash into three general rhetorical categories. In "Midrash as Paraphrase," the exegete discovers a new meaning in an old text through a rephrasing or rewriting of the source. When this occurs, "the fresh meaning is imputed by obliterating the character of the original text and rendering or translating it in a new sense" (WM 7). The result is that the "barrier between the text and the comment here is obscured and the commentator joins in the composing of the text" (WM 7). Paraphrase, in this strong sense, adopts the power and authority of the original even as it creates something unexpected from its source. In "Midrash as Prophecy," the reader turns to scripture "to explain meanings of events near at hand" (WM 7). By doing so, the reader "treats the historical life of ancient Israel and the contemporary times of the exegete as essentially the same, reading the former as a prefiguring of the latter" (WM 7). The prophetic reading of a text assumes that the meaning of history requires interpretation – it is not self-evident. Such a textual practice moves beyond treating the utterance as meaningful only in the past; instead, it views the historical text as an opportunity for present cultural intervention, something to be put to use. The homiletic tradition of midrash may be the clearest example of that practical use, an instance of new composition-as-revision emerging within a specific historical context. Finally, in "Midrash as Parable" the commentator "reads Scripture in terms other than those in which the scriptural writer speaks" (WM 8). According to Neusner, "the basic principle here is that things are never what they seem to be. Israel's reality is not conveyed either by the simple sense of Scripture or by the obvious realities of the perceived world" (WM 8). Like the prophetic mode, then, the location of the community within an unfolding, unpredictable time requires a re-visioning of the text, for continually transformed conditions demand new understandings of scripture.

In each of its three modes, midrash is a communitarian, adaptive practice characterized by a double vision, a point crucial for understanding DuPlessis's poetics. The practice is oriented toward the textual past, a tradition that traces its origins to Moses, and yet this historical sensibility is entangled within the present experiences of the community. The internal processes of meaning generated by midrash self-modify in response to unexpected conditions, anticipating many of the processes found in other complex adaptive systems: iterative and recursive repetition through the rereading of ancient texts, responsiveness to changing environmental pressures and historical realities, even structural coupling to other texts to generate new meanings, as midrash comments on midrash. To be sure, the cultural beliefs and values informing traditional midrash are fundamentally different from other emergent systems, and so we must use caution when drawing these connections. Nevertheless, the parallels are clear.

Due to its many modes and applications, midrash is a predominantly multivocal practice. The anthologies of midrash often reveal disagreement among the various commentators, presenting a diversity of interpretations that, while not necessarily contradicting each other, at least emphasize very different elements of a given passage.[16] Stern writes that "the presentation of multiple interpretations (often, though not always, prefaced by the formula *davar aher*, 'another interpretation') is probably [midrash's] most ubiquitous feature."[17] In staging these "other interpretations," the collections of midrash bring together various fragments of larger glosses, making visible the history of interpretative practice on the page itself, which includes commentaries on other commentaries. These many interpretations reveal a commitment to the polyvocality of language. According to Irving Jacobs, the midrashic commentators believed that because Scripture was the word of God, "the most common-place terms and expressions – even particles of speech indispensable to the functioning of Hebrew – were to be regarded as 'containers' of deeper meanings, which the interpreter was required to unlock."[18] Thus, words from one passage could be linked to other, distant uses of the same formulation, each occurrence of the term illuminating all of the others.[19]

Although midrash writers shared a common belief in the multiplying, productive potential of sacred language, scholars disagree on the philosophical and cultural implications of this interpretive practice. Susan A. Handelman reads Rabbinic thinking as inherently textualist, in contrast with a strain of Western and Christian metaphysics that degraded writing. Instead of critiquing language as a fragile imitation of the logos, in "the contingent world of Hebrew thought, one must not look to nature for ultimate reality, but to the divine creative word which simultaneously reveals and conceals the hidden God."[20] Significantly, the word's creativity becomes manifest through the new interpretation and textual production. Through commentary, "the text continues to develop each time it is studied, with each new interpretation, for the interpretation is an uncovering of what was latent in the text, and thus only an extension of it; the text is a self-regenerating process."[21] In this sense, the text guarantees its own fecundity, proliferating meanings as an essential element of its original yet still-emerging identity; indeed, Handelman's language of "self-regenerating processes" recalls the notion of autopoiesis within systems theory.

But what happens when that process of interpretation generates many different, perhaps even contradictory, readings of the same text? Here, Handelman affirms the potentially radical consequences of midrashic practice, arguing that Rabbinic principles "set up no hierarchy of interpretation, but call for a horizontal interplay; for since the text is a unity, all elements are potentially equal in the interpretive process."[22] As a result, "instead of geometrical organized patterns, the Talmud is composed of a cacophony of voices, arranged in a seemingly freely associative way."[23] The unity of the text includes its many possible, always accumulating, "self-regenerating" interpretations, and this potential for endless and emergent signification is a sign of the scripture's power. For Handelman, the willing embrace of that "cacophony of voices" stems from the Rabbinic commitment to a textualist metaphysics, one that does not abandon the written word for the univocality of the (Western) Logos.

Where Handelman reads midrashic multiplicity as a sign of Rabbinic openness to language's proliferating power, Stern, admitting that many voices can be found in midrash, shifts the focus to a projected social or historical solidarity that unites those different interpretations. Arguing against those who would see in midrash a precursor to poststructuralist interpretive play, Stern contends that midrash as a social practice had a precise and clear function of stabilizing the community. "Following the Temple's destruction [in C.E. 70]," Stern writes, "the text of the Torah became for the Rabbis the primary sign of the continued existence of the covenantal relationship between God and Israel, and the activity of Torah study – midrash – thus came to serve them as the foremost medium for preserving and pursuing that relationship."[24] No longer able to ground the sacred community in its proper home, the Rabbis turned to textuality to maintain cultural identity. In its social function, the willing acceptance of multiple interpretations into the midrashic text is "an attempt to represent in textual terms an idealized academy of Rabbinic tradition where all the opinions of the sages are recorded equally as part of a single divine conversation."[25] That idealized academy projects, in turn, "a fantasy of social stability, of human community in complete harmony, where disagreement is either resolved agreeably or maintained in peace," a fantasy that is all the more utopian in the face of actual historical conditions of persecution without and dissension within.[26] As a site of social dialogue, the interpretive multiplicity of midrash, in Stern's reading, does not arise as the product of textual indeterminacy. Instead, midrash's unity in difference signifies a (perhaps unconscious) historical reconciliation; writing is used to symbolically contain cultural processes and forms that could not otherwise be controlled or predicted.

Before returning to the specifics of *Drafts* as a secular, emergent adaptation of the literary system of midrash, it is worth adding another opinion to the conversation, one derived not from an emphasis on indeterminacy or the social function of commentary but from ethics. The philosopher Emmanuel Levinas, in contrast to more restricted definitions of midrash, extends the religious import of the practice of midrash into a general interpretation of all language. For Levinas, language offers a mediation between two people, and so constitutes an ethical situation that precedes ontology. While Levinas's stance is undoubtedly radical and occurs within a broader philosophical project, his assessment of midrash is relevant for understanding some of the central ethical imperatives of *Drafts*, particularly as the poem attempts to craft a post-Holocaust consciousness. For Levinas, language's multiplicity grants it an almost religious significance; as he asks, "is not inspiration the sublime ambiguity of human language?"[27] This polyvocal ambiguity in all language allows him to link Scripture with literature in general, and literature with the ethical recognition of an other:

> The latent birth of Scripture, of the book, of literature, and an appeal to interpretation, to exegesis, [is] an appeal to the sages who solicit texts. A solicitation of solicitation – Revelation. An appeal to the Talmud and to the infinite renewal of the Word of God in commentary, and commentary on commentary. There is a prophetism and a Talmudism preceding theological considerations: it is *a priori* (for it is doubtless also the very process of the coming of God to the mind) in the face of the other man.[28]

In this view, a text is a gift, a request for interpretation, which itself is asking to be heard – each text, original and interpretation, is both giver and recipient, neither able to fully determine its future meaning. Thus, for Levinas the "solicitation of solicitation" in this linguistic exchange is a form of "Revelation," the advent of the divine in the exchange with another person through the written word. Before any positive, propositional content there is an activity of transmission and transformation implicit in human language, that a priori Talmudism. As one of his commentators points out, "Levinas's project for escaping the totality of the Western philosophical tradition" includes a "recognition of the Talmud as a vehicle for exhibiting a literary discourse in which this escape is, in fact, accomplished."[29] Presupposing an ongoing writing instead of a concluding word, or, at best, a text that unites multiple voices, the practice of midrash, for Levinas, reflects the openness to alterity, an ethical stance preceding any positive utterance, and the implicit recognition of the face (or, more properly, the script as evidence of the face) of another.[30]

As these many interpretations suggest, the rich tradition of midrash offers several resources to DuPlessis as a writer of an emergent poem after modernism. Midrash is an open compositional practice born out of language's self-proliferation, the processes of social history, and the ethical demand of other voices. Like other forms of emergent textuality, it unites interpretation and exploration, composition and contemplation. Those shared values do not, however, overcome a fundamental difference between the poem and the historical practice, namely the rejection in *Drafts* of a divine perspective. Language is a purely human phenomenon in *Drafts*, an uncanny medium structurally coupled to history. The Rabbis may have been able to hope, despite their circumstances, in a God who had spoken and heard, albeit a God who had withdrawn in many other respects. DuPlessis admits only to human ears:

> If I were to cry out
> the questions why or how or
> who would hear us –
> I'd say the only ones to hear this
> are ourselves.
> Therefore it is scrupulous to listen.
> Especially to shadows.[31]

Writing in such a condition, and with such Levinasian ethical imperatives, becomes an act of perception, of listening and speaking to others. Such a task poses unique challenges and opportunities for poetic form.

II Midrash and Emergent Form

Midrash is an important precursor to the long poems we have already explored in this study, which challenge conventional measures of artistic form and their associations with closure, objecthood, completion, and symmetry. Writing at the intersection of these two practices, DuPlessis develops an adaptable poetic structure, substituting a "process of formation" for the stability of form. This approach is far from a rejection of form; instead, *Drafts* develops multiple techniques of provisional closure that never fully solidify into completed form. In doing so, *Drafts* maintains a formal capacity for future emergence. As DuPlessis puts it in "Midrashic Sensibilities," form in *Drafts* must be understood as "a kind of self-skepticism and praxis, not an iconic object" (MS 220). The practice of self-skepticism is directly stated in "Draft 19: Working Conditions":

> This is the work
> This is the work
> disfigured
> form as experienced
> struggle, over the mark.
>   (T 128–9)

"Disfigured" resists compositional strategies and also suggests damaged, torn, and defaced. Under this sign, form cannot achieve closure because it is an "experienced / struggle," something that occurs in time and yet comes out of an iteration of points, the mark encountered, debated, and contested. By implication, "work" must be read not as a thing but as an active task. The struggle "over the mark" is a hermeneutic process, where poetic form becomes the record of its conflicted emergence, vacillating, as DuPlessis puts it elsewhere, between "open and closed, A and not-A."[32] Like a system continually reestablishing itself, a disfigured poetic keeps the struggle open, unable or unwilling to capture the mark.

Elsewhere in *Drafts*, that mark is presented as a dot, letter, or word that bears social and historical significance. Moving between the past and the future, the meaning of the mark is established through its own iterations and recursions. This mark also originates in midrash; as DuPlessis puts it, the "dot" is "imagined as the smallest Hebrew letter 'yod,' as a pinhole through which 'it' all enters. The questions of the 'itness' of the world, its flooding plethora, are central" to *Drafts* (MS 211). Surveying the magnitude of existence by way of a pen stroke, the *yod* (ʼ) brings together history, phenomenological time, and language, a recurring motif throughout *Drafts*. The speaker describes herself as "a mite in the letter," one who "quiver[s] in [her] pinhole time / where bits of voice are buried" (T 27, 80). Privy to only a part and yet conscious of a larger whole, the *yod* affords a fragmentary perspective, eliciting powerful interpretive energy but unable to fully account for "all." That interpretive risk is evident elsewhere in the poem, where "Frenzied with mere pinholes of opening, letters / flooded into the space like paint / and soaked the site / with unreadable stain" (T 159). In an added midrashic twist, the *yod* as poem, like the speaker, generates its own autopoietic, recursive interpretive process, "a dot glossing itself inside existence" (T 253).

This endless struggle with letters – autopoietic, recursive, adaptive, and historically inflected – is made possible through a variety of midrashic techniques. One such technique is the rigorous attention to the smallest units of language. Through these discrete and often ignored elements of communication DuPlessis builds to her larger interests, ranging from art and social practice to the plethora of the "itness" of the world. Many of the individual Drafts are dedicated to these fundamental units: "Draft 1: It," "Draft 2: She," "Draft X: Letters," "Draft 11: Schwa," "Draft 41: Of This," "Draft 54: Tilde." These tests of language are accompanied by pictorial depictions of individual letters (T 1), experimentations with fonts and inks,[33] and even the blacked out blocks of text found in censored or classified documents (T 28–9, 31). The speaker points out that everything rests on these fundamental units of meaning:

> That the whole is strains "of"
>   thinking what the whole and its fractions
>   come to
>
> That it is –
> and I've said only this –
> a gloss on it
> a gloss on is   (T 238)

The most fundamental statement of ontology could be reduced to "it is," and to say "only this" is thus an effort to articulate all. However, the "it" and the "is" are first and foremost words, texts which can only be interpreted through more writing. The "whole," in turn, exists partially and inseparably from "'of / thinking,'" the quotation marks calling attention to the grammar of thought itself. "Strains" can be read as the whole's pressure on thought or as thought's "straining" out the "whole and its fractions," another instance of struggle. Thought, language, and "the whole" thus emerge from words like "of," "it," and "is." In this manner, a gloss on language's smallest units opens the door for ontological reflection.

Formally, glossing relies on a source and commentary structure, in which one text becomes the interpretation of another. On a visual level, DuPlessis adapts gloss into a spatial poetics, whereby the page becomes a field of composition, utilizing "sidebars, visuals, anything to create 'other-ness inside otherness,'" recalling a Spencer-Brownian logic of embedded distinctions.[34] From the very first Draft, DuPlessis works within this topic and comment form, at times through the use of two, independent poetic margins placed side by side. Her interest in marginality, the unspoken space next to and between any utterance, is visibly produced in the poem itself, as in this excerpt from "Draft 1: It":

It
is not surprising That.   This is the spoilage of
                                         presence   a condensation of
It's the little stuff that slips the wink   rot ick or
slides past phatic   split tingle
under all those sheets   "what
dog is woofing"   what shuttle
brights what warp?   WATER damage it really needs
                                         replacement

Can I heed   you, it?   This line, scrawl of a bird line
                                         tide line   (T 3)

By placing the two units next to each other in this way, DuPlessis unites a modernist poetics of disjunction and collage with midrashic marginal com-mentary. The concern with the marginal everydayness of "phatic" speech, the "warp" and "woof" of social communication (another manifestation, perhaps, of the *yod*), is placed next to an apparently informational utter-ance, the diagnosis of some form of damage that comes from an equally unnoticed water leak. "WATER" and language are loosely connected: the capitalization of the word calls attention to "water" *as* a word, while the "scrawl" of a bird line is linked to "tide line," and, in the context of the passage, both suggest the discrete order of these poetic lines. By extension, the two columns are undoubtedly joined thematically, not sim-ply visually; they deliberately echo each other, albeit in a rather distant way.

But which lines achieve priority? The many possible readings of the pas-sage, the associations and links evoked by the double margin, imply a text and gloss structure but deny the possibility of identifying which text is source and which comment. The left margin may be a gloss of the right, just as the right may be of the left. Neither text is originary or inspired, and thus the text can only be read as a feedback loop, where each col-umn is simultaneously text and gloss of the other. Metaphor cannot pro-vide much clarity, as the two columns do not share sufficient properties for us to see one as a representation of the other. Nor do the lines offer the flash of insight Pound assumed one would experience from the ideogram. At the same time, to argue for absolute disjunction fails as well, for we *can* discover likeness, shreds of meaning, echoes, or, in the multiple senses of the volume's title, tolls.

One implication of the two columns, the two interconnected yet disparate texts, is the necessary production of an unspoken, virtual *third* text; another gloss or commentary inevitably emerges from the two poetic columns (such as the one produced in the preceding paragraph). Furthermore, it is obvious that many potential "third texts" can be written out of the passage. The absence of the third text, its merely virtual possibility, leaves this particular secular midrash in that draftlike state, suggesting a process of formation without closure. This logic of "thirdness" offers space for the production of writing to come, generating formally the conditions of a yet-unwritten emergence.

The generative feedback loop of topic/commentary and the production of a virtual third text allow the poem to move itself forward in each iterative section, often unpredictably, while still remaining only a "draft." This poetics of gloss and commentary is also visible in the overall structure of *Drafts*. Perhaps DuPlessis's most important innovation, one she discovered in the midst of composition, *Drafts* is organized according to a repeating nineteen-poem sequence, in which each poem connects to, or "donates" to, its correlative poem in the following sequences, producing "doubled and redoubled commentary, poetry with its own gloss built in."[35] Thus, "Draft 1: It," "Draft 20: Incipit," "Draft 39: Split," "Draft 58: In Situ," "Draft 77: Pitch Content," and "Draft 96: Velocity" constitute what Du-Plessis refers to as the "line of 1." This particular example is telling, as one can see the titles morph into one another (most of the "lines" do not have as clear a connection in the individual titles): "It" expands to "Incipit," with "Split" and "In Situ" carrying the *s* and hard *it* sounds. DuPlessis explains that these correspondences between the various Drafts can exist in "some sensuous, intellectual, allusive, or even simple way," and that "this puts the responsibility for connection not on one central figure to settle the work's fullness, nor on any particularly gendered figure, but on numerous connectors dispersed all across the texture of the work, a mesh or net to hold fullness while honoring its enormous extent."[36] In this way, the poem is developed linearly (one poem written after the other), as well as across time, through the nineteen "lines" produced by the folds, establishing the poem's form as a grid with numerous connections and possibilities. Midrashic practice informs this structural device, as one can see that commentary is built into the logic of the fold: "It" produces the conditions of possibility for "Incipit." At the same time, and in keeping with DuPlessis's interest in the "ungraspable rush," the fold, like her use of the double margin, ultimately does not allow for a hierarchy among the texts. "It" is just as much a reading of "Incipit" as the latter is a commentary on the former. As the "line" extends through the addition of new poems, links and dispersals emerge, transforming the form of the whole.

In attempting to create a nontotalizing poetry in which "fullness" remains excessively untamable in its "ungraspable rush," DuPlessis also synthesizes the emergent aesthetic of ongoing composition with the traditional poetic desire for formal shape, developing a completed structure while still maintaining unwritten potential as an essential element of the work. With the publication of *Surge: Drafts 96–114*, DuPlessis brought *Drafts* to a completion. "Draft 114: Exergue and Volta" concludes the sixth nineteen-draft sequence, with each "line" now containing six poems. While "Draft 114: Exergue and Volta" brings her task of writing to a stopping point, the commentary logic of the "line" extends the poem into many possible "readings." Because each is essentially a commentary on all, the number of recursive echoes, "tolls," and interpretations the fold generates for future readers will continue to grow, along with the many meanings one encounters in a sequential reading of the entire poem. The "completion" of this poem does not necessarily run, then, against the poetics of ongoing and emergent formation that has animated her work (and the other long poems explored in this study). "With a number like 114," DuPlessis writes, "I declared 'term,' 'limit,' or 'bourne,' while at the same time evoking a number large enough to feel like an abyss."[37] Or, more appropriately, the poem, even beyond its 114th entry, continues to carry with it a (virtual) volume of blank pages that remain to be written, glossed, and rewritten.

DuPlessis's use of numerical systems to generate, constrain, and shape the interpretive energies of *Drafts* indicates a family resemblance with her contemporaries, particularly writers of Language poetry.[38] We can see a similar but contrasting logic of thirdness in a poet like Ron Silliman, a friend and interlocutor of DuPlessis and a major figure in the Language movement. Like *Drafts*, Silliman's life work *Ketjak* spans several volumes and includes many works that are produced through the use of numerical, grammatical, and other constraints. Perhaps the most influential of these poems, also called *Ketjak*, was written in 1974 and first published in 1978.[39] Composed of prose poetry paragraphs, each of *Ketjak*'s sections repeats previous sections while expanding according to a fixed pattern. Andrew Epstein summarizes Silliman's method: "(1) each paragraph has twice as many sentences as the previous paragraph; (2) the new paragraph repeats each sentence from the previous paragraph in the exact same order, although sometimes those earlier sentences are altered or expanded; and (3) the new sentences in each new paragraph are placed between the existing sentences."[40] The result of this procedure is a rapidly expanding text, with the use of repetition producing the iterative and recursive effects we have seen in a number of emergent poems. Here are the first three paragraphs, which show both repetition and variation:

> Revolving door.
>
> Revolving door. A sequence of objects which to him appears to be a caravan of fellaheen, a circus, begins a slow migration to the right vanishing point on the horizon line.
>
> Revolving door. Fountains of the financial district. Houseboats beached at the point of low tide, only to float again when the sunset is reflected in the water. A sequence of objects which to him appears to be a caravan of fellaheen, a circus, camels pulling wagons of bear cages, tamed ostriches in toy hats, begins a slow migration to the right vanishing point on the horizon line.[41]

The requirement that the sentences appear in each section in the same order and that the new sentences of each section appear between the previous sentences produces a logic of thirdness similar to that found in *Drafts*. Furthermore, as we saw in Lyn Hejinian's *My Life*, another Language work, the new contextual combinations of sentences suggest alternative, emergent meanings through the process of iteration. "Revolving door," for instance, when preceding "A sequence of objects which to him appears to be a caravan, a circus," suggests one kind of movement – migrant, itinerant, even perhaps the parallel between the revolutions of the caravan wheel and the "door." In contrast, "Revolving door. Fountains of the financial district" evokes an entirely different interpretation, with the door now quite literal (perhaps), reminding one of the revolution *without* change that also characterizes the movement of water through the decorative fountains of corporate America. Combined, then, the emergent meaning of "Revolving door" within the poem *Ketjak* would be both the combination of these two context-determined senses of the sentence as well as the other potential contexts generated by future iterations of the poem.

If these readings sound merely suggestive and largely speculative, such indeterminacy is one of the effects of Silliman's procedure. For a major difference between Silliman's and DuPlessis's thirdness is that *Ketjak*'s mechanisms never shape which sentences are to be added to the work, nor do they offer a robust interpretive framework for their environment. Consequently, the poem resists the emergence of *second order* formal procedures or processes. The new additions are not commentaries on the old, as in *Drafts*, nor new translations out of an emergent vocabulary, as in the *Cantos*, nor even annexes reshaped to fit within an adaptive, expanding form, as in *Leaves of Grass*. Indeed, one of Silliman's explicit aesthetic values is to create a poetry that resists orders of meaning beyond the immediate experience of the sentence as a linguistic artifact. At the most, "the new sentence," which he advocated in an important manifesto, would flirt with the logical or "syllogistic" movement of thought between sentences without ever solidifying into a higher order claim, pattern, narrative, or form. Silliman does not deny relationships between sentences entirely; in writing that takes this approach, "each sentence plays with the preceding and following sentence," thus generating more than a mere "heap of fragments."[42] However, "any attempt to explicate [such works] as a whole according to some 'higher order' of meaning, such as narrative or character, is doomed to sophistry, if not overt incoherence. The new sentence is a decidedly contextual object. Its effects occur as much between, as within, sentences. Thus it reveals that the blank space, between words and sentences, is much more than the 27th letter of the alphabet. [The new sentence] is beginning to explore and articulate just what those hidden capacities might be."[43]

In articulating an interest in the "hidden capacities" between sentences, Silliman appears to indicate virtual, emergent effects made possible by the relationships between sentence units. And yet his dismissal of a "higher order" – what systems theorists might call second-order patterns or global effects – indicates a resistance to the poem as a self-organizing, adaptive system generating a larger system of meaning. Such an approach has its advantages and motivations. As Epstein argues, Silliman seeks to create a text of maximal "openness," where any sentence can enter in, producing "a kind of raw feed of the polymorphic everyday itself as it constantly unfolds."[44] *Ketjak* is thus a textual system producing elusive moments of simple emergence without generating self-reflexive feedback loops to stimulate larger formal transformation and second-order, complex emergence. In other words, Silliman's work simultaneously invites and resists emergence.

Oren Izenberg has argued that Language poetry on the whole can be read as "an endlessly productive faculty for generating a potentially endless array of 'New Sentences,'" using Chomsky's generative grammar as a model for this fundamental human linguistic capacity.[45] For Izenberg, linguistic capacity is akin to a system or procedure "independent of context," in contrast to "intentionality, which is always contextual."[46] *Ketjak* does not remove context entirely; instead, the primary context of each sentence is the immediate sentences surrounding it, generating the syllogistic "play" that Silliman praises in "The New Sentence." At the same time, Izenberg's argument suggests an important distinction relevant for understanding emergent poetics: that poetries can use iteration and recursion while differing in their degree of structural coupling to an environment and thus in their degree of complex emergence. *Ketjak* is an iterative system that produces internal emergent effects but largely lacks the hermeneutic edge of a practice like midrash. Consequently, subsuming these different long poetries – each with their own values and aesthetics – under broad generalizations about multiplicity, expansion, addition, and endlessness would be a mistake. Systems theory gives us a more flexible and precise vocabulary capable of revealing these distinctions.

Comparing Silliman and DuPlessis's long poems thus illustrates the way emergent effects do not take a single form; like different organisms, each poem establishes degrees of environmental entanglement. Both poems generate a poetics of "thirdness" and thus produce the internal emergence of the closed system. At the same time, DuPlessis's poem uses these internal operations to pointedly engage her changing environment to a degree that Silliman's work, at least in *Ketjak*, does not.[47] This comparison returns us to the question of formation as process, the experience of fractured, contested moments that characterize DuPlessis's cultural, poetic, and "creolized" stance. The porous nature of the fold refuses form as icon, but it still implies a flexible hermeneutic procedure that allows the poem to make "the grain of grid stand in for loss" (D 204). Like the Rabbis and their exiled consciousness, *Drafts* insists that the process of composition is an act of social comprehension, even a moral imperative. For this reason, developing a poetic form that acknowledges historical displacement while attempting to ethically comprehend it is a recurrent task in *Drafts*, a poetic ambition made all the more poignant in light of the historical erasures of subjects and cultures that preoccupy DuPlessis throughout the poem. DuPlessis thus deploys an emergent sensibility to dialogue with these obliterated pasts and invisible futures.

III Glossing Adorno

The feedback loops of commentary that constitute the form of *Drafts* allow DuPlessis to engage an endless number of outside texts in an ongoing dialogue. This communication without totality DuPlessis names "the ethics of poetry," a sentiment that recalls Levinas (T 233). Such ethical concerns are particularly apparent in the "Line of 14," which questions the role of writing in an apocalyptic world.[48] I end this analysis of DuPlessis's emergent poetics by offering a reading of some of the poems in the "Line of 14," demonstrating how the logic of the fold produces emergent connections between poems while also creating the conditions for a sustained commentary on outside texts, in this case the work of Theodor Adorno.

"Draft 14: Conjunctions" begins with an audacious yet mournful description of poetic ambition: "To write with the formidable consciousness of loss *thus*: / repeatedly emphasized under cross-examination: skin, sky, fog, silence, *and* humility" (T 92). The verse continues to argue for a "posthumous" poetics, one conveying an awareness of failure, destruction, and future catastrophes in which the world of the poem is lost forever. In that future, what scraps of language might remain, and what would they offer? In part, fragmentation itself would be characteristic of those scraps, tenuously linked by language's conjunctive potential. Such joints through language offer one explanation for the title of the poem, and for the simple device of italicizing each conjunction throughout the verse, highlighting the linking properties of language as both arbitrary and necessary.

The poem concludes by pivoting from command to question:

> What, then, is the size of the loss?
> The size is a triumph.
> A chemical glue drying askew
> bares the device.
> It is called "anguage."
> It won't be the same, ever-where
> *or* far away since.
>
> . . .
>
> Anarchist *and* pleasuring
> a flowered surface
> a surwind on the flood of the sea
> splintered bountiful marks.
>
> I throw it all *as* far *as* I can,
> *and* it blows back, blows black,
>
> "a certainty based on the acceptance of doubt"
> in "texts at once perfect *and* incomplete."
>
> (T 99)

To say that the size of the loss is a "triumph" undermines any positive definition of poetic accomplishment. The misapplied glue (another conjunction) that deliberately "bares the device" marks the loss of the illusion of wholeness, even the loss of individual letters, so that we are left with "anguage," a nonword recalling anguish, anger, even measurement ("gauge") in the absence of a complete language. The embrace of that loss, that partial, posthumous condition, allows the poem to accept that there is no absolute "ever-where" by which a poem could establish hermeneutic certainty.

In light of this uncertain reality, a poetics of loss can afford nothing but a pleasurable anarchy, a fragmented tossing of scraps into an unfriendly sea to acknowledge that chaos. The speaker throws words as "bountiful marks" into history, which, although they blow back, generate a text "perfect [because] incomplete," certain in its doubt. The fully secular perspective of this poetic stance is unmistakable: no final utterance will guarantee that fertility or validate the poem. DuPlessis "accepts" that doubt through the language of another speaker, another text, thus enacting the fragmentary, iterative, and structurally coupled textuality the poem declares. And, appropriate for a poem of conjunctive commentary, we are told in the notes that these final words come from scholar Reneé Bloch's analysis of midrash (T 271).

The interest in loss, "anguage," and a posthumous poetics creates space for a later poem in the "line of 14," "Draft 52: Midrash," which takes as its epigraph and central concern Adorno's infamous statement that "To write poetry after Auschwitz is barbaric."[49] By addressing this claim, DuPlessis interrogates the role of poetry in the contemporary world, a subject, as her own notes to the poem admit, that has inspired significant debate among contemporary writers (D 231). For DuPlessis, Adorno issues a challenge and a warning, evoking a textual response in the very form – poetry – that Adorno forbids. The poem's early sections are dominated by deliberately naïve and yet pointed questions that attempt to tease out the implications of Adorno's statement. "What," the poem asks, "is the specific vulnerability of 'poetry,'" as opposed to the other arts (D 142)? These queries prompt her to interrogate Adorno's claims about poetry in the most literal of terms: "Does poetry ignore crisis . . . / accept the normal / prettify hegemony?" and, if that is its only possible function or legitimate provenance, "should it therefore be forbidden?" (D 143). The questions are simultaneously ironic and sincere. *Drafts* has persistently self-critiqued any simplistic "prettifying of hegemony," thus challenging through its practice the accusation it poses. At the same time, the poem's rigorous self-examination suggests that ideological complicity is a constant risk.

When trying to answer these questions, one cannot ignore the events of the Holocaust, the fact that "[these] Deaths have altered thought" (D 145).

The dilemma is restated in its clearest terms in section 20. If "All culture, / after Auschwitz, including its urgent critique, / is garbage," one is left with the following impossible decision:

> Acting to maintain this "guilty and shabby culture"
> you are criminal, "Accomplice."
> Yet to reject this culture is precisely
> "furthering the barbarism
> that culture
> showed itself to be."
>
> The interstice is a stark revolting site.
> We are not frightened enough, nor enough engaged
> to be riven by this, to live by this. (D 153)

In light of Auschwitz, contemporary poets are faced with a (by now well-known) dialectical challenge. One can choose neither to affirm culture, which has shown itself to be no protection against barbarism, nor to reject culture, an impossible withdrawal from the social world that often perpetuates barbarism by other means. By posing this dialectic in the baldest of terms, DuPlessis suggests that the writer of modernity is a traumatically torn subject, "a stark revolting site" one can barely "live by." Such a torn subject speaks and does not speak, articulates in a barbaric tongue. One both cannot and cannot *but* write poetry.

Accepting, for the moment, such an impossible position, the problem of how to compose "riven" poetry, has yet to be solved as a formal problem in "Draft 52." In the posthumous world of those who remember the Holocaust, each "mourner is a black Letter unwritten," an image DuPlessis develops to conclude that "there is no accurate lexicon" to describe either the mourning or the tragedy (D 148). This linguistic inadequacy validates Adorno's decision to single out poetry for peculiar attention and also highlights the problem of composition. If "Language [is] not equal to itself" then "[the] only poem is blackened, barred-out lines," a device DuPlessis in fact utilizes at a number of points in the work (D 148). The reader then must "imagine the rest of this writing as black blocks. / But this, then, would be indistinguishable / from the 'censored,' from the 'erased'" (D 149). The "riven" poem thus achieves a new level of irony. In confessing to the failures of language in mourning, one may succumb to the tempting notion that to deny linguistic meaning is the purest "post-Auschwitz" poetic gesture. But, in doing so, one replicates in kind a device that contributed to the destruction in the first place, a censored silence that denied voice to the victims.

Toward the poem's end, DuPlessis offers one possible formal gloss on Adorno, Auschwitz, and poetry, but in a way that opens the burden of responsibility within the work to another text to come, responding with an unfinished answer and pointing to future, emergent writing. The most demanding section of the poem, this passage evokes her double-column commentary form but more radically intertwines the texts:

> . . . It was the   endlessly overwritten
> erosions of the book,   specificities
> of book, and the voice of the traveler-   detail
>   poem by its edgy sentence
> its ontological intransigence to Let
> Be   austere hermetic readable urgency.
> Smoke and billows salient
> shifting so that one is caught in
>   hypnogogic shakedowns
> their whorled resonance,   their dark bars, even access blocked.
>
> (D 156)

The section challenges interpretation and opens itself to emergent possibilities, demanding an "austere hermetic readable urgency" (D 156). The passage contains hints of midrash ("endlessly overwritten"), of decay ("erosions of the book"), of modernist difficulty and precision ("specificities," "edgy sentence," "ontological intransigence"), of wandering ("traveler- / poem"), of the actual details of the Holocaust ("Smoke and billows"), of marginality, imprisonment, and unreadability ("their dark bars, even access blocked"). The gaps, both spatially and grammatically, thus toll with innumerable culturally specific and historically significant details, none of which are ever fully articulated but exist as virtual possibilities on the cusp of emergence. The poem is a commentary broken off, a margin brought to a porous center.

Such a passage, simultaneously demanding and open, conveys the "riven" subject bound to neither affirm nor reject culture. This alternative, as DuPlessis imagines it, embodies the ethics of unfinished work by pointing toward another scene of writing made possible by the poem:

> The beyond is in the surface.
> Walking through the dead as partly dead
> – it must only be
> an impossible draft of half-built, half-crumbled
> all-suspicious poetry.   (D 156)

The poem, doubtful, questioning, and centerless, already falling apart, becomes a witness to its historical fracture. The half-dead poet writes only so that the poem can be rewritten.

One cannot easily take leave of that situation or accomplish that task. The structure of *Drafts* does not require DuPlessis to do so, and the work returns, reglossing, and reinterpreting, the problems of "Draft 52: Midrash," with "Draft 71: Headlines . . . ," "Draft XC: Excess," and "Draft 109: Wall Newspaper." The response to Adorno's claim, and the historical realities that it reflects, takes the form of more writing, a secular example of the self-regeneration Handelman identifies with midrash. At the same time, the projected social stability Stern emphasizes is here transformed into a measure of social lack. The many voices referenced in DuPlessis's poem are acknowledged in their silence, that "formidable consciousness of loss." At that point, where "deferral [is] intermingled with a helix of hope and doubt" (MS 220), the social work of secularized midrash and emergent writing most powerfully coincide. As DuPlessis learned from Oppen, the long poem is a powerful mechanism for discovering how to "speak where / rare earth riddles / have no end,"[50] even if, or because, as Oppen himself admitted, one cannot offer total or complete judgment. A poetic response must necessarily arise by way of a "turn, a fold, / a pitch, a bend,"[51] or, in other words, "another interpretation."

By exploring in detail how DuPlessis draws on the resources of both modernist aesthetics and midrash, *Drafts* exemplifies a moment of literary evolution, adapting and extending the literary system of emergent poetics and offering another interpretation of writing in real time. Her work uses an emergent sensibility to stage a recursive, restless social history, while, at the same time, her formal innovations extend and critique the practices of her modernist precursers. DuPlessis demonstrates that midrash was an unrecognized potential for American poetry, an element within the linguistic environment, as it were, that the literary system of emergent poetics had not yet adequately engaged. *Drafts* thus combines creation and interpretation on the level of literary history, offering a new practice that simultaneously critiques, recalls, and transforms the "system memory" of the long poem.

In these ways, midrash provides not only a textual and formal model, a mode of composition, but also a cultural consciousness, a "sensibility," as DuPlessis calls it, which is significant for understanding how *Drafts* moves through the history of the present and the literary past. Perhaps midrash's peculiar appeal comes from the fact that, as Stern argues, it is neither of nor apart from the Western literary tradition, but, instead, is "a marginal presence on its borders, a tradition that developed by drawing on Western categories and transforming them without becoming wholly absorbed by them."[52] Or, in systems-theoretical terms, midrash is a complex adaptive system in its own right structurally coupled to the developments of Western literature and thought. As a midrash on emergent poetics, *Drafts* presents, in its unfolding, another reading of both traditions, a "creolized" hermeneutic which the struggles of contemporary history seem to demand. The "creole" is also an important term for Nathaniel Mackey, who, like DuPlessis, is concerned with the historical potential of the unwritten and erased. As we will see in the next chapter, Mackey uses writing in real time to hazard a utopian leap, imagining a future hope without definitive expectations.

CHAPTER 6

Emergent Sounds
Nathanial Mackey's "Post-Expectant Futurity"

For Nathaniel Mackey, poetic language has everything to do with music, and music has everything to do with loss. The loss of home, kinship, and identity – these absences are central to a story told by the Kaluli people of Papua New Guinea, a myth used to explain the origins of music. In the tale, which Mackey summarizes in one of his essays, a brother and sister go out to gather crayfish. When the brother is unsuccessful, he asks his sister to share her catch, which she refuses. Eventually, the boy catches a crayfish and places it on his nose, which transforms into a beak. As he is morphed into a Muni bird and flies away, Mackey writes that the "sister begs him to come back and have some of the crayfish but his cries continue and become a song, semi-wept, semi-sung: 'Your crayfish you didn't give me. I have no sister. I am hungry. . . .'"[1] Mackey uses this story to claim that music and poetic language emerge out of the "orphan's ordeal." In declaring its alienated condition, music is "wounded kinship's last resort" (DE 232), both an acknowledgment of a ruptured past and a cry for healing. The "wounded" speaker represents disrupted boundaries within the self and the social that point to a future reconstitution, a new identity not yet visible. Loss thus carries an undertone of possible hope.

The tones that Mackey draws on most directly in his poetics is what he calls "Black music," notably jazz but ranging broadly to include blues, reggae, gospel, soul, hip hop, and flamenco, among many others.[2] For Mackey, "Black music" is a "music whose 'critique of our concept of reality' is notoriously a critique of social arrangements in which, because of racism, one finds oneself deprived of community and kinship, cut off" (DE 234). As the boy-turned-Muni bird sings/mourns the broken kinship relationship, he refuses to accept either victimhood or autonomous agency – indeed, agency requires articulating the traumatic past in a certain kind of tone that calls attention to the disequilibrium in the structurally (de)coupled relationship. Within this framework, emergent writing practices take on a new sound, making possible a formal space capable of welcoming a "post-expectant futurity," a phrase that comes from one of Mackey's novels that could be a gloss on his entire work: "Post-expectant futurity stood accused of harboring hope. Nonetheless we stood by it, one and all."[3] In other words, this aesthetic articulates hope while abandoning concrete prescriptions for that awaited future of healing and reconnection. The future hope will necessarily be emergent, arising out of the present conditions of woundedness, rupture, break, and incompleteness while transforming those conditions into a new system of relationships. An emergent textuality thus becomes a correlative to a new kind of politics, where one writes to uncover, in Paul Naylor's phrase, "the holes in history,"[4] making hope inseparable from surprise.

In his recent study of black experimental poetry, Anthony Reed argues that such poetry "'speaks' to what is at once a singular and plural 'voice,' and through that act it lays claim to yet unfigured visions of a liberated future."[5] Drawing on the grammatical figure of the future anterior, Reed explores the way such writing reconstitutes our relationship to time, collectivity, and individuality through active poetic constructions, emphasizing the work of *poiesis*. Reed argues that Mackey's work develops an unknown future through a "poetics of the cut," using the term "cut" to designate break, rupture, and difference but also individual articulation and performance, as in the "cut" of music on an album, stressing the way in which Mackey's cuts disrupt and reconfigure time.

As the previous chapters have demonstrated, emergence offers another way to conceptualize the dynamic relationship between time, poetic practice, and form. Complex adaptive systems develop meaning both linearly and recursively, transforming the text's capacity for historical memory. Emergent texts make time newly visible by developing forms that could not have been anticipated in advance, adapting themselves through their self-organization, their iterative processes, their acts of provisional closure, and their structural coupling to an environment. As an alternative to Reed's "cut," this chapter uses the systems-theoretical concept of "distinction" to explore the emergent qualities of Mackey's utopian futurity, where form is both coming to be within time while also creating the conditions for unexpected poetic and social possibilities. Mackey's emergent poetic forms make possible on the level of *poiesis* the kind of historical, social, and political creativity that Reed celebrates.

After all, in the tradition of black music, form and social critique are inseparable. Born out of this tradition, each movement in Mackey's poetry is continually reconstituted in a process of improvisational, active thinking, restlessly reinventing itself through iteration and recursion. Like a

John Coltrane solo, which Amiri Baraka once compared to "watching a grown man learning to speak," Mackey's poetry relearns or "unlearns" its own terms to generate a new articulation that opens up thought (DE 45). While the critical discussion of the musical quality of Mackey's work has been rich, a thorough assessment of Black music as the structural ground for an emergent poetics is essential for understanding the cultural work of this practice.[6] I thus begin this chapter in a descriptive mode, outlining the many distinctions, subsystems, networks, and forms that constitute Mackey's project.

The forms of emergence that Mackey deploys to articulate a "post-expectant futurity" also provide an alternative perspective on the historical sensibilities of late twentieth-century art, particularly the received discourses of postmodern aesthetics. As the name "postmodernism" suggests, the artworks grouped under this sign possess a vexed relationship with history, whether expressed through the anxiety of Thomas Pynchon's paranoid characters or the deliberate play of historical spaces in Frank Gehry's Santa Monica home. In the 1980s, when Mackey began his project, theorists like Frederic Jameson criticized this aesthetic development for its apparent rejection of both teleology and strong hermeneutics: the world of postmodernism became flat and noisy, with an excess of contradictory meanings. Thus, Jameson argued that a critical position or a utopian perspective could not be sustained by these artworks, which were content to surf the "total flow" of consumer capitalism.

Instead of challenging this characterization of "postmodernism" tout court, the second part of this chapter argues that emergence offers an alternative to both Jameson's strong hermeneutic and his postmodern flat time. Emergent systems respond to the complexity of their environment by generating an interpretive perspective *within* time: they thus organize and interpret that environment by attuning themselves to the meaningful patterns that they identify and cause to appear. A model of depth hermeneutics cannot adequately account for these unpredictable patterns, while a model of total flow does not explain the critical and historical perspective generated by an emergent system. By writing in real time, Mackey's poetry offers what I call a weak hermeneutic position, parallel to Walter Benjamin's notion of messianic history, positing a meaningful future out of a traumatic past without claiming an authoritative position on what will bring that future into being.

As a spatial correlative to that temporal movement, this chapter concludes with an analysis of one of Mackey's key tropes: travel by sea, often a forced voyage, wherein characters are caught in dangerous weather and damaged boats, following partial maps. These images indicate Mackey's self-conscious relationship to the long poems of writers like Pound and Olson, who used sea imagery to characterize the writing process. At the same time, we can triangulate the oceans of the American long poem with the aesthetics of what Paul Gilroy has called the "Black Atlantic," a "transcultural, international formation" that networks Africa, Europe, and the Americas.[7] Given the violence and loss of the Middle Passage, critics have begun to extend Gilroy's model by speaking of a haunted Atlantic. Read alongside the vast aesthetic range that constitutes long poems of the haunted Atlantic, such as M. NourbeSe Philip's *Zong!* and Derek Walcott's *Omeros*, the emergent temporality of Mackey's oceans become newly legible. Unable to embrace positions of craft and control, Mackey's speakers are left measuring loss, attempting the dangerous work of imagining a world that could be constructed from the ruins of a ship. Singing at sea, Mackey's poem approaches history as a series of wrecks making possible alternative formations and cartographies. Shipwreck is thus the precondition for a new emergent practice, calling into being an unpredictable world.

I Musical Distinctions

In his use of form, Mackey's poetry both mimics and extends a famous dictum in the discourse of systems theory. As discussed in the introduction, George Spencer Brown begins his calculus in *Laws of Form* with the command to "draw a distinction,"[8] to carve out a space with an inside and outside, a frame that makes visible an orientation within a world that the distinction has caused to appear. For Spencer Brown, a "universe comes into being when a space is severed or taken apart. The skin of a living organism cuts off an outside from an inside."[9] This skin makes other actions and new distinctions possible; the accumulation of these distinctions allows a complex adaptive system to emerge. For Mackey, distinction is a promise and a threat. On the one hand, an oppressive social history has taken the form of exclusionary race and class distinctions; at the same time, drawing distinctions can in turn make another world possible, whether by criticizing oppression or by establishing alternative modes of life. His poetry further uses distinction as a formal strategy to transform past articulations, including prior moments in his own project: the poetry adaptively breaks open and rewrites its own language while also engaging external materials. In this way, Mackey's work reflects the sensibility that he detects in Edward Kamau Brathwaite, who "announces the emergence of a new language and acknowledges the impediments to its emergence, going so far as

to advance impediment as a constituent of the language's newness."[10] Each
of Mackey's compositional units, ranging from the line to the bound volume, is marked by these distinctions that simultaneously block and enable
the poem's development. Impediment becomes a condition for adaptive
possibility.

In the history of Black music, distinction, repetition, and expansion
have long been used to generate aesthetic form. Works can be adaptive,
even deliberately unfinished, allowing the musical performance to remain
aesthetically unresolved.[11] Mackey deploys these bent notes, cracks in the
voice, and repetitive, self-transforming tendencies in his writing, a strategy Brent Hayes Edwards describes as "a necessary cohabitation of origi-
nality and flow, mobility and limp, articulation and stammer."[12] This aesthetic, performative and innovative while socially and culturally hindered,
has been read as an example of "trickster poetics" by Megan Simpson,
generating a "cross-cultural identity, neither essentialist nor assimilation-
alist, but improvisational."[13] In the case of jazz, such improvisations often
arise from a deliberate engagement with unfinished sounds or phrases. As
Mackey puts it, "[obliquity] or angularity (a word used frequently in reference to the music of Thelonious Monk, Andrew Hill, Eric Dolphy, and
others) challenges the epistemic order whose constraints it implicitly brings
to light . . . by insisting upon the partial, provisional character of any proposition or predication, by advancing a vigilant sense of any reign or regime
of truth as susceptible to qualification" (DE 43). Improvisation as Mackey
enacts it becomes a stance of watchfulness and suspicion, a willingness to
offer statements that include the capacity to be subsequently revised, transformed, modified, or recontextualized. One might call this an expectation
of emergence, a realization that the adaptations of the poem will generate surprise within the space of distinctions that it has generated. Every
angular approach provides the ground for another attempt, an alternative
take, the new articulation that will only emerge from the system's prior
states. Mackey characterizes this endless predication as "the ongoingness
of an attempt that fails but is repeatedly undertaken to insist that what it
fails to capture nonetheless exists" (DE 255). Thinking within the music,
improvising a tune in the face of failure, bending the note to attest to a lost,
displaced condition: only such an angular formal approach can account for
what Mackey calls elsewhere the "rickety floor, boarded house known /
as history."[14]

Informed by this ontology of Black music, Mackey's writing develops an
expansive, recursive structure, posing a radical challenge to generic or formal categories. His work is divided into three major open sequences, each

of which is structurally coupled with the others. *"mu,"* the first of these sequences was begun in the chapbook *Septet for the End of Time* (1983), later reprinted in *Eroding Witness* (1985). *"mu"* has been sustained, in one form or another, through each of Mackey's subsequent books of poetry: *School of Udhra* (1993), *Whatsaid Serif* (1998), *Splay Anthem* (2006), *Nod House* (2011), *Outer Pradesh* (2014), and, most recently, *Blue Fasa* (2015). The sequence is marked by an explicit attention to sound as a principle of composition, resulting in a highly musical poetic language. Thematically, the work persistently connects musical tone, the body, and the rough, jagged material world, a common triad in Mackey's work echoed in the sequence's title, which evokes "music," "muse," and "amusement," among other things.

An older musical source becomes the foundation of Mackey's second sequence, *Song of the Andoumboulou*. This sequence, also begun in a chapbook and continued through the remainder of Mackey's books of poetry, takes its title from a funeral song performed by the Dogon people of West Africa. The mythical, cosmological address to the spirits is linked, in the first poem of the sequence, to language and music:

> The song says the
> dead will not
> ascend without song.
>
> That because if
> we lure them their names get
> our throats, the
> word sticks.[15]

Here, the living owe a debt to the dead that can only be paid out in song, and yet the very dalliance with the dead becomes risky, catching the word in the throat and disrupting articulation. As the poem unfolds, this risk is inseparable from history, a form of memory which, to borrow from Benjamin, "flashes up at a moment of danger."[16] The speakers in Mackey's *Song* travel through a geography of diasporic spaces, returning and recollecting the traumatic past through new songs. Indeed, the songs make a form of imaginative travel possible; many of the poems focus attention on shifting environments, generating a cross-geographic and transhistorical memory.

While these two sequences share the space of three individual volumes of poetry, they are brought together structurally in Mackey's fourth book of poems, *Splay Anthem*. He declares in the introduction that the sequences are "two and the same, each the other's understudy. . . . By turns visibly and invisibly present, each is the other's twin or contagion, each entwines the other's crabbed advance."[17] This structural coupling becomes self-reflectively explicit in the first four titled poems of the volume, designated "*mu*" parts 15–18, followed by "Song of the Andoumboulou: 40." The attentive reader of *Whatsaid Serif*, the volume preceding *Splay Anthem*, would note that the last iteration of "Song" was number 35. At the end of "'*mu*' part 18," a metapoetic passage informs us that we have been reading the missing poems without realizing it, a disoriented position shared by the poems' "we":

> 39 was what it was we
> were in, "mu" no more itself
>   than Andoumboulou, both,
> '8, '7, '6 gone by unbeknown
>   to
>   us   (SA 18)

Mackey here disrupts the confines of the sequence and poem, not by succumbing to formlessness but by creating a recursively complex structure in which an element's "boundaries permeate and are permeated by other . . . works,"[18] so that each poetic sequence becomes a distinction disrupting the other and, in doing so, allowing a new, second-order form in the poem to emerge. The resulting "text" – if we can still use the term for a multivolume, multisequential system – demands an improvisatory reading correlative to a writing that is in the process of discovering its own terms, "learning to speak" through the possibilities enabled by its earlier forms. Encountering *Splay Anthem*, in other words, prompts one to return to the previous volumes, rereading them with a new sense of their twinned formal identity, recognizing that each proposition has now become part of a new, emergent structure.

While "*mu*" and *Song of the Andoumboulou* are explicitly structural twins, the full extent of Mackey's emergent project includes a third component, the prose work *From a Broken Bottle Traces of Perfume Still Emanate*. Also a multivolume composition (five to date), Mackey relies on the epistolary form to sustain the open-ended narrative, as the novels are a series of letters from "N." to "Angel of Dust" (who, throughout the series, never directly composes a letter of his or her own, thus making the novels a one-sided correspondence). The connection between the poems and the novels is stronger than it may first appear, however, because readers of Mackey's work initially encounter a letter from N. to Angel of Dust in *Eroding Witness*, as "Song of the Andoumboulou: 6" and as part three of "Song of the Andoumboulou: 7." In the former, to add one more compositional twist,

N. opens the letter by noting that Angel of Dust "wrote in response to *Song of the Andoumboulou: 3*" (EW 50). Later in the correspondence N. sends Angel of Dust numerous musical and textual compositions, and one could therefore read the letter as a suggestion that N. is the fictionalized composer of the *Song*.[19] Alternatively, given that N. and Angel of Dust often discuss other novels and albums, it could be that they are an imagined audience to the series, whose reflections throughout the novels can be read as indirect responses to the development of the poetic sequences.

The distinctions and convergences between these sequences are not the only lines drawn by Mackey's text, as most of the volumes contain a deliberate structure, further making the work "discrete *and* continuous."[20] *Whatsaid Serif*, for instance is divided into two parts, "Strick" and "Stra," suggesting thematic or tonal units both making up the book and dividing the sequence. Similar formal distinctions occur on the level of individual poems, fracturing them into various overlapping units and wholes. Beginning in *School of Udhra*, Mackey relies on an "under the line" device, whereby poems are often, but not always, accompanied by one or more passages appearing on the bottom half of the page beneath a solid black line. Simultaneously a repetition, a response, and a marginal comment, the poems below the line are not individually titled, although they appear in the table of contents of each volume.

Brent Hayes Edwards suggests that these lines, both impediment and repetition, mimic the jazz "reprise" or "retake," a term that evokes "contesting articulations wrestling for a single space," as well as an unwillingness to abandon a musical or spiritual journey:

> [The reprise] is the way the music "holds" or carries the hearer and the performer alike. In the African-American church, one often finds a version of reprise, where, after a spiritual ends, the organist or the congregation falls back into the groove, revisiting the thread of song. It is as though the momentum of the music – its *transport* in every sense – demands it be taken up again, and taken elsewhere.[21]

Unwilling to abandon its difficult search, unable to let the composition rest, and yet acknowledging the hopeful prospects of a future articulation, a poetics of reprise, as Edwards reads it, is the expression of a spirituality that admits its own dissatisfaction as it presses toward another world. Such a poetics is necessarily difficult because the meaning of a given articulation is not contained by the single work but occurs *within*, *between*, and *through* the distributed network of performance and the environment with which it is entangled. Indeed, as Norman Finkelstein points out, Mackey's poems "may not be readable as individual poems at all."[22] Instead, the poems should be approached as moments in the process of surprising, and still unfolding, compositional, aesthetic, and conceptual movements. N., quoting from Victor Zuckerkandl's *Sound and Symbol*, makes a similar point when he notes that "[listening] to music, we are not first *in* one tone, then in the next, and so forth. We are always *between* the tones, *on the way* from tone to tone; our hearing does not remain with the tone, it reaches through it and beyond it" (FBB 15). Mackey's writing attempts to create that movement between tones, each poem one reprise on the way to a not-yet-articulate future, each distinction creating its own new possibility for future emergence. The use of tone to create expectation and movement clarifies Mackey's complex use of sonic patterns, through which, as Robert Zamsky notes, the "excesses of sound, structure, and organization" and "manifest material identity" differentiates from yet emerges out of everyday language, producing a form in process by attending to "the desire-laden moments between . . . beats."[23] In keeping these moments alive, and always seeking for the next tone that can provide a sonic extension, Mackey's music maintains a constant ear to the ground, as it were, for sonic as well as semantic significance.

As an example of Mackey's complex and emergent sonic patterns, consider the following excerpts from an under-the-line reprise:

> Day of the new dead or a new day
> of the dead, La Catrina had we been
>   farther south . . . [. . .]
>   Day
>   of the new dead a new day of the
>   dead . . .
> Wind in off the water blew us there.
>
> A beat before. Beginning's beginning.
> Never to be there again . . . Beginning beaten
> back, aboriginal. [. . .]
>   Grudge or its
>   ghost, grudge against going, grudge to've
> been anywhere at all . . . Gnostic hostages
>   down
>   on all fours, then-again's beginning, beat
>   before
> beginning be-
> grudged[24]

In the "main movement" of the poem, "Lone Coast Anacrusis," ("*mu*' fifty-third part"/ "Song: 74"), we discover that "Some new Atlantis known as Lower / Ninth we took leave of next,"[25] informing us that the poem has turned to its attention to the events of Hurricane Katrina. I return at the end of this chapter to this emergent element of Mackey's work and its feedback loop relationship to historical, social, and environmental pressures. For now, I want to focus primarily on the poem's sonic effects, keeping in mind that those sounds can never be divorced from material and cultural history when employed in a poem of the flooded New Orleans, a city of profound musical and cultural hybridity.

The title "Anacrusis" suggests a rhythmic connection between poetry and music, as it is a term used to describe the use of opening beats before the introduction of the measure proper, the "beat / before beginning." The predominance of a nine-syllable line in this poem offers Mackey many potential variations in metrical patterning, which he uses throughout to emphasize sonic (and semantic) discontinuities, different beginnings and endings, like a "new day of the dead." For instance, the anacrusis extra beat, interestingly enough, occurs either at the beginning or end of the opening line, depending on how it is scanned. "Day of the new dead or a new day" can be read as a series of trochees and iambs, with a final, orphaned beat on "day." At the same time, the regular use of alternating trochaic and iambic patterns throughout the poem has a tendency to create anapestic sounds, as in "of the dead," "of the new," "on all fours," effects that are particularly pronounced in Mackey's live performances of the poem.[26] When read as an anapest line, then, the opening becomes an alternation of accented, single syllables and anapests, with unattached beats on the first, middle, and last syllables. These overlapping meters underscore the loss of a stable beginning and end, leaving us waiting for a patterned regularity that does not quite arrive and yet surprising us when other patterns take its place. It is as if the orphaned syllable of the anacrusis is always looking for a "beginning's beginning," establishing the metrical possibility for shifting, emergent rhythmic forms.

Woven into the metrical play is further sonic patterning, using repetition with slight variations to generate melodic force and movement. "Day of the new dead or a new day / of the dead" repeats both consonant and vowel sounds with slight semantic shifts, calling attention to the difference and repetition between the "new dead" and a "new day." Similarly, the labial sounds in lines 10–12 produce a rhythmic force: "A *beat* before. *B*eginning's *b*eginning. / Never to *be* there again. *B*eginning *b*eaten / *b*ack, a*b*original." To borrow a phrase from Simon Jarvis, here melodics courts "the limit of explicability,"[27] and any interpretation of the many possible connections in the poem will inevitably fall short, as the sound links beginnings, being, an aboriginal origin, and the physical beatings associated with (and protested against by) musical beats. And one cannot help but hear echoes of the previous line, when "Wind in off the water *b*lew us there," not only sonically, with another labial, but also conceptually and perceptually, the beating of the water and wind against the buildings of the Lower Ninth. Additional sonic phrases can be found throughout the verse, as in the "grudge" / "ghost" / "gnostic" play in 16–19.

With the variability of the nine-syllable line, the multiple metrical patterns, and the repetition of sounds, the poem achieves that "manifest material identity" Zamsky identifies in Mackey's earlier work. Indeed, the poem exists almost as much as a sonic display of its own compositional structure as it does anything else, as the narrative is fragmented and elliptical at best. Reflecting the establishment, dissolution, and reestablishment of metrical and sonic patterns in the text, the poem offers an emergent configuration of specific identities and geographic spaces, bridging the Lower Ninth and "La Catrina," the skeletal icon of Mexico's Day of the Dead celebrations. At the same time, cultural references are never divorced from the sound, the two levels interacting as counterpointing partners or even rasping twins. One might suggest that the musicality of this representative verse becomes an improvisatory measure of the social conditions under which the semantics of its language are continually – and surprisingly – reproduced.

Clearly, this complex line between sound and sense, the sociality of music implied in an anacrusis poem about Hurricane Katrina, is central to Mackey's poetic thinking. As his verse creates distinctions, generates new spaces, and then inhabits those spaces through improvisatory compositions, the poem enacts an engagement with the present that is at once abstract and yet grounded in material and social history. The simultaneous interplay between the music of the lower Ninth and the fate of its people offers an unfinished beat, pregnant with possibility and looking for a future to produce a resonant tone. This tentative, uncertain yet insistent orientation within time enables a mode of critical futurity, one that challenges some of our established theoretical narratives about the historical aspirations of art in the late twentieth century.

II   Historiography of a Possible Future

Mackey's ontology of Black music – with its emphasis on strained distinctions, improvisatory spaces, cultural displacement, and the shifting sounds of language – refuses to separate the aesthetic from the social. However, Mackey's work is not simply a representation of a lost condition, a broken sociality: it is also an interpretation of that condition. In generating this interpretive perspective, Mackey's poetic hermeneutic reframes our understanding of some of the critical debates current when he began his work – namely, the arguments surrounding postmodern literature and culture. Mackey's poetry shares qualities associated with a postmodern aesthetic – fractured subjectivity, formal self-reflexivity, cultural hybridity, ontological instability, and a radical assimilation of diverse materials – and yet his work sits uncomfortably within the label, not least because of his attempt to bridge the past and the future, what I will call here, following the work of Benjamin, a weak messianism.

The unique relationship to the past that Mackey's poetry develops can be contrasted with Frederic Jameson's influential arguments about modernism, postmodernism, and art's capacity to offer a utopian or critical perspective on historical processes. In *Postmodernism, or, the Cultural Logic of Late Capitalism*, Jameson explores the way history functions as a "present absence" in postmodern literary production, a trove of images and styles evacuated of their content and given up to an aesthetic play symptomatic of late capitalism itself. That is, postmodern history by Jameson's account is devoid of hermeneutics: history is *used* by postmodern artists but never *interpreted*. In contrast to the hermeneutics versus postmodernism binary that Jameson presents, Mackey's poetry offers a third possibility, neither caught up in free play nor reducing the multiplicity of history to a single code or narrative. Like the shifting, unpredictable movement of a flock of birds, Mackey's poetry reveals the contours of an equally unpredictable, changing world. His work demonstrates that the framework of emergence provides a powerful conceptual alternative to postmodern temporality and historiography.

Of the various permutations of Jameson's thinking across *Postmodernism*, two concepts are important for understanding Mackey's emergent poetics, namely the anti-teleological character of postmodern art and the cultural experience of "total flow" (a term Jameson borrows from Raymond Williams).[28] Jameson further theorizes the anti-teleological in two ways. First, he detects a break between modernist notions of progressive art and the postmodern rejection of the new. "[In] art, at least," Jameson writes, "the notion of progress and telos remained alive and well up to very recent times indeed . . . in which each genuinely new work unexpectedly but logically outtrumped its predecessor (not linear history, this, but rather [Viktor] Shklovsky's 'knight's gambit,' the action at distance, the quantum leap to the undeveloped or underdeveloped square)" (PCL xi). The leap of the new, and its attendant ideological beliefs in progress, genius, and the monumental artwork, is no longer pursued in the postmodern era. Instead,

as Jameson argues, all styles are simultaneously present, all artistic practices more or less suitable for cultural production in postmodern culture.
Such a condition internal to art reflects another mode of anti-teleology: the
distrust of social progress and the decline in the revolutionary imagination.
As the spread of global capital becomes more complete, and its systematic
power seen as inevitable, the future new is replaced, instead, with an ideology of "ends" (PCL 1). By abandoning pretensions of innovation, according
to this account, postmodern artists reflect an ideological exhaustion represented by the "end of history" arguments that appeared in the early 1990s,
most famously in Francis Fukuyama's *The End of History and the Last Man*
(1992).[29]

These antiprogressive elements indicate for Jameson the interpretive
limitations of postmodern art, which is characterized by "a new depth-
lessness" and a "weakening of historicity" (PCL 9). Jameson's models of
"depth," which he contrasts with postmodern "surface," are the powerful hermeneutic schools of modernity: psychoanalysis, existentialism, and
Marxist dialectics (PCL 12). The postmodern replaces such interpretive
frameworks with "surface," within which there is nothing to interpret, no
latent causes underlying the manifest. A rejection of hermeneutic depth
sets the stage for the second characteristic of postmodern art, a "weak"
historicism, "the random cannibalization of all the styles of the past, the
play of random stylistic allusion" (PCL 18). Such a "play" of allusion
acknowledges past styles but does not try to work them into a formal, self-
sustaining, or rigorous whole that could offer a critical alternative to the
contemporary.

The lack of depth and the random consumption of historical styles give
way to the experience of "total flow," which Jameson considers to be the
characteristic experience of postmodernity. The total flow of streaming
information "without interruption" makes "'critical distance' seem obso-
lete" (PCL 70). Immersive experiences, according to this logic, cannot be
interpreted, and we return, once again, to the loss of the hermeneutic: "The
postmodernist text . . . is defined as a structure or sign flow which resists
meaning, whose fundamental inner logic is the exclusion of the emergence
of themes as such in that sense, and which therefore systematically sets out
to short-circuit traditional interpretive temptations" (PCL 91–2). Such an
aesthetics, and, indeed, consciousness, may offer the chance for some "joyous intensities," as Jameson argues in his controversial comments on Bob
Perelman's poem "China" (PCL 28–9), but ultimately the postmodern loss
of the hermeneutic, and the subsequent loss of meaningful history, is a clear
cornerstone of Jameson's argument.

Jameson's theorization provides a useful context for analyzing the relationship between interpretation and multiplicity in Mackey's work, as a writer of a long poem coming out of the postmodern period. While *Song of the Andoumboulou* and *"mu"* share some postmodern characteristics, Mackey's poetry offers a model of historical interpretation and utopian desire that evades both modernist mastery and postmodern surface. Instead, his texts dramatize a weak messianism, which comes from writing so that one's text remains open to as yet unanticipated meanings. Emergent poetic form makes possible an orientation toward a future world that the poem will cause to appear and yet that it cannot at present imagine or fully anticipate. Form resists full interpretation in Mackey not by way of a hermeneutic "short-circuit" but through its ongoing processes of provisional closure and recursive recreation, establishing a perspective on both the present and the future that interprets, projects, and courts a progress whose end result the poet is unable to name. In this sense, the interpretive work of a complex adaptive poetic system comes from its capacity to establish, develop, and extend patterns within the world. Such texts are thus not "centerless"; instead, they generate a continually enactive and adaptive "domain of significance out of the background of [their] random milieu," as Varela describes it.[30] Emergent writing is not an undifferentiated flow, a superficial multicultural pastiche, but instead a weak messianic gesture generating a utopianism without mastery.

This ethos of humble utopianism can be traced back to the original "Song of the Andoumboulou." According to the Dogon myth, the Andoumboulou were an early version of humanity, condemned to live underground. Mackey writes that he "couldn't help thinking of the Andoumboulou as not simply a failed, or flawed, earlier form of human being but a rough draft of human being, the work-in-progress we continue to be. . . . The song of the Andoumboulou is one of striving, strain, abrasion, an all but asthmatic song of aspiration" (SA xi). That abrasion and aspiration appears in Mackey's *Whatsaid Serif*, when the speaker confesses that the tribe "Wondered where the we we / were after would come / from."[31] The poem as a work-in-progress becomes, here, a metaphor for a broader anthropology. To write as an Andoumboulou is to measure a past continuous with the present state of affairs while acknowledging our "drafted" condition. Thus, the Andoumboulou writer affirms a future that by definition cannot be entirely understood, yet whose possibility is still palpable. Similarly, the past from which the song is born can only be interpreted through new performances, an attitude that calls to mind Benjamin's claim that "[History] is not simply a science but also and not least a form of remembrance [*Eingedenken*]. . . . Such mindfulness can make the incomplete . . . into something complete, and the complete . . . into something incomplete."[32] Benjamin's memory becomes both the extension and transformation of the past. In this sense, imagining history in the form of an active, creative memory is itself a historical event, neither deterministic nor entirely free yet manifesting the possibility of an emergent future.

Benjamin's approach to historical interpretation offers a theoretical correlative to Mackey's project. Methodologically, Benjamin's practice of citation, most radically manifest in the *Arcades Project*, echoes Mackey's own writing practices. Hannah Arendt understands this method as the "modern equivalent of ritual invocations": a materialist reanimation of the dead in the hope of discovering and absorbing their power,[33] and, in that act, generating a historical self-consciousness which, in the Hegelian tradition of *Aufhebung*, is necessarily something new. This relationship among citation, active memory, and future potential explains Benjamin's own weak messianism as it appears at the end of his "Theses on the Philosophy of History." The historical materialist, Benjamin argues, seeks to supply "a unique experience with the past" by "[grasping] the constellation which his own era has formed with a definite earlier one. Thus he establishes a conception of the present as the 'time of the now' which is shot through with chips of Messianic time."[34] Here, the language of arrest and imagistic constellation is counterbalanced by the utopian undercurrent of "Messianic time," suggesting a dialectical relationship between a present form and the future transformation of that form. The final section of the "Theses" clarifies this tension, employing the language of a ritual address inseparable from the past:

> We know that the Jews were prohibited from investigating the future. The Torah and the prayers instruct them in remembrance, however. This stripped the future of its magic, to which all those succumb who turn to the soothsayers for enlightenment. This does not imply, however, that for the Jews the future turned into homogenous, empty time. For every second of time was the strait gate through which the Messiah might enter.[35]

If we read this passage in light of Benjamin's earlier claims, then it becomes clear that direct manipulation of the future (the actions of the "soothsayers") is a suspect, perhaps even blasphemous activity. Instead, the Messianic future occurs *in the way of memory*, an engagement with the past that becomes the articulation of a future promise. To take some liberties with Benjamin, a secularized version of the Messianic "strait gate" could be the act of memory itself: remembering is the weak messianic gesture, a performance that enlivens time even as it opens it up.

Mackey's speakers share Benjamin's commitment to historical performance as an act of transformational memory, taking "act" as both the artifice of fiction and the activity of the artistic process. In *Bedouin Hornbook*,
Benjamin's theses are cited directly, in the middle of a complex solo performance by Lambert, a member of N.'s band. Taking up the harmonica for
a solo "worthy of the Delta blues at its visceral best," Lambert addresses N.
and the rest of the band:

> Before blowing into it [Lambert] raised his right forefinger and said some-
> thing which, had I been walking, would've stopped me 'dead' in my tracks.
> 'To articulate the past historically,' he said, 'means to seize hold of a memory
> as it flashes up at a moment of danger. This danger affects both the content
> of a tradition and its receivers: that of becoming a tool of the ruling classes.'
> I could hardly believe my ears. It sounded like a quote, but he neglected to
> name its author. (FBB 119)

Lambert's anonymous and partial quotation functions as a nod to Benjamin's methods while testifying to Mackey's own engagement with Benjamin's thought. Of equal interest is the sentence Lambert skips: "Historical materialism wishes to retain that image of the past which unexpectedly
appears to man singled out by history at a moment of danger."[36]

Lambert generates one of these fleeting, dangerous moments later in
his own piece, using the music to establish an emergent transhistorical and
transgeographic community. N.'s characterization of this performance calls
attention to this transformation:

> I'm not sure I've made it sufficiently clear that what Lambert was up to was
> in no way, strictly speaking, a solo performance. The more or less overt allu-
> sions he made throughout to the [John] Coltrane/[Rashied] Ali duets, as well
> as to [Archie] Shepp's teaming up, on "The Magic of Ju-Ju," with a five-man
> percussion choir, had the effect of conjuring a rhythmic umbilicality, if you
> will, an implied polity or a mystico-accentual assembly dealing in alchem-
> ized, neo-Africanized 'weight' (i.e., duration and pulse). The conspicuously
> absent drums, I mean, had a way of making their 'presence' felt, giving yet
> another dimension to the concern with *skin* which was so inescapable a part
> of the piece. (FBB 121)

Musical allusions and citations of past performances interpret history while
bringing it back to life. Dallying with the dead, the performance becomes
dangerous for all participants, Lambert's work necessarily changing the
music he evokes while the history embedded within the music, its "neo-
Africanized" post-diasporic conditions, implicates the new work into the
shared "polity." The dangers of that "time of now" are evoked by the term
"skin," suggesting the politics of racialized appearance, the rhythm of the
drum's skin (an instrument that was banned at points in the history of

American slavery), the relationship between the body and identity, even perhaps vulnerability and eros, the skin as edge between body, world, and other bodies. And, to return us to Spencer Brown's terminology, the skin is a primary distinction through which a world is brought into being.

Lambert's Benjaminian, diasporic performance, in other words, offers a fictional dramatization of Mackey's humble, but no less forceful, messianic aspirations: "The song says the / dead will not / ascend without song" (EW 33). Such an approach toward historical interpretation and utopian hope is a far cry from postmodern historiography and pastiche, which Jameson characterizes as "the imitation of dead styles, speech through all the masks and voices stored up in the imaginary museum of a now global culture" (PCL 18). The voices of the dead are not simply museum sets in Mackey's work, painless masks to be adopted and set aside at whim. Instead, "their names get / our throats, the / word sticks" (EW 33), and the responsibility toward those names and voices requires an endless effort, a play that continually acknowledges its own debt to a still-unsatisfied past while watching for those who will come after the Andoumboulou.

The reanimation of the dead, the attention to moments of danger, the communion of performance – all of these historigraphic attempts give way to, and are implied in, Mackey's figures of journey, voyage, and travel. Indeed, to return to Jameson's terms, Joseph Allen, writing of *From a Broken Bottle*, suggests that "Mackey's narrative seems to operate as one of Jameson's new cognitive maps by ceaselessly pushing toward a fresh narrative space."[37] In light of the fractured, broken, and contingent temporality evident throughout Mackey's work, however, what would such a cognitive map look like? What coordinates could adequately reflect spatially that which is temporally in the process of being transformed? Or, as N. asks, "what about rescue? What, that is, could free the future from every flat, formulaic 'outcome,' from its own investment in the contested shape of an otherness disfigured by its excursion thru the world?" (FBB 95). The structure, form, and potential of music, when coupled with a weak messianic historiography, that "contested," "disfigured" shape, give way to a third emergent principle in Mackey's text: the cartography of a disaster.

III   Emergent Forms of the Haunted Atlantic

In *Bass Cathedral*, the fourth volume of *From a Broken Bottle*, N. offers some reflections on the West African "deification of Accident." N. speculates that there may be a complicit link between an all-powerful originary being and the mythological trickster who usurps that being in many of the traditional tales, illustrating the point through the story of Ogo-Yurugu, the "Dogon diviner-trickster" whose "first rebellious act, his assault on the earth's fiber skirt, takes place while Amma, the Supreme God, is asleep." N. comments on this strange state of affairs: "What, that is, is a Supreme God doing falling asleep? Could a charge of ineptitude be laid at Amma's feet? But if a Supreme God, by definition, never sleeps, surely Amma slept, if such it can be called, with one eye open."[38] The God who blinks, deliberately allowing the usurpers to act in any number of unpredictable ways, is both frightening and liberating. In such a world, the potential for accidental, unexpected events does not exist as an exception to the cosmic order but as its paradoxical rule. Where God sleeps, albeit with one eye open, there is an ontological gap waiting to be filled, a potentiality as well as a lack.

N.'s penchant for anagrammatic wordplay translates this insight into a new idiom: "a mapping I'd instead call m'apping to accent intimacies between 'map' and 'mishap,' a crossed or contracted rapport we otherwise overlook (mishap→m'ap)."[39] Mishaps become a necessary precondition for the m'ap as it attempts to communicate the world's unpredictable, self-transforming order. Similarly, any chart will also be a record of accident, mishap, even trauma. If the figure is extended to include time as well as space, history, as we have seen, must be conceived of as a series of false starts, incomplete projects, and broken trajectories. Throughout Mackey's work, the figure of the shipwreck is used to illustrate that historical and social fracture. The shipwreck and the m'ap are thus paired concepts, figuring the network of distinctions that constitutes Mackey's poetry.

In the context of the long poem, ships and maps appear regularly, harkening as far back as Homer's Catalogue of the Ships in *The Iliad* and, more immediately, recalling Whitman's figures of travel. Pound's mapping figure was "periplum," the geographical perspective of one traveling at sea, while Olson referred to *The Maximus Poems* as a "mappemunde," and moments of navigation appear throughout their respective works.[40] Both poets treat maps and ships as a tool to be used responsively, wielded with an intimate knowledge of the ocean and with precise (although adapting) skills that enable one to work within one's environment. References to oceanic travel in emergent textuality can thus be read as a sign of self-consciousness, a way for the poem to measure its own ambitions as well as imagine the human journey that the text purportedly represents.

However, not all oceans share the same language, as Brathwaite notes, speaking of the Caribbean experience: "like the hurricane, our seas don't usually speak in pentameters."[41] There is no single metric for the sound of the waves. Indeed, the long poem's tradition of ships intersects with another

world-historic oceanic space, namely the Atlantic slave trade and its generation of what Paul Gilroy calls the "Black Atlantic," a diasporic identity
triangulating Europe, Africa, and the Americas. Oceanic navigation takes
on a different sense when read through the lens of what Erin Fehskens has
called, building on Gilroy, the "haunted Atlantic."[42] This haunting is not
simply the result of remembering the past dead but also arises through the
loss of the record itself, the erasures of memory. The voyages of the Middle Passage suppressed or destroyed cultural memory, and, in many cases,
submerged the names of the victims, both literally and figuratively. Consequently, the haunted Atlantic is a linguistic, textual phenomenon as well
as a material, geographic, political, and cultural state of affairs.

Within this framework, the haunted Black Atlantic offers poets a vexed
and conflicted field of ships, sails, and voyages. Mackey is not alone in
his interest in the m'ap, and other long poetries of the Black Atlantic use
a range of formal tactics, from the experimental to the conventional, to
make the ghosts palpable. For instance, M. NourbeSe Philip's *Zong!* cuts,
rearranges, and rewrites one of the legal decisions surrounding the slave
ship *Zong*, an infamous case from 1781 that acutely represents the tangled
contradictions of the slave trade.[43] Claiming that the ship was running
out of water, the captain of the *Zong* ordered approximately 150 slaves to
be thrown overboard. The owners then attempted to collect insurance for
the dead slaves, arguing that their cargo had been lost due to the unpredictable dangers of sea travel. When the insurance company refused to
pay, the *Zong* case went to trial; instead of a murder prosecution, the case
turned on matters of liability and commercial risk. The dead themselves
remain unnamed, unnoted, hidden behind the legal language of the court
record.

Philip's haunted Atlantic is poetically represented through the iterative deployment of fragments that bridge the material, linguistic, and historical. Her work thus uses local emergent effects to make palpable the
historical ghosts. *Zong! #1* opens with a meditation on water, using the
page as a field that divides and repeats the word as individual letters and
phonemes (with visual effects I cannot replicate here): "w w w w a wa /
w a w a t / er."[44] Sonically, the repetition of "w" simultaneously suggests
questioning, crying, and the rhythm of the waves, making the physical
properties of the word and their echoes with human experience visible
and audible through the splitting of the word. Later in the text, a similar
strategy crosses time and language, drawing the distress signals of modern mariners into the Latin for bone: "died es es es / oh es / oh oh es
es oh / . . . os / *os* / bone."[45] SOS becomes os (an echo of "us") becomes

os, the bone hidden beneath the surface of the body and, in the case of the *Zong* victims, beneath the surface of the Atlantic. The haunting of Philip's ocean thus arises as a ghostly articulation established between and behind the constituent elements of words iterated across the page. Deforming the words of the *Zong* trial becomes the occasion for reforming a spectral presence hovering over the Black Atlantic as both text and geographic space.

We can triangulate Philip and Mackey's work with Derek Walcott's *Omeros*, a long poem of the haunted Black Atlantic written in a traditional epic register. Walcott's text is explicitly intertextual, establishing ties with the European epic, most notably Homer, whose name is echoed in the title of the poem and whose characters – Hector, Achilles, Helen – are recast in Walcott's native St. Lucia.[46] Walcott links the Homeric tradition to the Caribbean and Africa by way of a ghostly ocean, a connection made explicit early in the poem with a gloss on its title: "I said 'Omeros,' / and *O* was the conch-shell's invocation, *mer* was / both mother and sea in our Antillean patois, / *os*, a grey bone, and the white surf as it crashes / and spreads its sibilant color on a lace shore."[47] Like Philip's "*os*," Walcott connects the bone to the ocean both in color and sound, but death gives way to visual, metaphoric, and sonic aesthetic pleasure, with the "sibilant color" of the hissing ocean echoed in the sibilant sounds of the line. Simultaneously haunted and hauntingly beautiful, the *mer* Walcott discovers in *Omeros* is never simply a site of disorder or trauma, suggesting that poetic practice can ameliorate both social and literary history.

Formal mastery is one of the conditions of renewal in *Omeros*, which is written in a loose terza rima pattern and twelve-syllable line, forms associated with both Dante and the Greek epic. The poem's display of its own virtuosity – its spreading sibilant color – attempts to guarantee its literary status as masterpiece while also proclaiming the African diaspora to be one of the great epic stories of human history, or History, to use the language of the text. One epic convention – the journey to the underworld – becomes, in Walcott's text, a visionary journey to Africa, where the fisherman Achille meets his ancestor Afolabe and encounters a past he never knew. As Srila Niyak argues, this passage is not a nostalgic claim for a return to Africa but another act of synthesis and spectral hybridity: "This tension between stereotypical repetition and an irrepressible poetic urge to figure Africa as the source of New World black identity is apparently resolved by Walcott's translation of epic episodes of reunion and parting in the underworld from *The Aeneid* and *The Odyssey*, advancing an anti-colonial synthesis of derivativeness and creative expansion of the genre. By borrowing Western epic devices, Walcott depicts an African journey that restores connections, both significant and perishable, with ghostly figures."[48]

Formally, thematically, and narratively, then, Walcott offers a poetic ocean simultaneously haunted and yet capable of literary refashioning. We can read his St. Lucian fisherman as extensions of the poet himself, new avatars of the epic aesthetic. Like Walcott, Achille and Hector are represented as craftsmen, capable of constructing and navigating their own canoes; the poem begins with a scene of boat-building, and many passages throughout the narrative emphasize their connection to the ocean. Isabella Zoppi suggests that Hector, for instance, is "in his true essence . . . a creature of the sea," so much so that his choice to leave his life of fishing for a job as a transport driver ultimately results in his death.[49] Reading these characters as figures for the identity that Walcott attempts to forge in his poem suggests that craft, whether poetic or oceanic, becomes an opportunity to reclaim the disaster of the Middle Passage. In this sense, Philip and Walcott can be read as two contrasting responses to the same historical and literary condition. Philip's use of fragmentation, repetition, and disarticulation attempts to make visible the ghosts of the past by unwriting dominant texts, while Walcott transforms the literary forms of the Western past to stake a claim for a new, hybrid present actualized by his poetic performance.

These instances of the haunted long poem of the Black Atlantic provide an important framework for reading Mackey's oceanic figures, which are characterized by a deliberately "post-expectant" orientation, an attempt to m'ap that reclaims ghosts of the past while generating an emergent interpretation of the present. Mackey's characters and scenes of ocean travel are more fraught than those of Walcott; in contrast to Achille and Hector's canoes, Mackey's ships are too damaged to adequately get one home, at least not with precision or control, and thus the ocean becomes an environment both hostile and transformational. Mackey's work also contrasts with Philip's in his aesthetic generation of material literary spaces for new m'aps and iterations of the poem, the ongoingness of his improvisatory writing. Thus, instead of the completion and closure of poetic craft as a kind of compensation for loss or the fragmentation of the word as a recollection of ghosts, Mackey's ships tack for a linguistic and cultural destination yet to come.

An early ship is found in "Ohnedaruth's Day Begun," an independent lyric that offers an imaginative precursor to *Song of the Andoumboulou* and "*mu*." The poem borrows from George Oppen the subtitle "Bright light of shipwreck," which, for Oppen, is the shipwreck "of the singular," through whose light we attempt to discover the meaning "Of Being Numerous."[50] Mackey's speaker, in turn, figures numerousness in the flotsam of that shipwreck:

> [my muse's] thread of words a white froth at our
> feet as I forget myself,
> limbs as
> though they were endlessly afloat,
> a flood of
> wreckage barters wood against incestuous
> dust.
> Her splintered ships clog the sea of new
> beginnings. Beyond waking, walking
> legless down where dreams unbottom our sleep,
> soaked ruins of a raft on which
> the world outlived itself to
> bear the Heartbreak Church . . .   (EW 73–4)

The wreckage affords, at best, the consolation of a raft, bobbing among the remains of an "outlived world." Such a seascape cannot be navigated with the keels of Pound's swart ship, the speed of Olson's Gloucester sailors, or the joyous affirmations of Walcott's Hector; instead, the poetic imagination swims with a shipwrecker of a muse left inextricably adrift on the "ruins of a raft," seeking to extend the world beyond its own "heartbreak."

This "light of shipwreck" returns in "Dogon Eclipse," the final poem of *Eroding Witness*. The speaker awakes, ambiguously under guard, on another boat, "So like a refugee's tilted boat, / white / light of shipwreck" (EW 98). Whether refugee or prisoner, the ship could also be a vessel of liberation, as the speaker tells us that he feels that he has "boarded one of Marcus' / erratic ships, aborted Black Star Line, / prophetic / ark of unrest" (EW 98). Marcus Garvey's Black Star Line sought to actualize a return to Africa, reversing the westward motion of the Middle Passage for a journey to an unremembered home. The ambivalence of Mackey's treatment of the Black Star Line is telling: a prophetic ark speaks of unrest, a return, and yet one cannot simply go back to the beginning. Unrest implies loss, even, at the same time, affording a refuge. Still, the attempt is aborted, incomplete, at sea, as is implied by the word "erratic," with its roots in "error" and wandering.

Compounding the disorientation evident throughout the poems, the historical events are themselves only communicated indirectly. There is no complete memory of a time before that catastrophe, which is why Mackey's travelers do not know to what or where they are returning. Shipwreck thus functions as an original condition. "Song of the Andoumboulou: 40" reads: "What we read said / there'd been a shipwreck. We / survived it, adrift at sea" (SA 21). The book from which the report comes is not coincidental. Language, bearing broken remnants of the historical record, can indicate but not adequately explain the wreckage through and around which the speakers' float. This record, in turn, points to other ships, the mechanisms by which the cultural catastrophe occurred. Later, in "On Antiphon Island," for instance, the poem's "we" are forced to dance a "limbo" that eventually becomes "The hold of a ship we were / caught / in," the "Soaked wood" keeping them barely afloat (SA 64). Lying on one's back in the hold of a ship, the Middle Passage here is evoked in distant yet unmistakable terms, a "ghostly reference," in Finkelstein's phrase.[51]

Far from the mastery of craft, then, Mackey's ships – wrecked, historical, broken, discontent, and looking for an elsewhere – reveal that his poem journeys, at best, elliptically, from the side, unable to directly approach the future world that it is seeking to make possible. He comments that "[the] poems' we, a lost tribe of sorts, a band of nervous travelers, know nothing if not locality's discontent, ground gone under" (SA x). This discontentment has a material origin. Mackey continues: "Glamorizations by the tourist industry not withstanding, travel and migration for the vast majority of people have been and continue to be unhappy if not catastrophic occurrences brought about by unhappy if not catastrophic events" (SA x). Mackey's understanding of travel as catastrophe echoes Jeffery Gray, who points out that as "[a] variant of *travail*, *travel* derives from *tripaliare* (to torment) and *tripalium*, a device of torture consisting of three stakes between which the victim was stretched."[52] Against the critical interpretations of travel that view it from the perspective of colonial mastery, Gray suggests "an alternative model, perhaps a return to 'travel''s unsavory roots: a view of travel not as mastery, hegemony, acquisition, penetration, pollution, rapine, and centripetal force, but, instead, as vulnerability, diminution, incoherence, disorientation, and centrifugal force."[53] In Mackey's hands, the bright light of shipwreck illuminates that vulnerable disorientation.

Due to this cultural shipwreck, poetry's humble messianic potential becomes even more essential. Indeed, emergent poetic writing *becomes* a projection of the future, the work of the m'ap. If we unite Gray's definition of travel as "vulnerability and disorientation" with Mackey's point that most human journeys are the result of displacement and trauma, generating "a lost tribe of sorts, a band of nervous travelers," then it is clear that the mishaps which make up N.'s m'ap are as much historical and social as they are cosmological. At the same time, a m'ap is a record as well as an unfolding mechanism for travel, a device through which a fraught journey can occur. The m'ap thus sits between agency and disorientation, a testimony of the tribe's lost condition as well as a potential tool for finding one's way elsewhere, wherever that may be, even, in fact, creating that elsewhere. Mackey's m'ap attends to gaps, generating the disorientation necessary for a utopian imagination, and thus making visible the spaces necessary for an emergent future.

To give a sense of that emergent imagination, I conclude by following out some of the reprisal links emerging from "Song of the Andoumboulou: 34" in which the theme of m'apping is poetically dramatized. "Song: 34" appears toward the end of "Stra," the second half of *Whatsaid Serif*. *Whatsaid Serif* offers a sustained mythic travelogue across the globe, in which the speakers do not know precisely where they are going nor, at times, what their mode of travel actually entails. At times on boat, others on train, the characters encounter material, historical, and physical spaces as well as cosmic, mythological entities. In "Song: 34," one such entity emerges from a sexual encounter as a "two-headed / twin," evoking the beast with two backs as well as an androgynous identity, in which "one head would be Eronel, the / other / Lenore" (WSS 99). The erotic coupling occurs within a cosmic voyage:

> They lay in our boat looking out at
> the earth, flat but for the relief
> love gave it. They lay on their backs
> looking out at the sky. Whatever it was it
> was a boat we were on, bus we were
> on, sat on a train orbiting abject
> Earth . . .
> (WSS 99–100)

Whether by boat, bus, or train, the group exists only in transit over a bleak and destitute landscape. On the one hand, the erotic encounter at the beginning of the poem may be an example of the love that affords some relief to the earth, a human illumination of what otherwise feels alien and unfamiliar. On the other, that relief can only be temporary and transitory because the speaker's troupe never rests, and love itself is fleeting in the poem.

The fact that rest is impossible is further implied in that they are looking for an "arkical / city soon to be founded we thought" (WSS 100). The

post-apocalyptic adjective "arkical" evokes their transitory condition yet
suggests that any future human habitation will itself be only another displaced boat. Desire, hope, and loss are inseparable in this search, as the
speaker acknowledges:

> That it wasn't there or that it was
> but unreachable,   hard to say
>   which was worse,   the Soon-Come
> Congress no sooner come than gone
>   (WSS 100)

Unable to assume that they will ultimately arrive at that "post-expectant"
future city, the group is left with two equally difficult prospects: either the
city they are seeking is only an illusion or it exists in an impossible-to-
discover location. Echoing (or reprising) the poem's erotic concerns, the
pun on "Soon-Come / Congress" reinforces the suggestion that desire will
characterize that as yet invisible future, whether in the form of a human
political establishment or in the less permanent mode of human coupling.
In either case, the poem ends by uniting the political, cosmic, and erotic
movement in music, reflecting the verse's own attempts at m'apping further
displacement:

>   Posthumous
>   music made us almost weep, wander,
>   Soon-Come Congress we'd otherwise have
>   been, sung to if not by Lenore by
>   Eronel,
>   every which way, on our way
>   out   (WSS 100–1)

The song of their joining and departing is voiced "every which way," by
either partner in the male/female twinning. Recalling the reprise, the song's
repetition on the "way / out" accompanies them on their unfinished journey. One gets a sense, here, of the historical function of that music. Black
song attempts to manifest this displaced yet utopian quality, accompanying actual, historic wanderers into the world while promising a potential
glimpse of another, the future recognition of who "we'd otherwise have /
been."

The theme of the transformed world relates to both the Andoumboulou
as "rough draft" and the Kaluli myth of the Muni bird, the latter a key allusion in one of the four "under the line" reprises of "Song: 35" which reiterate
the concerns of the original text: "Wept adhesion, the way of the Kaluli. /
Remanent water, whatsaid salt . . . / Whatsaid rise into inclement wind"

(WSS 104). "Wept" implicates "adhesion" – either as kinship, coupling, or community – and desires it. Whoever is weeping could be mourning both the loss of social adhesion and kinship relations, in the "way of the Kaluli," or adhesion's eventual decay. And yet, from another perspective, the weeping can also produce community, generating an alternative connection through the loss. Weeping and song, by way of the Kaluli, occurs in the ongoing journey through difficult weather, another recollection of the "abject / Earth" in "Song: 35." The wind and salt, as the poem continues, tear at the "book," scratch the "voice," leaving the travelers in a condition of broken and bent articulation, at best, bringing us back to the provisional distinctions of music. That return, which is also an ending (recall that the traditional "Song of the Andoumboulou" is a funeral dirge), brings the short reprise poem to its provisional closure while pointing to another iteration to come:

> Rough, andoumboulouous draft whose we
> they were, who lay on their backs wrapped in
> burlap it seemed. Rough weave
> and as rough an unwinding,
> rough
> turn finding themselves so drawn . . .
> Tropic
> wind out of nowhere, world a magnetic
> rock,
> clung to, the better to be let go, they
> insisted, beginning, they said again,
> to
> say goodbye   (WSS 104)

Gone is the more leisured displacement of "Song: 35," where coupling affords momentary consolation. The "rough draft" who is "we" wears rags that are in the process of being created and destroyed. Just as the cloth is being unraveled, presumably by the rough conditions at sea, so too the "andoumboulouous we" are being pulled apart. The destructive transformation of the we/they is highly ambivalent, for if we are a rough draft, then surely we must be remade in some fashion, continuing to be drawn in places and erased in others. The rough draft's only hope is to be transformed into something else, a necessarily painful process that threatens the identity of the one being re-created while still retaining continuity with that earlier, provisional form. The human emerges, at times painfully, always surprisingly.

The dialectic between danger and promise continues when the "Tropic / wind" blows across the "magnetic / rock" that is the world. A tropic wind may be the hope of better weather, a warm wind, presumably, although "Tropic" in this context also evokes the Caribbean's history of slavery, as well as the figurative "trope," a poetic device. Thus, hope, history, geography, and poetry are combined and equated, a complex weave. That ambivalence finally brings the poem's they/we to a point of crisis, clinging to the rock of the world but "insisting" that it is "the better to be let go." To let go of the rock could be to give up on the world entirely, or it could be simply to abandon *this* world, to strike out for another. But they/we are not insisting on "letting go" but "to be let go": it is a request for release, a declaration of liberation. "Better to be let go" can thus be read as a cry of the oppressed claiming that the world could be other than it is, that another history can be imagined if not yet actually visible. And yet, to push the two possibilities even further, one could argue that the poem is suggesting that liberation from history, were such a condition possible, would be a terrifying risk, a necessary "letting go" of one's grip on things to welcome an alternative. The still-deferred promise of such an escape is implied in the "beginning, they said again / to / say goodbye" of the poem's end. They/we repeat the act of farewell, as if this act has occurred before and, implicitly, will continue beyond the confines of the poem. This "say again" returns us to the end of "Song: 35," with its evocation of song as leave-taking, song ceaselessly carrying the characters on into their interminable journey. The insistent repetition of the "andoumboulous we" – iterative, recursive, provisionally closed, only to be reopened – becomes its own reprise.

Or its own anacrusis, to return to Mackey's later poetic exploration of Hurricane Katrina in *Nod House*. The figures of lost, shipwrecked, dissatisfied travelers recollect past experiences, such as the Middle Passage and slavery, while anticipating new ones, like the images of the floating bodies from the Lower Ninth. In many respects, then, "Song: 35," composed in the 1990s, demonstrates that Mackey's emergent textuality was always already a Katrina poem, generating a grammar, tone, and imaginative repository that establishes an adaptive feedback loop with present events and making their historical meaning palpable. The reciprocity between "Song: 35" and "*mu*' fifty-third part," not to mention the network of relationships between these seas and the many strains of shipwreck and m'apping throughout Mackey's work as a whole, thickens our cultural memory through the activity of writing in real time, of responding with and through the text as a complex adaptive system to the material conditions of our historical world. In this sense, an emergent text can show us precisely, and painfully, how Katrina becomes a new weave in the unfinished story of the Andoumboulou known as the United States.

In no sense does this anticipation of Katrina suggest soothsaying or prophecy; instead, it attests to the potential force of emergent writing as a historically and environmentally entangled process. Mackey's own investigation of the past, and the working of the past into poetic language, focuses his attention, and the structures and terms he has generated enable the poem to identify new events in the world as meaningful elements within that larger, adaptive form. One can only say it is "as if" *Song of the Andoumboulou* anticipated Katrina, as contingency and change are always essential to an improvisatory interpretive process. Still, this particular example perfectly illustrates a central assumption and claim of this study: that emergent poetics is a textual practice to think *with* and *in* time, that a self-modifying and self-transforming poetic process makes possible adaptable and yet critical cognition. Mackey's text, and his readers, participate in a practice in which thought, loss, and hope are inseparable, learning to speak again in order to declare that "we knew there was / a world somewhere" (WSS 28). The poetics of emergence opens the possibility, although never the guarantee, that one may articulate that world on some unforeseeable day, in some unknown place.

CHAPTER 7

Conclusion
Emergent Poetics and the Digital

Writing in real time has become a characteristic practice of the digital era. We are endlessly composing, shaping our tweets, blog posts, and status updates in response to events as they occur. This textual productivity has accompanied the advent of what Alan Liu calls "social computing," also known as "Web 2.0," characterized by "the migration of social experience . . . into the network."[1] As one would expect, this social transformation also recalibrates the literary environment. With the rise of new information technologies, all poets, as Marjorie Perloff puts it, find themselves "writing in an environment of hyperinformation, an environment, moreover, where we are all authors."[2] It is this complex environment, shaped by Big Data, instantaneous global news cycles, and social networking (not to mention the servers, wireless signals, and high-tech manufacturing facilities that make these networks possible), that I lump, somewhat imprecisely, under the concept of "the digital." By way of conclusion to this study, I want to examine the ways emergent poetics can shape our understanding of the digital, offering a literary framework for responding aesthetically and imaginatively to that environment of hyperinformation.

If the imperative of the digital in its present instantiation is writing in real time, the threat of that imperative is, paradoxically, a form of illegibility. In the endless writing of the digital age, our aggregately composed texts are overwhelmingly large, and thus, to a certain extent, unreadable by traditional means. The accumulative size is certainly colossal; in some strange digital variation of industrial logic, the textual output of the network has begun to be measured by rates of production, such as Twitter's "Year in Review," which includes a timeline noting the most "Tweets per Second." Such a metric emphasizes the mechanical act of composition over the production of meaning. To take 2011 as a recent representative year, we see that posting news of Steve Jobs's death (6,049 tweets per second) or celebrating Beyoncé's pregnancy (announced at the MTV Video Music Awards; at 8,868 tweets per second, the most tweeted event of 2011) becomes far more significant as an act of cultural collaboration than what one might actually say about these events.[3] Production, not content, is central to digital composition. By writing at a particular moment, we participate in a rapidly moving history, partnered with others who are also composing our time, a complex joining of practice and temporality that undermines conventional literary assumptions about meaning, language, and interpretation, not to mention form.

In recent years, another dynamic has emerged, in that individuals are being endlessly written and interpreted by the network, in quite literal terms. The revolution of Big Data challenges our agency in tangible ways, whether through the invasions of privacy, like the National Security Administration's PRISM program, or through uncanny predictions of our behavior, as when the retailer Target discovered that it could mine purchasing patterns to anticipate when customers had become pregnant.[4] The data we produce is easily taken against our will; at the same time, given enough data and the right kinds of algorithmic tools, our will seems to dissolve into patterns of statistical probability. Life under Big Data poses obvious challenges to traditional notions of privacy, agency, and choice. Perloff's point that now we are "all authors" only tells half of the story, as we are both the producers and subjects of writing in real time, a writing/being-written that provokes, on the one hand, feelings of digital community and technofuturistic pleasure and, on the other, a legitimately anxious consciousness, where the borders of self-possession are repeatedly permeated by the network.

What might poetry have to say about this condition? Such a question may appear somewhat anemic, as spying on citizens or the commercial use of personal data are best addressed through regulatory policy, not a revolution of the poetic text. Yet as early as 2001, Jerome McGann argued that "understanding the structure of digital space requires a disciplined aesthetic intelligence,"[5] a claim even more relevant today, when the network is becoming pervasive and complex. Poetry's unique relationship to language, cognition, and affect can generate precisely the kind of aesthetic discipline necessary for a critical understanding of digital space; its role in our era of hyperinformation is essential, not peripheral. Still, one might object that turning to literature is a retrograde move, missing the core dynamic of the contemporary moment. As Adalaide Morris argues, our contemporary experience "is conditioned by a technoenvironment" while "what we think is conditioned by concepts developed, for the most part, in a world of print."[6] Because of this lag between concept and lifeworld, Morris wants us to develop new ways of understanding our relationship to technology, asking "[what] would the early twenty-first century look like if we did not conceptualize it in categories developed in the heyday of Fords, silent film, prop planes, and typewriters?"[7] As provocative as Morris's question may be, what happens when we take the opposite approach, turning to older poetic practices but reading them in a new way, thus establishing a new framework for investigating both our contemporary moment and our aesthetic past? Or, alternatively, perhaps our stories about print – its purported closure and stability – are themselves in need of revision. Print, as Ammons, Hejinian, Whitman, Pound, Olson, DuPlessis, and Mackey demonstrate, can become mobile and transformative through certain kinds of poetic practices. In other words, the world of (older media) poetry still has undiscovered resources to help us imagine – and interpret – our contemporary moment. Facilitating this interaction is, after all, one of the tasks of criticism.

In particular, emergent textual practices are unique in their ability to offer a compelling alternative to digital memory, where so often historical consciousness, as Liu notes, disappears into the constantly replicating present. In the information age, "our craving for instant data binds us to an ever more expansive, yet also vanishingly thin, present."[8] The resulting historical consciousness, if we can still call it this, may be trapped in a "*Now* [that] is the order of the day": "*Now* is history as it really *is*, with no *was* in view more extensive than – on a typical Web 2.0 screen – just a handful of entries ordered by most-recent at top. Beyond is only the black hole of an archive or history page of interest just to researchers."[9] While Liu is being deliberately hyperbolic, this description recalls Plato's *Phaedrus*, where Socrates recounts the legend of Teuth and the invention of writing: the technology purported to protect or aid memory actually leads to forgetfulness.[10] The digital technoenvironment courts a similar risk. As the documents of history become universally accessible, their significance may become more obscure, their value for both the past and the present forgotten.

Liu himself rejects the notion that social computing lacks historical awareness, preferring instead a kind of tempered digital triumphalism by claiming that the unfinished revolution of "Web 2.0 . . . is a libertarian pygmy standing on the shoulders of a tyrant ogre. As a result, spatial-political barriers that once took muscular civilizations centuries, if not millennia, to traverse . . . are now overleaped in milliseconds by a single finger pushing 'send.'"[11] Such celebrations of technology's triumph, as Liu admits, run the risk of assuming that the old historical work is behind us, a dubious claim given the persistence (and acceleration) of economic inequality and the inevitable social disruptions that will attend climate change. More to the point, recognizing digital media as an emergent development within the historical process is not the same as developing a positive model of historical consciousness within Web 2.0. Liu recognizes this point, suggesting that digital communication networks like Web 2.0 need supplements to reclaim a historical sensibility – alternative, complementary methods for fostering a sense of cultural memory and a connection to the past.[12]

Liu's interest in the historical consciousness of Web 2.0 reflects recent discussions in poetics of creativity, memory, and ethical engagement. As Brian Reed puts it in a study of twenty-first-century avant-garde poetry, "[how] does a person – can a person – achieve 'ethical habits of selected gathering' and 'other forms of advanced attention' in the age of iPads and iTunes?"[13] To pose the question somewhat differently: to what extent might "advanced attention" and "ethical habits of selected gathering," phrases Reed borrows from the poet Andrea Brady, require both creativity and memory? To answer these questions, one must conceptualize creativity and memory in such a way that it does not mimetically replicate the habits of mind already present in the iPad. But neither does creativity in the age of the iPad require older ideals of authorial expression or formal autonomy. Creativity in the present would need to be distinct from the dominant modes of attention, consumption, and cognition privileged by the digital but still capable of interacting with that stream of information. A creative work – say, a poem – would need to be self-sustaining while also interactive, or, in the language of systems theory, autopoietic yet structurally coupled. As for memory, we might look for mechanisms that would allow us to resist Liu's restless NOW, where history is either forgotten or transformed into another simulacrum for contextless consumption. In other words, we need a creative memory that offers a critical engagement with what we might call the *digital imaginary* – the imagined relations to the real conditions of the information age.

Emergent poetics offers one model for that kind of creative memory, but to contextualize its potential, consider some of the alternative approaches to literary production that have arisen alongside the network, most notably the work affiliated with conceptual poetry.[14] As a conceptual writer committed to investigating the digital imaginary, Kenneth Goldsmith's work most acutely articulates the challenge to creativity posed by a world of infinite textual production. Goldsmith posits that in a world with an "unprecedented amount of digital text, writing needs to redefine itself in order to adapt to the new environment of textual abundance."[15] Goldsmith's core redefinition: poets should abandon creativity as an aesthetic value, following in the path of the conceptual and pop artists of the 1960s.

From conceptual art Goldsmith borrows the compositional strategy of recontextualization, so that "context becomes the new content," while with pop art he embraces both a cool detachment and a faux-populism, joyfully writing about the "daily encounters" of life in a corporate, networked society.[16] And, indeed, Goldsmith's writer is perfectly at home in the world of fast capital and neoliberal organization: "Having moved from the traditional position of being solely generative entities to information managers with organizational capacities, writers are potentially poised to assume the tasks once thought to belong only to programmers, database minders, and librarians, thus blurring the distinction between archivists, writers, producers, and consumers."[17] Given Goldsmith's track record of irony and cheek, we should not, as Reed warns, read him and other conceptual poets "straight,"[18] and a parody of contemporary techno-utopianism can be detected in this passage. At the same time, Goldsmith's model for literature in the digital imaginary is clear: simultaneously democratic and uncreative, the writer becomes a flexible "manager" of preexisting text, ideally suited to the contemporary marketplace. Like a Web 2.0 user, Goldsmith's poet generates the very textual commodities that he in turn consumes (and, along the way, producing surplus value in some form or another).[19]

However, Goldsmith's grand pronouncements about uncreative writing in the digital are not entirely consonant with his practice. Both Reed and Perloff have demonstrated that Goldsmith's work in fact involves creative choices, despite the roteness of his procedures. For Perloff and Reed, the aesthetic effects of these texts are not simply found in the concept by which they were constructed but within the reading experience. For Perloff, a text like Goldsmith's *Traffic* (2007), purportedly a word-for-word transcription of New York City traffic reports broadcasted by the WINS radio station, is "hardly passive recycling." Instead, the book is shot through with gaps and lacunae that "[transform] the intersection of time and space into a wholly surreal situation."[20] The poem is thus an example of "fluid text" removed from its original context but also "spliced to produce a new construct" with legible, and literary, effects.[21] In detecting this new construct, Perloff concludes that Goldsmith and other practitioners of "unoriginal genius" are, in fact, producing works whose end product is "ultimately carried out *according to taste*," "always the product of choice – and hence of individual taste."[22]

For Reed, Goldsmith's practice is less about his own taste than it is about the institution of poetry and our contemporary sensibility. Reed's thoughtful analysis of *The Weather* (2005), another purported transcription of radio broadcasts, shows that an attentive reading offers literary experiences on several levels. The text "gathers ephemeral floating media-speak and re-presents it as a series of alternately absorbing and disturbing rhythms and flows," where close reading allows one to better understand "weather reporting and the flawed mechanisms for transcribing speech."[23] But the text also prompts "a different kind of reading," one that brings us closer to the digital imaginary, "a means of taking in and processing information," a "semi-distracted variety of textual engagement [that] both rewards and troubles this twenty-first-century modality of attention":

> *The Weather* might teach lessons about the nature of poetry, the vocation of the poet, and the inadequacy of available channels for learning about the contemporary world, natural and human alike. It also, though, reconfigures an audience's experience of perusing poetry. Moreover – and here it is unlike more conventional verse – its 'structure of desire' belongs to a new digital era in which, just as all information is reducible to bits, so too all content can be frictionlessly integrated into a horizonless, everlasting present-focused flow.[24]

Goldsmith's text has merit both as linguistic artifact and as the production of a new kind of literature. The remediation of language from radio weather report to poetry enacts an avant-garde institution critique, expanding the definition of poetry. At the same time, Goldsmith's text generates a reading experience that more adequately channels the phenomenological experience of a digital era bound to a constant stream of information, recalling the postmodern aesthetics of "total flow" theorized by Jameson.

Goldsmith's "uncreativity" is thus revealed by Perloff to be another way of reflecting a cultivated sensibility, while Reed shows it to be a (creative) development in the tradition of avant-garde practice for the digital age. Indeed, Goldsmith himself, although possibly in jest, ultimately affirms subjective and creative elements within "uncreative" writing. Recalling Perloff's "taste," Goldsmith suggests that "the suppression of self-expression is impossible. Even when we do something as seemingly 'uncreative' as retyping a few pages, we express ourselves in a variety of ways."[25] Elsewhere, he articulates the belief that "it is impossible, working with language, not to express oneself."[26] Although it would be a mistake to collapse expression into creativity, it is clear that Goldsmith's possible tongue-in-cheek claims illustrate Perloff's ultimate reaffirmation of sensibility: the uncreative, appropriative "language manager" has snuck in subjective, creative activity, wherein the activity of choosing what and how to copy becomes an expressive act. Goldsmith admits that this mode of literary practice is not entirely new. James Joyce, for instance, "presages uncreative writing by the act of sorting words, weighing which are 'signal' and which are 'noise,' what's worth keeping and what's worth leaving."[27] Texts like *Ulysses* and *Finnegan's Wake* are thus an articulation of sensibility that pluck meaning from the pool of language, a fount that has become even more vast and accessible in the digital age.

But how new is this conceptualization of artistic practice? And is the best response to the challenge of the digital an affirmation of uncreativity that surreptitiously brings in creativity by other means? As thoughtful as critics like Perloff and Reed can be in their assessment of Goldsmith, the conclusion is finally, and somewhat strikingly, conservative: the artist is someone with taste or one who mimetically replicates the flow of information that already surrounds us, albeit with potentially critical gestures through the framing of this information as "poetry." In either case, the work of Goldsmith's poetry in the digital age, despite its aspiration to provoke, remains consonant with traditional conceptions of expression, creativity, and representation. Alternatively, and more problematically, Goldsmith's work is affirmed for its capacity to replicate the "structure of desire" that already exists in the network's flow – the poetry does not, then, offer a substantive alternative to our contemporary modes of attention, but, instead, joins itself to the flow, dispersing itself into its environment.

To return to Goldsmith's evocation of the cybernetic concepts of "noise and signal," what is missing in this formulation is a mechanism explaining how the writer can actually distinguish between the two. Goldsmith has no articulate way of telling the difference between signal and noise, and thus it is unsurprising to find him falling back on claims about expression or to see Perloff's turn to taste.[28] Ultimately, in a somewhat hidden romanticism, the artist becomes the differential, the ghost within the machine separating out signal from noise, but the criteria by which those choices are made is unclear. Similarly, the creativity present in his work, yet disavowed, is obscured by the uncreative appropriation of endless information. What Goldsmith ends up producing looks very much like the same flow of information from which he derived his text. In the language of George Spencer Brown (whose *Laws of Form* could certainly be useful for thinking about the best work in conceptual art), the distinction being drawn by the poem may be too weak to adequately distinguish between signal and noise.

Emergent poetics offers an important alternative to this creative-uncreative confusion, providing an actual conceptual and aesthetic framework for separating signal from noise while also responding to the potentially infinite flow of information. As complex adaptive systems, emergent literary texts use their internal processes – iteration, recursion, provisional closure, and feedback loops – to engage the external languages of the networks to which they are structurally coupled. In this sense, the complexity and unpredictability of our current informational environment is no different from the other changing environments we have seen throughout this study, whether Whitman's Civil War or Mackey's Katrina-ravaged New Orleans. In each case, the capacity to transform formal processes in response to environmental pressures allows emergent texts to both incorporate and interpret the world of surprising information. This model of creation doesn't rely simply on "taste" to separate signal from noise; instead, the interpretive orientation emerges from the poetic system itself, through the complex adaptive interactions of its functions and processes. Similarly, such a model of self-organization does not eliminate the subjectivity of the poet, the unique human capacities for experience. Instead, subjectivity is a process connected to (and powerfully transformed by) the emergent system: it is not the unacknowledged ghost in the artistic machine nor the controlling consciousness executing a foreordained plan. Instead, the consciousness of the poet – and, by extension, the reader – is structurally coupled to the poem's own adaptive movement. We might say that *Leaves of Grass* is writing Walt Whitman, that *My Life* is generating Lyn Hejinian's "taste," even as these living, breathing persons are necessary constituents of the poem itself. Thus, emergent texts develop aesthetic processes where both expression and subjectivity are retained yet networked to the poetic process. These processes, in turn, establish meaning within a changing environment, including the surprising pressures of our digital era.

To illustrate the potential value of emergent poetic strategies within the flow of digital media, I want to conclude with a brief reading of Juliana Spahr's 2005 volume *This Connection of Everyone with Lungs*. Made up of two poems, "Poem Written after September 11, 2001" and "Poem Written from November 30, 2002 to March 27, 2003," the book manifests, in a restrained fashion, all of the formal properties characteristic of emergent texts: iterative and recursive elements, moments of provisional closure, structural coupling to outside environments, internal and external feedback loops, and emergent meanings that arise out of these processes. Complementing these formal structures, Spahr's purpose in the poem is to comprehend the network of connections that comprise the world, a network whose noise is overwhelmingly present in an era of continuous, digital global information. In Spahr's hands, emergent poetry allows us not simply to repeat or surf the flow of information but to creatively remember and inhabit that network of connections in which we are inevitably, hopelessly entangled.[29]

We can see an emergent sensibility in the opening figure of "Poem Written after September 11," which begins with an image of Spencer-Brownian division, describing the "cells, the movement of cells and the division of cells" developing into the organism of the body as "a shape / a shape of blood beating and cells dividing. / But outside of this shape is space."[30] Drawing a distinction, Spahr's body is a system of subsystems creating new spaces, including the spaces between hands, rooms, bodies, and cells. These spaces are not neutral or abstract, however. As Spahr continues, space becomes a life-sustaining example of environmental entanglement through the act of breathing: "Everyone with lungs breathes the space" (CEL 5). Combined, "everyone with lungs" and "space" become the iterative elements in an expansive, recursive structure, as each stanza of the poem repeats and adds to the stanza that came before. As a result, the poem's form shows that this "connection of everyone with lungs" is an inextricably entangled and growing network:

> as everyone with lungs breathes the space between the hands and the space around the hands and the space of the room and the space of the buildings that surrounds the room and the space of the neighborhoods nearby and the space of the cities in and out (CEL 5)

Divided space offers a way to conceptualize the interaction between bodies, domesticity, the city, and, ultimately, the planet.

The formal strategies of "Poem Written after September 11, 2001" sets the stage for the more complex, adaptive explorations of "Poem Written from November 30, 2002, to March 27, 2003," a text that writes the real time developments leading up to the second Iraq war. Composed of fifteen dated sections, "Poem Written from November 30" is a twenty-first-century extension of the "write every day" approach taken by A. R. Ammons in *Tape for the Turn of the Year*, explored in the introduction of this book. Of equal importance, the poem offers a profound alternative to Goldsmith's treatment of information. Spahr writes (nearly) every day, using the poem as a space to identify and engage patterns within the flux of quotidian life and the flow of information. Replacing Ammons's typewriter with the complex sociality of the computer, the first section of the poem, titled "November 30, 2002," includes an anticipation of the "morning to come, mundane with the news of it all," when the speaker and her Beloveds (the addressees of the poem) turn "to our separate computers and the wideness of their connections and the probably hourly changes of temperature between 79 and 80 degrees that will happen all day long with winds that begin the day at 12 mph and end it at 8 mph" (CEL 17). As we saw in the introduction, Ammons used the materiality of the receipt tape as a physical space of provisional closure within his long, thin poem, relying on the type-writer's capacities to add another dimension to his text. In contrast, Spahr finds a disorientation of space in the computer's simultaneous closeness and distance; physically together, three people at their "separate computers" are also plugged into a networked, global space, where the "news refreshes every few minutes on the computer screen and on the television stream" (CEL 33). Spahr's evocation of weather alongside the computer, then, speaks to the multiple spaces of connection, physical and virtual, material and repre-sentational, that draw us together on a shared planet. While her professed desire is to use the poem "to tie it all up and tie up the world in an attempt to understand the swirls of patterns," she recognizes that "there is no effi-cient way" to accomplish this task (CEL 32). At the same time, the poem's apparent inefficiency, its feedback loops and unpredictable acts of provi-sional closure, offers a mechanism by which those swirls become visible and multiply.

Indeed, "Poem Written from November 30" creates its own network of formal structures to register these environmental patterns. Along with the provisional closure of each section, further distinctions are created through several iterative and recursive devices appearing within and across each sec-tion. These devices range from the mode of address, the "Beloveds" to whom the poem is written, to the use of "I speak," through which the poem self-reflexively draws attention to its own performative operations. Both structures are visible in the opening lines of "December 1, 2002":

> Beloveds, yours skins is a boundary separating yous from the rest of yous.
> When I speak of skin I speak of the largest organ.
> I speak of the separations that define this world and the separations that
>   define us, beloveds, even as we like to press our skins against one
>   another in the night.
> When I speak of skin I speak of lighting candles to remember AIDS and
>   the history of attacks in Kenya.
> I speak of toxic fumes given off by plastic flooring in a burning nightclub
>   in Caracas.
> I speak of the forty-seven dead in Caracas.
> And I speak of the four dead in Palestine.
> And of the three dead in Israel.   (CEL 19)

Here, the capacity to "speak" is simultaneously an act of poetic atten-tion as well as a self-reflexive claim for the shifting, expanding, and emer-gent meanings of the textual utterance. Each "speak" is singular as a unit of meaning while the accumulation of these "speaks" suggests that each utterance is also determined by all of the others. "I speak" thus serves two purposes, functioning as an iterative form capable of ongoing predications as well as a self-reflexive, recursive operation generating a network of meanings between the individual "states" of the poetic system, each instance of "I speak" and its connection to all of the other instances that comprise the text. We might say that "speaking" connects the Beloveds' skins to all other elements in the environment of which one can speak. Further expanding the meaning of the volume's title, "I speak" combines poetic discourse with a physical capacity dependent on the breath, another connection of everyone with lungs.[31]

Through this insistent use of "I speak," Spahr's text testifies to its own interpretive desires even as it establishes "swirls of patterns" out of the chaotic complexity of the world that the poem encounters through the digital news feed. "December 1, 2002" later comments that reports of troop movements give the impression of a game, where armies "are massed on a flat map of the world," the same world where there is a "memory of four floating icebergs off the coast of Argentina and thirty thousand dead salmon in the Klamath River this year" (CEL 20–1). The poem combines these facts into a second-order, emergent claim only to note the necessary insufficiency of this containment: "I speak of the intimate relationship between salmons and humans, between humans and icebergs, between icebergs and salmons, and how this is just the beginning of the circular list" (CEL 21). Spahr uses the poem to establish its own network of meaning while insisting that this network also has a correlative within the world of bodies and spaces, those "moments when we do not understand why we must remain separated or joined only in the most mundane ways" (CEL 21). In many respects, the poem generates that moment of "not understanding" through its form, the accumulation of speaking to and with Beloveds making palpable the intimacy of our many structural couplings, even though, as Charles Altieri puts it, the poem cannot "achieve a position where it can reconcile" these conflicting and connected forces.[32] The human skin is both an organism within an environment that includes icebergs, salmon, and soldiers as well as an environmental force that transforms organisms. The poem here asserts a bewildered relationship to a world whose networked complexity it has helped make visible.

Given her interest in intimacy and connection, Spahr's use of "I speak" as an iterative form cannily bridges the long poem and the conventions of the lyric.[33] In her note to "Poem written from November 30," Spahr claims that she found the "lyric – with its attention to connection, with its dwelling on the beloved and on the afar – suddenly somewhat poignant, somewhat apt, even somewhat more useful than I usually find it" (CEL 13). The address to the "Beloveds" owes an obvious debt to the lyric, although the plural form creates a condition of multiple identifications that recalls Whitman's use of "you," an intimacy that both establishes and disrupts boundaries between selves and relies upon the mobility of language. More significantly, Spahr's "I speak" directly engages the ideology of lyric as "voice," a topic that has been hotly debated for decades in both experimental and mainstream contexts.[34] At the same time, "I speak" is also a convention of the long poem, evoking the "I sing" of the classical epic with its public, declamatory rhetoric. As an emergent text bridging the long poem and the lyric, *This Connection of Everyone with Lungs* is an appropriate place to end this study by pointing beyond its ending to other possibilities that come with reading for emergence. Spahr's work suggests that the models of emergent form that I have examined in these chapters might be usefully adapted to reading other poetries, including the lyric. Perhaps by attending to the network of relationships between poetic practices, we might establish critical vocabularies that articulate connections between forms like lyric and long poem without collapsing their differences.

If nothing else, through its processes of attention and articulation, its lyric intimacy and its environmental entanglement, Spahr's work offers a striking version of creativity, literary form, and cultural memory responding to the disorienting flow of the digital. Her text does not uncreatively surf the digital flow nor fall back on the psychology of taste or a hidden ideology of expression. Instead, the writing process becomes a distinctively poetic interpretive process allowing her – and us – to reimagine the network of relationships in which we are embedded. Undoubtedly, Spahr's interpretive activity has limitations; as she suggests in an introductory note to the poem, the knowledge gained for herself through the writing process was not entirely satisfactory. She writes that the impending war prompted her to "sort through the news in the hope of understanding how this would happen. I thought that by watching the news more seriously I could be a little less naïve. But I gained no sophisticated understanding as I wrote these poems" (CEL 13). This last statement appears, at first glance, to contradict the broad hermeneutic orientation of my argument here, as I have claimed that emergent poems become interpretive systems in their own right. But if, following systems thinkers, we expand "interpretive" to include the establishment and identification of meaningful patterns, the development of an orientation of interest or purposiveness within an environment, then Spahr's poem clearly satisfies this demand, developing a humble hermeneutic posture similar to that of DuPlessis or Mackey. Indeed, where Goldsmith's *Day* "uncreatively" frames the language of the newspaper and deliberately abandons much of the interpretive potential of literary form, Spahr's work creatively and adaptively interacts with the flux of news and the historical events behind those reports, engaging the digital imaginary with all of its material pressures and disorientating virtuality. While the causes and cures for these events may remain unknown, the poem's work is essential to bring that world into appearance. Consequently, *This Connection of Everyone with Lungs* illustrates the unique capacity of emergent writing practices to articulate a critical subjectivity within the digital imaginary of infinite, immersive information. In doing so, emergent practices challenge Goldsmith's poetics of the uncreative, offering a meaningful but no less contemporary alternative to conceptualism's claims. Indeed, Spahr's deployment of conventions from both the long poem and the lyric further demonstrates that inherited practices of literary form and imagination can still be a valuable resource for understanding the flow of new media experience.

Flow, after all, was where *Writing in Real Time* began, with Ammons's metaphor of "occupying the stream" of the present, bobbing creatively within the movement of a changing environment. Ammons's *Tape for the Turn of the Year* could not anticipate the developments in global communication and textual proliferation of our current era, and yet the rolling of receipt tape through his typewriter perhaps dramatizes *avant la lettre* the flow of tweets and status updates that constitute the digital avatar of a contemporary person. But unlike the absence of history that can so often characterize the temporality of Web 2.0, emergent texts generate a more complex relationship to time and memory. To remember, in such a system, is to (re)create, and thus historical memory is not unique to the subject but arises out of the subject-poem-environment relationship. The poem thus affords a supplement or tool for cultural memory, operating according to a prosthetic economy. The prosthetic, as Brian McHale notes, following David Wills, is that which "combines natural and artificial, human and mechanical, the spontaneous and the contrived, overriding the distinction between these categories."[35] McHale uses the concept of prosthesis to conceptualize machine-written poems (including those composed with the help of a computer), but then extends this concept to re-read poetic tradition, suggesting that formal devices like rhyme and meter might be understood as serving a prosthetic function.[36] In the realm of the prosthetic, agency and action are dispersed, the human and the artificial functioning in a systematic relationship with one another. Emergent form, from this perspective, prompts a kind of memory that might otherwise be lost, if not entirely impossible, a prosthetically imagined past and future.

McHale suggests that thinking of poetry as prosthesis figures a kind of cyborg subjectivity, theorized as early as 1985 by Donna Haraway. This link brings us back to the mid-twentieth-century intellectual history of systems-thinking, as the "cyborg is a cybernetic organism, a hybrid of machine and organism, a creature of social reality as well as a creature of fiction."[37] As a coupling of actuality and fiction, Haraway posits the cyborg's significance as "the condensed image of both imagination and material reality."[38] Thus, the cyborg is a potent figure for an emergent imaginary, lacking, according to Haraway, a traditional Western myth of originary unity, wholeness, or self-presence. The cyborg, like the emergent text, is actively functional and yet still to come, capable within its form of further modification and adaptation.

The cyborg and the prosthetic are far removed from the accounts of poetic form that have shaped criticism for decades, even centuries. Through re-reading the long poem as a complex adaptive system, I hope that this study makes a small contribution to new ways of thinking about literary form as such. Perhaps literary form becomes an active force in the world precisely through its entangled, embedded, structurally coupled, complex, and adaptive operations. The long poem has always seemed to know this truth, but, as Spahr's work in particular demonstrates, there is still much to explore in the couplings of the long poem and the lyric, or, for that matter, in the larger network of interactions that we call literature. Moving beyond the concerns of literary criticism, I also believe that literature is essential for understanding other forms of complex adaptive systems. Far from systems theory being the key to literature, I hope that these chapters have shown how literature can provide essential insight into our intimacy with other meaningful systems.

Despite these promises, reading for emergence has definite risks. The emphasis on newness, creativity, and the unexpected recurring throughout the chapters of this book might leave the impression that emergent poetry is a literary equivalent of the neoliberal cult of innovation or perhaps even a proxy for "creative capitalism." If so, the poetics of emergence, one might argue, is simply another instance of the cooptation of change and transformation by capital, a problem that haunts any progressive or radical politics. Instead of discounting emergent poetics for advocating adaptation, I prefer Haraway's own double vision, which she uses to wrest the dream of a liberatory cyborg from the destructive forces that have brought it into being. Acknowledging that the hypertechnical systems that generate the cyborg may also be read as a sign of the total dominance of Western power, Haraway argues that the "political struggle is to see from both perspectives at once because each reveals both dominations and possibilities unimagin-able from the other vantage point."[39] Similarly, emergent poetics does not itself generate a politics. Such texts, instead, provide a powerful mechanism for political imaginations that wish to remain fluid, projective, and experi-mental. In the social and cultural world of Web 2.0, the need to foster that kind of adaptive imaginary while retaining an acute cultural and historical memory seems essential.

This study's journey from Whitman's leaves to the poem-as-cyborg may appear somewhat unexpected in its own right. Nevertheless, reading for emergence both within an individual text and in the broader network of literary production brings these synergies into sharper focus, offering a new critical and literary-historical vision. It would be tempting to close by sug-gesting how emergent poetics will develop in the future, but that predic-tion goes against the spirit of the unexpected that these texts enact. Perhaps poets of the future will wish to extend and transform the possibilities of iter-ation, recursion, and structural coupling; or perhaps an entirely new model of conceiving both the past and the future through literary form will arise. Until then, I would suggest that reading for emergence powerfully shapes our current imaginary, cultivating McGann's "disciplined aesthetic intelli-gence" required by digital spaces – and indeed, required by any complex ecology, including our physical and social worlds. If nothing else, the aes-thetic intelligence generated through emergent poetry includes the capacity to imagine the world as a place of both unexpected surprise and recogni-tion, historical continuity and radical change. The consequences of that imaginary are yet to be determined.

Notes

CHAPTER 1

1. John Holland, *Emergence: From Chaos to Order* (Reading, MA: Perseus, 1998), 2. See also Steven Johnson, *Emergence: The Connected Lives of Ants, Brains, Cities, and Software* (New York: Scribner, 2001).

2. Holland, *Emergence*, 2. For more on "complex adaptive systems," see John H. Miller and Scott E. Page, *Complex Adaptive Systems: An Introduction to Computational Models of Social Life* (Princeton: Princeton University Press, 2007).

3. Understanding a poem as a self-organizing system is not new; we can trace this notion to Coleridge's discussion of organic form. Other critics have shown that self-organization can occur in surprising ways. See, for instance, Margaret Holley's claim that Marianne Moore's stanza structure generates a "formal tension which a wholly organic or wholly mechanical arrangement could not raise" ("The Model Stanza: The Organic Origin of Moore's Syllabic Verse," *Twentieth Century Literature* 30.2–3 [1984], 188). I am grateful to an anonymous reader for pointing me to Holley's essay.

4. T. S. Eliot, "Tradition and the Individual Talent," in *The Sacred Wood* (London: Methuen, 1920), 50.

5. A. R. Ammons, *Tape for the Turn of the Year* (New York: Norton, 1993), 1. Hereafter cited parenthetically as TTY.

6. Ted Gioia, *The Imperfect Art: Reflections on Jazz and Modern Culture* (Oxford: Oxford University Press, 1988), 61. Gioia's distinction between the "retrospective" and "blueprint" also appears in Edgar Landgraf's work on improvisation, discussed subsequently.

7. Ibid., 60–1.

8. Ibid., 60.

9. We see the New Critical lyric in Cleanth Brooks, *The Well Wrought Urn* (New York: Harcourt, Brace, 1947); the structuralist lyric in Roman Jakobson and Claude Lévi-Strauss, "Baudelaire's 'Les Chats,'" in *Language in Literature*, ed. Krystyna Pomorska and Stephen Rudy (Cambridge: Belknap, 1987), 180–97; the deconstructive lyric in Paul De Man, *The Rhetoric of Romanticism* (New York: Columbia University Press, 1984); and the Frankfort school lyric in Theodor Adorno, "Cultural Criticism and Society," in *Prisms* (1967), trans. Samuel and Shierry Weber (Cambridge: MIT Press, 1997), 17–34.

10. Marjorie Levinson, "What Is New Formalism?" *PMLA* 122.2 (2007), 558–69.
11. Derek Attridge, *The Singularity of Literature* (London: Routledge, 2004); Rita Felski, *Uses of Literature* (London: Blackwell, 2008); Gayatri Chakravorty Spivak, *An Aesthetic Education in the Era of Globalization* (Cambridge: Harvard University Press, 2012).
12. Stephen Best and Sharon Marcus, "Surface Reading: An Introduction," *Representations* 108 (2009), 1–21. For a brief reprise of the "descriptive turn," see Best, "Well, That Was Obvious," response to *Denotatively, Technically, Literally,* special issue of *Representations* 125 (2014), no pagination, www.representations .org/responses.
13. Levinson, "New Formalism?," 561. One cannot talk about the long poem without talking about form, but recent work on form and the long poem rarely considers form as a theoretical problem. Important exceptions include as Rachel Blau DuPlessis, "Notes on Silliman and Poesis," *Journal of Poetics Research* 2 (February 2015), no pagination, http://poeticsresearch.com/article/ rachel-blau-duplessis-notes-on-silliman-and-poesis-2, and Simon Jarvis, "The Melodics of Long Poems," *Textual Practice* 24.4 (2010), 607–21.
14. Rita Felski argues that Bruno Latour's actor-network theory can be a valuable model for rethinking literary agency. For a brief summary of her position, see "Latour and Literary Studies," *PMLA* 130.3 (2015), 737–42. For a thoughtful expansion of the notion of "form," which includes a discussion of "network" as form, see Caroline Levine, *Forms: Whole, Rhythm, Hierarchy, Network* (Princeton: Princeton University Press, 2015).
15. Cary Wolfe, "The Idea of Observation at Key West, or, Systems Theory, Poetry, and Form beyond Formalism," *New Literary History* 39.2 (2008), 259–76.
16. Marjorie Levinson, "Lyric: The Idea of This Invention," unpublished manuscript, University of Michigan (2015).
17. Virginia Jackson, *Dickinson's Misery: A Theory of Lyric Reading* (Princeton: Princeton University Press, 2005).
18. Frederic Jameson, *A Singular Modernity* (London: Verso, 2002), 169–72. Clement Greenberg's position was given its most programmatic form in "Avant-Garde and Kitsch" (1939), reprinted in *Art and Culture: Critical Essays* (Boston: Beacon, 1965), 3–21.
19. Jameson, *A Singular Modernity*, 207.
20. Ibid., 207–8.
21. Edgar Allan Poe, "The Poetic Principle," in *Selected Poetry and Prose of Edgar Allan Poe*, ed. T. O. Mabbott (New York: Modern Library, 1951), 383.
22. Aristotle, "Poetics," trans. by Ingram Bywater, *The Basic Works of Aristotle*, ed. by Richard McKeon (New York: Modern Library, 2001), 1450a 36–40.
23. Jacques Derrida, "The Laws of Genre," trans. Avital Ronell, *Critical Inquiry* 7.1 (1980), 55–81.
24. M. L. Rosenthal and Sally M. Gall, *Modern Poetic Sequence: The Genius of Modern Poetry* (New York: Oxford University Press, 1986), vi–vii.
25. Ibid., 9, 7.

26. Ibid., 6, emphasis in the original.
27. Ibid., 227.
28. Ibid., 341.
29. Michael André Bernstein, *The Tale of the Tribe: Ezra Pound and the Modern Verse Epic* (Princeton: Princeton University Press, 1980), 11, 14.
30. Ibid., 23. For another example of the epic approach, see Jeffery Walker, *Bardic Ethos and the American Epic Poem: Whitman, Pound, Crane, Williams, Olson* (Baton Rouge: Louisiana State University Press, 1989). Peter Baker's *Obdurate Brilliance: Exteriority and the Modern Long Poem* (Gainsville: University of Florida Press, 1991) argues that the modernist long poem is neither epic nor lyric because it lacks a "traditional epic hero" and the poets do not "center on their own internal feelings or experiences" (2).
31. Bernstein, *Tale of the Tribe*, 265.
32. James E. Miller, *The American Quest for a Supreme Fiction: Whitman's Legacy in the Personal Epic* (Chicago: University of Chicago Press, 1979), 36.
33. Similar to Miller, Thomas Gardner's *Discovering Ourselves in Whitman: The Contemporary American Long Poem* (Urbana: University of Illinois Press, 1989) cites Whitman as the figure "who most clearly identified and exploited the distance between an individual voice and the larger world" (1). Margaret Dickie's *On the Modernist Long Poem* (Iowa City: University of Iowa Press, 1986) does not rely on the model of "personal epic," yet her approach could also be called something of a third way, arguing that these long poems point beyond themselves to a narrative of their own composition. A recent example of lyric/epic hybrid criticism is Daniel Gabriel's *Hart Crane and the Modernist Epic: Canon and Genre Formation in Crane, Pound, Eliot, and Williams* (New York: Palgrave Macmillan, 2007).
34. Rachel Blau DuPlessis, "Considering the Long Poem: Genre Problems," *Readings Webjournal* 4 (2009), no pagination, www.bbk.ac.uk/readings/issues/issue4/duplessis_on_Consideringthelongpoemgenreproblems.
35. Ibid., no pagination.
36. Joseph M. Conte, *Unending Design: The Forms of Postmodern Poetry* (Ithaca: Cornell University Press, 1991), 1, hereafter cited parenthetically as UD. In what follows, I use the term "postmodern" in a provisional, deliberately undertheorized manner. A more detailed discussion of the concept appears in Chapter 6.
37. Bruce Clarke and Mark B. N. Hansen, "Introduction: Neocybernetic Emergence," in *Emergence and Embodiment: New Essays on Second-Order Systems Theory*, ed. Bruce Clarke and Mark B. N. Hansen (Durham: Duke University Press, 2009), 11.
38. Brian McHale, *The Obligation toward the Difficult Whole: Postmodernist Long Poems* (Tuscaloosa: University of Alabama Press, 2004), 3. Hereafter cited parenthetically as ODW.
39. DuPlessis, "Considering the Long Poem," no pagination.
40. For some of the many applications of emergence and complexity theory, see Stephen Wolfram's *A New Kind of Science* (Champaign, IL: Wolfram Media,

2002) and Harold Morowitz's *The Emergence of Everything: How the World Became Complex* (Oxford: Oxford University Press, 2002), in addition to the works already cited by Holland and Johnson. For a recent use of complex adaptive systems to rethink the role of the imagination in philosophy and neuroscience, see John Kaag, *Thinking through the Imagination: Aesthetics in Human Cognition* (New York: Fordham University Press, 2014), 165–91.

41. Niklas Luhmann, *Introduction to Systems Theory*, trans. Peter Gilgen (Cambridge: Polity, 2013), 25.
42. Bernard Dionysius Geoghegan, "From Information Theory to French Theory: Jakobson, Lévi-Strauss, and the Cybernetic Apparatus," *Critical Inquiry* 38.1 (2011), 100.
43. Ibid., 101.
44. Lydia H. Liu, *The Freudian Robot: Digital Media and the Future of the Unconscious* (Chicago: University of Chicago Press, 2010).
45. Norbert Wiener, *Cybernetics, or Control and Communication in the Animal and the Machine*, 2nd ed. (Cambridge: MIT Press, 1961), 11.
46. An overview of the Macy Conferences can be found in N. Katherine Hayles, *How We Became Posthuman: Virtual Bodies in Cybernetics, Literature, and Informatics* (Chicago: University of Chicago Press, 1999), 50–83, hereafter cited parenthetically in the text as HBP. For a longer history, see Steve Joshua Heims, *The Cybernetics Group* (Cambridge: MIT Press, 1991).
47. Luhmann, *Introduction to Systems Theory*, 26.
48. Wiener, *Cybernetics*, 6–7.
49. Ibid., 43.
50. Bernadette Mayer, "Sonnet: you jerk you didn't call me . . . ," in *A Bernadette Mayer Reader* (New York: New Directions, 1992), 93.
51. Humberto Maturana and Francisco Varela, *Autopoiesis and Cognition: The Realization of the Living* (Dordrecht: D. Reidel, 1980), 79. For an early application of autopoiesis to literature, see Jerome McGann, *The Textualist Condition* (Princeton: Princeton University Press, 1991), 15.
52. For more on openness and closure, see Luhmann, *Introduction to Systems Theory*, 38.
53. Ibid., 82.
54. This description of neuroplasticity is necessarily oversimplified. For a more thorough discussion, see Kaag, *Thinking through the Imagination*, 176–81.
55. George Spencer Brown, *Laws of Form* (London: George Allen and Unwin, 1969), 3.
56. Luhmann, *Introduction to Systems Theory*, 51.
57. Ibid., 52.
58. I borrow the concept of "affordance" from Levine, *Forms*, 6–11.
59. Rachel Blau DuPlessis, "Manifests" *Diacritics* 26.3–4 (1996), 51. Brian McHale builds on DuPlessis's model in "Beginning to Think about Narrative in Poetry" *Narrative* 17.1 (2009), 14–15.
60. N. Katherine Hayles, *My Mother Was a Computer: Digital Subjects and Literary Texts* (Chicago: University of Chicago Press, 2005), 25.

61. Francisco Varela, Evan Thompson, and Eleanor Rosch, *The Embodied Mind: Cognitive Science and Human Experience* (Cambridge: MIT Press, 1993). For more on cellular automata, see Hayles, *My Mother Was a Computer*, 25, and Wolfram, *A New Kind of Science*, 23–50.
62. Varela, et al., *Embodied Mind*, 89.
63. Ibid., 89.
64. Ibid., 151.
65. Ibid., 156.
66. Noam Chomsky, *Aspects of the Theory of Syntax* (Cambridge: MIT Press, 1969).
67. Fred Karlson, "Syntactic Recursion and Iteration," in *Recursion and Human Language*, ed. Harry van der Hulst (Berlin: De Gruyter Mouton, 2010), 43.
68. Allen Ginsberg, *Howl and Other Poems* (San Francisco: City Lights, 1956), 9.
69. Muriel Rukeyser, *The Life of Poetry* (Ashfield, MA: Paris Press, 1996), 186–7.
70. Jack Burnham, "System Esthetics," *ArtForum* (September 1968), 31.
71. Ibid., 31.
72. Ibid., 32.
73. Niklas Luhmann offers an extensive discussion of this relationship between perceptual and communicative systems in the first chapter of *Art As a Social System*, trans. Eva M. Knodt (Stanford: Stanford University Press, 2000), 5–53.
74. Ibid., 105.
75. Ibid., 118.
76. Edgar Landgraf, *Improvisation as Art: Conceptual Challenges, Historical Perspectives* (New York: Continuum, 2011), 5.
77. Ibid., 36.
78. Mark Hansen takes this relationship between openness and closure a step further, arguing that neocybernetic interactive emergence opens the possibility for system-environment hybrids, wherein the environment and the system share creative agency. See "System-Environment Hybrids," in *Emergence and Embodiment: New Essays on Second-Order Systems Theory*, ed. Bruce Clarke and Mark B. N. Hansen (Durham: Duke University Press, 2009), 125.
79. Lyn Hejinian, *Writing Is an Aid to Memory* (Los Angeles: Sun & Moon, 1996).
80. See Ron Silliman, "The New Sentence," in *The New Sentence* (New York: Roof, 1987), 63–93.
81. Lyn Hejinian, *My Life and My Life in the Nineties* (Middletown, CT: Wesleyan University Press, 2013), 118. Hereafter cited parenthetically as ML.
82. "Para-, prefix," OED Online (Oxford University Press, March 2015).
83. Hejinian articulates a similar point in an introductory note to her influential essay "The Rejection of Closure" (1985): "[The] world [is] vast and overwhelming; each moment stands under an enormous vertical and horizontal pressure of information, potent with ambiguity, meaning-full, unfixed, and certainly incomplete. What saves this from becoming a vast undifferentiated mass of data and situation is one's ability to make distinctions. The open text is one which both acknowledges the vastness of the world and is formally differentiating. It is form that provides an opening" ([Poetry Foundation: 2015], no pagination, www.poetryfoundation.org/learning/essay/237870?page=1).
84. Clarke and Hansen, "Introduction," 11.

85. Barrett Watten, "New Meaning and Poetic Vocabulary: From Coleridge to Jackson Mac Low" *Poetics Today* 18.2 (1997), 150.

86. Edward Brunner, *Cold War Poetry: The Social Text in the Fifties Poem* (Urbana-Champaign: University of Illinois Press, 2004).

87. I am grateful to an anonymous reader for pointing out these novelistic links.

CHAPTER 2

1. Ralph Waldo Emerson, "The Poet," *Essays and Lectures* (New York: Library of America, 1983), 450.

2. Samuel Taylor Coleridge, *Coleridge's Criticism of Shakespeare: A Selection*, ed. R. A. Foakes (London: Athlone Press, 1989), 53.

3. Immanuel Kant, *Critique of Judgment*, trans. J. H. Bernard (New York: Prometheus, 2000), 187.

4. Ibid., 187.

5. Recent reassessments of Whitman's historical context include Michael Robertson, *Worshipping Walt: The Whitman Disciples* (Princeton: Princeton University Press, 2008) and Ted Genoways, *Walt Whitman and the Civil War: America's Poet during the Lost Years of 1860–1862* (Berkeley: University of California Press, 2009). Kenneth M. Price's *To Walt Whitman, America* (Chapel Hill: University of North Carolina Press, 2004) unites race, sexuality, transnationalism, and American studies in an analysis of Whitman's influence, while *Whitman Noir: Black America and the Good Gray Poet*, edited by Ivy Wilson, focuses on Whitman's complex relationship to blackness (Iowa City: University of Iowa Press, 2014). For a reading of class in Whitman, see Andrew Lawson, *Walt Whitman and the Class Struggle* (Iowa City: University of Iowa Press, 2006). Transnational approaches include Laure Katsaros, *New York-Paris: Whitman, Baudelaire, and the Hybrid City* (Ann Arbor: University of Michigan Press, 2012) and M. Wynn Thomas, *Transatlantic Connections: Whitman U.S., Whitman U.K.* (Iowa City: University of Iowa Press, 2005). On the ecological Whitman, see M. Jimmie Killingsworth, *Walt Whitman and the Earth: A Study in Ecopoetics* (Iowa City: University of Iowa Press, 2004). New work in textual studies includes Ed Folsom, *Whitman Making Books, Books Making Whitman: A Catalog and Commentary* (Iowa City: Obermann Center for Advanced Studies, University of Iowa: 2005) and Matt Miller, *Collage of Myself: Walt Whitman and the Making of Leaves of Grass* (Lincoln: University of Nebraska Press, 2010). The single most important resource for the digital Whitman is the *Walt Whitman Archive*, ed. Ed Folsom and Kenneth M. Price, Center for Digital Research in the Humanities (Lincoln: University of Nebraska—Lincoln, 2016), www.whitmanarchive.org.

6. Andreas Weber and Francisco Varela, "Life after Kant: Natural Purposes and the Autopoietic Foundations of Biological Individuality," *Phenomenology and the Cognitive Sciences* 1 (2002), 102; emphasis in the original.

7. Ibid., 117.

8. Walt Whitman, *Poetry and Prose* (New York: Library of America, 1996), 5, hereafter cited parenthetically in the text as PP. Unless otherwise noted, all poetry citations are drawn from the 1891–2 edition of *Leaves of Grass*.

9. Roy Morris, Jr., *The Better Angel: Walt Whitman in the Civil War* (Oxford: Oxford University Press, 2000), 47. For more on Whitman's war years, see Genoways, *Walt Whitman and the Civil War*.

10. Morris, *The Better Angel*, 61.

11. Or seven, depending on how one treats the 1891–2 "deathbed" edition, which, as the editors of the *Walt Whitman Archive* note, is primarily a reprinting of the 1881–2 with new annexes; see comments at www.whitmanarchive.org/published/LG.

12. By poetic thinking, I mean composition as a form of thought itself. See J. H. Prynne, "Poetic Thought," *Textual Practice* 24.4 (2010), 596.

13. For a more complete account of the relationship between Whitman the printer and Whitman the poet, see Folsom, *Whitman Making Books*.

14. Whitman, *Leaves of Grass* (1856), 362, page image available at the *Walt Whitman Archive*, www.whitmanarchive.org/published/LG/1856/whole.html.

15. Cristanne Miller, "Drum Taps: Revisions and Reconciliations," *Walt Whitman Quarterly Review* 26.4 (2009), 173.

16. The exact page number depends on which version of the 1871–2 edition you consider. As Luke Mancuso relates, the fifth edition of *Leaves* has a "complicated publishing history" that "includes at least three rearrangements of the book" ("Leaves of Grass, 1871–1872 Edition," *Walt Whitman: An Encyclopedia*, ed. J. R. LeMaster and Donald D. Kummings [New York: Garland, 1998], 368).

17. Miller, "Drum Taps," 180.

18. According to Alain Badiou, "an event is always extracted from a situation, always related back to a singular multiplicity," "The Event as Trans-Being," *Theoretical Writings*, ed. and trans. Ray Brassier and Alberto Toscano (London: Continuum, 2004), 98.

19. George Kateb, "Walt Whitman and the Culture of Democracy," *Political Theory* 18.4 (1990), 551.

20. Allen Grossman, "The Poetics of Union in Whitman and Lincoln: An Inquiry toward the Relationship of Art and Policy," *The American Renaissance Reconsidered*, eds. Walter Benn Michaels and Donald E. Pease, *The English Institute* n.s. 9 (Baltimore: Johns Hopkins University Press, 1985), 184, 192.

21. James Perrin Warren, *Walt Whitman's Language Experiment* (University Park: Pennsylvania State University Press, 1990), 114; W. C. Harris, "Whitman's *Leaves of Grass* and the Problem of the One and the Many," *Arizona Quarterly* 56.3 (2000), 32. See also Grossman, "The Poetics of Union," as well as Diane Kepner, "From Spears to Leaves: Walt Whitman's Theory of Nature in 'Song of Myself,'" *American Literature* 51.2 (1979), 179–204.

22. The characterization comes from Whitman's posthumously published *An American Primer* (Cambridge: 1904), viii.

23. Warren, *Walt Whitman's Language Experiment*, 114.

24. Charles Altieri, "Spectacular Antispectacle: Ecstasy and Nationality in Whitman and His Heirs," *American Literary History* 11.1 (1999), 36.

25. I refer to Louis Althusser's well-known interpretation of the "you" as the ground of ideology in "Ideology and Ideological State Apparatuses," trans. Ben Brewster, in *Critical Theory Since Plato*, eds. Hazard Adams and Leroy Searle, 3rd ed. (Boston: Thomson Wadsworth, 2005), 1304.

26. Mitchell Breitwieser, "Who Speaks in Whitman's Poems?" *The American Renaissance: New Dimensions*, eds. Harry R. Garvin and Peter C. Carafiol, *Bucknell Review* 28.1 (London and Toronto: Associated University Press, 1983), 132.

27. Grossman, "The Poetics of Union," 193.

28. Ibid., 189.

29. Frank McConnell, *The Confessional Imagination: A Reading of Wordsworth's* Prelude (Baltimore: Johns Hopkins University Press, 1974), 2.

30. Kenneth R. Johnston, *Wordsworth and* The Recluse (New Haven: Yale University Press, 1984), xiv–xv.

31. For a summary of the relationship between Wordsworth and Milton, see Robin Jarvis, *Wordsworth, Milton, and the Theory of Poetic Relations* (London: Macmillan, 1991).

32. M. H. Abrams, *Natural Supernaturalism: Tradition and Revolution in Romantic Literature* (New York: Norton, 1971), 76.

33. Anne K. Mellor, "Writing the Self/Self Writing: William Wordsworth's Prelude," *William Wordsworth's* The Prelude*: A Casebook*, ed. Stephen Gill (Oxford: Oxford University Press, 2006), 294–5.

34. William Wordsworth, *The Prelude 1799, 1805, 1850*, eds. Jonathan Wordsworth, M. H. Abrams, and Stephen Gill (New York: Norton, 1979), II.351–5. Unless otherwise noted, all citations are to the 1805 version of *The Prelude*; subsequent references will be cited parenthetically in the text as P.

35. Barbara Herrnstein Smith, *Poetic Closure: A Study of How Poems End* (Chicago: University of Chicago Press, 1968), 99.

36. Ibid., 99.

37. For Pound's definition of "periplum," see *ABC of Reading* (New York: New Directions, 1960), 43–4.

38. Smith, *Poetic Closure*, 100.

39. Miller, *The American Quest*, 43.

40. Robert Duncan, *Fictive Certainties* (New York: New Directions, 1955), 200.

CHAPTER 3

1. The canonical account of the modern dynamo comes from Henry Adams in *The Education of Henry Adams* (New York: Library of America, 2009). On music machines, see Paul K. Saint-Amour, "*Ulysses* Pianola," *PMLA* 130.1 (2015), 15–36. On reading machines, see Jessica Pressman, "Machine Poetics and Reading Machines: William Poundstone's Electronic Literature and Bob Brown's Readies," *American Literary History* 23.4 (2011), 767–94. On writing

machines, see Brian McHale, "Poetry as Prosthesis" *Poetics Today* 21.1 (2000), 1–32. On driving machines, see F. T. Marinetti, "Manifesto of Futurism," (1909), trans. R. W. Flint and Arthur A. Coppotelli, in *Manifesto: A Century of Isms*, ed. Mary Ann Caws (Lincoln: University of Nebraska Press, 2001), 187–9. On flying machines, see Robert Wohl, *A Passion for Wings: Aviation and the Western Imagination, 1908–1918* (New Haven: Yale University Press, 1994).

2. Marinetti, "Manifesto of Futurism," 187.

3. William Carlos Williams, "Author's Introduction to *The Wedge*" (1944), in *Selected Essays of William Carlos Williams* (New York: New Directions, 1969), 256.

4. Ibid., 256.

5. W. K. Wimsatt and Monroe C. Beardsley, "The Intentional Fallacy" (1954), *The Critical Tradition*, ed. David H. Richter, 3rd Ed. (Boston: Bedford/St. Martins, 2007), 811.

6. Walter Benjamin, *The Work of Art in the Age of Its Technological Reproducibility, and Other Writings on Media*, ed. Michael W. Jennings, Brigid Doherty, and Thomas Y. Levin (Cambridge: Belknap Press, 2008). For recent work in modernist media studies, see Mark Goble, *Beautiful Circuits: Modernism and the Mediated Life* (New York: Columbia University Press, 2010).

7. Scholars are beginning to look more closely at the link between modernism and cybernetics; see, for instance, Heather A. Love's "Cybernetic Modernism and the Feedback Loop: Ezra Pound's Poetics of Transmission" *Modernism/Modernity* 23.1 (2016), 89–111.

8. *Blast* 1, edited by Wyndham Lewis (1914) (Santa Rosa: Black Sparrow Press, 2002), 8.

9. Ibid., 36.

10. Ibid., 39, 41.

11. For one biographical account, see A. David Moody, *Ezra Pound: Poet. A Portrait of the Man and His Work. I: The Young Genius 1885–1920* (Oxford and New York: Oxford University Press, 2007).

12. McHale, "Poetry as Prosthesis," 3.

13. Ibid., 3.

14. Ibid., 3.

15. Ibid., 21.

16. Watten, "New Meaning and Poetic Vocabulary," 150.

17. Ibid., 150.

18. Ibid., 155.

19. Ibid., 171.

20. Ibid., 171–2.

21. Ibid., 172.

22. The first half of *"A-9"* was published in 1940. Zukofsky and Pound's relationship was understandably complex; for the authoritative account of Zukofsky's life and influences, see Mark Scroggins, *The Poem of a Life: A Biography of Louis Zukofsky* (Berkeley: Counterpoint, 2007).

23. Franco Moretti, *Modern Epic: The World-System from Goethe to García Márquez*, trans. Quintin Hoare (New York: Verso, 1996), 96.
24. Ibid., 97.
25. For general discussions of Pound's politics, see Robert Casillo, *The Genealogy of Demons: Anti-Semitism, Fascism, and the Myths of Ezra Pound* (Evanston, IL: Northwestern University Press, 1988) and Tim Redman, *Ezra Pound and Italian Fascism* (Cambridge: Cambridge University Press, 1991). Peter Nicholls's *Ezra Pound: Politics, Economics and Writing* (London: Macmillan, 1984) specifically addresses the ideological implications of *The Cantos*.
26. Ezra Pound, *The Cantos* (New York: New Directions, 1996), 3, hereafter cited parenthetically in the text as C.
27. Hugh Kenner, *The Pound Era* (Berkeley: University of California Press, 1971), 349.
28. Hugh Kenner, "Leucothea's Bikini: Mimetic Homage," in *Ezra Pound: Perspectives*, ed. Noel Stock (Chicago: Henry Regnery, 1965), 28–9.
29. Ibid., 27.
30. Ibid., 36.
31. Edgar Landgraf, *Improvisation as Art*, 24.
32. Ibid., 38.
33. Ronald Bush, *The Genesis of Ezra Pound's* Cantos (Princeton: Princeton University Press, 1976), 5–6.
34. Bernstein, *The Tale of the Tribe*, 32.
35. Stephen Sicari, *Pound's Epic Ambition: Dante and the Modern World* (Albany: State University of New York Press, 1991), x–xi.
36. James E. Miller offers a helpful survey of such negative critics in *The American Quest*, 77.
37. Marjorie Perloff, *The Poetics of Indeterminacy: Rimbaud to Cage* (Princeton: Princeton University Press, 1981), 181.
38. Ibid., 182.
39. Ibid., 188.
40. Joseph Riddel, "'Neo-Nietzschean Clatter' – Speculation and/on Pound's Poetic Image," in *Ezra Pound: Tactics*, ed. Ian F. A. Bell (London: Vision, 1982), 197.
41. Ibid., 203.
42. One sees these multiple passageways in Carroll Terrell's essential *A Companion to* The Cantos *of Ezra Pound* (Berkeley: University of California Press, 1993), which begins each section of annotation with a list of Pound's many source texts.
43. Pound, *ABC of Reading*, 37.
44. William Cookson, *A Guide to the* Cantos *of Ezra Pound* (London: Croom Helm, 1985), 6.
45. Ibid., 5–7.
46. Ezra Pound, *Selected Poems* (New York: New Directions, 1957), 35.
47. Lawrence Rainey, *Ezra Pound and the Monument of Culture: Text, History, and the Malatesta Cantos* (Chicago: University of Chicago Press, 1991), 43.

48. Bernstein, *The Tale of the Tribe*, 40.

49. Guy Davenport, *Cities on Hills: A Study of I–XXX of Ezra Pound's* Cantos (Ann Arbor: UMI Research Press, 1983), 69.

50. T. S. Eliot, *The Waste Land and Other Writings* (New York: Modern Library, 2002), 51.

51. Joseph Frank, *The Idea of Spatial Form* (New Brunswick: Rutgers University Press, 1991), 11.

52. In *The Post Card*, Jacques Derrida is preoccupied with the necessary condition of accident inherent in every act of writing. "Le Facteur de la Vérité" could be read as a poetics of Pound's purloined letters. See *The Post Card: From Socrates to Freud and Beyond*, trans. Alan Bass (Chicago: University of Chicago Press, 1987), 413–96.

53. N. Katherine Hayles, *Writing Machines* (Cambridge: MIT Press, 2002), 25.

54. Jerome McGann, *Towards a Literature of Knowledge* (Oxford: Clarendon, 1989), 106.

55. The iterative evolution of "The Waste Land" and Pound's influence on its final shape can be seen in *The Waste Land: A Facsimile and Transcript of the Original Drafts*, ed. by Valerie Eliot (New York: Harcourt Brace Jovanovich, 1971).

56. Donald Hall, "Ezra Pound: An Interview," in *Ezra Pound's* Cantos*: A Casebook*, ed. Peter Makin (Oxford: Oxford University Press, 2006), 252.

57. The term comes from Lawrence Rainey, who writes that "[perhaps] no poet, and perhaps no poem, has ever been so firmly welded to the realm of secular time, to the present as history *in statu nascendi*" ("Introduction," in *A Poem Containing History: Textual Studies in* The Cantos, ed. Lawrence S. Rainey [Ann Arbor: University of Michigan Press, 1997], 2).

58. Christine Froula, *To Write Paradise: Style and Error in Pound's* Cantos (New Haven: Yale University Press, 1984), 2.

59. Ibid., 7.

60. Ibid., 153, 151.

61. Hall, "Ezra Pound: An Interview," 258.

62. Frederick K. Sanders, *John Adams Speaking: Pound's Sources for the Adams Cantos* (Orono: University of Maine Press, 1975), 6.

63. Ibid., 18.

64. Ibid., 58.

65. My reading of Cadmus as an instance of an emergent poetic vocabulary parallels earlier interpretations of Pound's "ideogrammic method." See, for instance, Girolamo Mancuso, "The Ideogrammic Method in *The Cantos*," trans. Peter Makin, in *Ezra Pound's* Cantos*: A Casebook*, ed. Peter Makin (Oxford: Oxford University Press, 2006), 78–9.

66. Michael Alexander expresses an early critical commonplace that *The Cantos* first become "openly autobiographical" in *The Pisan Cantos*, and that "any strong semblance of overall architectural plan ... now breaks down" (*The Poetic Achievement of Ezra Pound*, Berkeley: University of California Press, 1981, 194). Ronald Bush would later make a more nuanced argument,

seeing some of the tensions in Pound's aesthetic and political commitments in *The Pisan Cantos* as consistent throughout the work ("Modernism, Fascism, and the Composition of Ezra Pound's *Pisan Cantos*," *Modernism/Modernity* 2.3 [1995], 83). More recently, Ayon Maharaj, while offering a reassessment of the lyrical values of *The Pisan Cantos*, still separates them from the rest of the work (Maharaj, "Why Poetry Matters: The Transpersonal Force of Lyric Experience in Ezra Pound's *The Pisan Cantos*," *Arizona Quarterly* 66.4 [2010], 71–92).

67. Cookson, *A Guide to the* Cantos, 53.
68. Olga Nikolova argues that we must expand our account of the visual aesthetics of *The Cantos* by examining early deluxe editions of the poems, which were published with illustrations and special fonts that did not make it into later collections. See Nikolova, "Ezra Pound's Cantos De Luxe," *Modernism/Modernity* 15.1 (2008), 155–77.
69. Jacques Derrida, *Of Grammatology*, trans. Gayatri Chakravorty Spivak (Baltimore: Johns Hopkins University Press, 1974), 92.
70. Cookson, *A Guide to the* Cantos, 120.
71. Ibid., 121.
72. Cookson, glossing Pound's citation of *The Odyssey* on returning to the land of the Phaekians, cites Martin Heidegger: "The vocation of the poet is homecoming" (*A Guide to the* Cantos, 121).
73. Wallace Stevens, "Notes Toward a Supreme Fiction," in *The Palm at the End of the Mind* (New York: Vintage, 1972), 207, 209, 212. Hereafter cited parenthetically in the text as SF.
74. Froula, *To Write Paradise*, 166.
75. McGann, *Towards a Literature of Knowledge*, 97.
76. Ibid., 125.

CHAPTER 4

1. These photos were taken by George Butterick and are housed in the Charles Olson Research Collection at the University of Connecticut. Digital reproductions are available online at http://charlesolson.uconn.edu/Photographs/selectphotos.cfm?SeriesID=6.
2. Charles Olson, *The Maximus Poems*, ed. George F. Butterick (Berkeley: University of California Press, 1983), 378. Hereafter cited parenthetically in the text as MP.
3. Brunner, *Cold War Poetry*, xiv.
4. Robert Lowell, *Life Studies* (New York: Farrar, Straus, and Cudahy, 1959), 5, 59, 63, 76.
5. Ibid., 24.
6. While *Life Studies* presents an imaginative domestic closure, other works by Lowell reflect a more expansive, exploratory practice. See, for instance, *Notebook* (New York: FSG Classics, 1995).
7. Lowell, *Life Studies*, 12–13.

8. The traditionally gendered associations of housekeeping will not be directly addressed in this chapter, although that history informs my reading. For a detailed study of the complex role of masculinity and gender formation in the New American Poetry, see Rachel Blau DuPlessis, *Purple Passages: Pound, Eliot, Zukofsky, Olson, Creeley, and the Ends of Patriarchal Poetry* (Iowa City: University of Iowa Press, 2012).

9. Shahar Bram, *Charles Olson and Alfred North Whitehead: An Essay on Poetry* (Lewisburg, PA: Bucknell University Press, 2004); Miriam Nichols, *Radical Affections: Essays on the Poetics of Outside* (Tuscaloosa: University of Alabama Press, 2010); Don Byrd, *Charles Olson's* Maximus (Urbana: University of Illinois Press, 1980); Robert von Hallberg, *Charles Olson: The Scholar's Art* (Cambridge: Harvard University Press, 1978); Robin Blaser, "The Violets: Charles Olson and Alfred North Whitehead," in *The Fire: Collected Essays of Robert Blaser*, ed. Miriam Nichols (Berkeley, University of California Press, 2006), 196–228.

10. Stephen Fredman, *The Grounding of American Poetry: Charles Olson and the Emersonian Tradition* (Cambridge: Cambridge University Press, 1993). Whitehead's work also emerged from pragmatism; as Don Byrd notes, William James was "the philosopher after Plato to whom Whitehead was most indebted" ("The Emergence of the Cyborg and the End of the Classical Tradition: The Crisis of Alfred North Whitehead's *Process and Reality*," *Configurations* 13 [2005], 105).

11. Charles Olson, *Collected Prose*, ed. Donald Allen and Benjamin Friedlander (Berkeley: University of California Press, 1997), 240. Hereafter cited parenthetically in the text as CP.

12. Joshua Hoeynck, "Introduction," *The Principle of Measure in Composition by Field: Projective Verse II*, by Charles Olson, ed. Joshua Hoeynck (Tucson: Chax Press, 2010), 12.

13. Olson, *Principle of Measure*, 15.

14. Ibid., 35.

15. Alfred North Whitehead, *Modes of Thought* (New York: Macmillan, 1938), 12, 15. Whitehead's language of interest and perspective anticipates Weber and Varela's autopoietic reinterpretation of Kant; see Chapter 2 of this text.

16. Ibid., 119.

17. Ibid., 122–3.

18. Ella Csikós, "Emergence and Reference in Whitehead's *Process and Reality*" *Semiotica* 170 (2008), 58.

19. For an explication of Olson's historical allusions in this passage, I draw on George Butterick, *A Guide to* The Maximus Poems *of Charles Olson* (Berkeley: University of California Press, 1978), 72.

20. Rosemary George, *The Politics of Home: Postcolonial Relocations and Twentieth-Century Fiction* (Cambridge: Cambridge University Press, 1996), 2.

21. Bernstein, *The Tale of the Tribe*, 235.

22. Charles Olson, *The Special View of History*, ed. Ann Charters (Berkeley, CA: Oyez, 1970), 42.

23. My account of Olson's historiographic poetics parallels those of other scholars. See in particular Gary Grieve-Carlson, "Charles Olson and the Poetics of Postmodern History," in *Olson's Prose*, ed. Gary Grieve-Carlson (Newcastle upon Tyne, England: Cambridge Scholars Press, 2007), 89–120; Anne Day Dewey, *Beyond Maximus: The Construction of Public Voice in Black Mountain Poetry* (Stanford: Stanford University Press, 2007); and Susan Vanderborg, "'Who can Say Who are Citizens?': Causal Mythology in Charles Olson's Polis," *Modern Language Quarterly* 59.3 (1998), 363–84.

24. Butterick, *Guide to* The Maximus Poems, 275.

25. "Economy," *The Oxford English Dictionary Online*, 2nd ed., 1989.

26. Barış Gümüşbaş, "Charles Olson's Poetical Economy," *Journal of American Studies of Turkey* 5 (1997), 82.

27. Ibid., 84. Robert Von Hallberg makes a similar point, arguing that "[Olson] preferred a stable economy in which men work for their own satisfaction and see their families' modest keep, not for the future, not for the prospect of their money eventually working for them" (*Charles Olson: The Scholar's Art*, 32).

28. Olson was perversely prescient here, as Gümüşbaş demonstrates in his reading of a Gorton fish-stick package marketed during the 1990s ("Charles Olson's Poetical Economy," 82).

29. See Vanderborg on Olson's use of the public record in this passage ("'Who can Say Who are Citizens?,'" 370).

30. Sherman Paul, *Olson's Push: Origin, Black Mountain, and Recent American Poetry* (Baton Rouge: Louisiana State University Press, 1978), 149.

31. Byrd, *Charles Olson's* Maximus, 104.

32. Ibid., 68.

33. Ibid., 104.

34. Paul, *Olson's Push*, 148.

35. Ibid., 144.

36. Enikó Bollobás, *Charles Olson* (New York: Twayne, 1992), 124.

37. Ibid., 124.

38. Philip L. Barbour, "Introduction," *The Complete Works of Captain John Smith*, ed. Philip L. Barbour, vol. 2 (Chapel Hill: University of North Carolina Press, 1986), 27, 32.

39. John Smith, *The Complete Works of Captain John Smith*, ed. Philip L. Barbour, vol. 2 (Chapel Hill: University of North Carolina Press, 1986), 400. Hereafter cited parenthetically in the text as CW.

40. For a brief history of the Dorchester and Plymouth conflict, see Christine Leigh Heyrman, *Commerce and Culture: The Maritime Communities of Colonial Massachusetts, 1690–1750* (New York: Norton, 1984), 31–3.

41. For clarification of the Melville allusion, see Butterick, *A Guide to* The Maximus Poems, 180.

42. Cornelius Castoriadis, *Figures of the Thinkable*, trans. Helen Arnold (Stanford: Stanford University Press, 2007), 196.

43. Olson, *Special View of History*, 28.

44. Walter Benjamin, "Theses on the Philosophy of History," in *Illuminations*, trans. Harry Zohn (New York: Schocken, 1969), 257–8.
45. Olson, *Special View of History*, 22.

CHAPTER 5

1. Yuri Tynyanov, "On Literary Evolution," trans. C. A. Luplow, in *The Critical Tradition*, ed. David H. Richter (Boston: Bedford/St. Martins, 1998), 727–35; Franco Moretti, "On Literary Evolution," in *Signs Taken for Wonders: Essays in the Sociology of Literary Forms*, revised ed., trans. Susan Fischer, David Forgacs, and David Miller (London: Verso, 1983), 262–78.
2. Luhmann, *Art as a Social System*, 235.
3. On the relationship between Oppen and DuPlessis, see Ann Vickery, "From Being Drafted to a Draft of Being: Rachel Blau DuPlessis and the Reconceptualisation of the Feminist Avant-Garde," in *Avant-Post*, ed. Louis Armand (Prague: Literaria Pragensia, 2006), 138–40. For the influence of Duncan, see Keller, *Forms of Expansion*, 244–52.
4. Rachel Blau DuPlessis, *Blue Studios: Poetry and Its Cultural Work* (Tuscaloosa: University of Alabama Press, 2006), 250.
5. Ibid., 249–50.
6. George Oppen, *New Collected Poems* (New York: New Directions, 2002), 181–2.
7. Rachel Blau DuPlessis, *Pitch: Drafts 77–95* (London: Salt Publishing, 2010), 63.
8. Ibid., 63.
9. Rachel Blau DuPlessis, "*Pater*-daughter: Male Modernists and Female Readers," in *The Pink Guitar: Writing as Feminist Practice* (New York: Routledge, 1990), 44.
10. Rachel Blau DuPlessis, "Midrashic Sensibilities: Secular Judaism and Radical Poetics (A personal essay in several chapters)," in *Radical Poetics and Secular Jewish Culture*, eds. Stephen Paul Miller and Daniel Morris (Tuscaloosa: University of Alabama Press, 2010), 204, 210. Hereafter cited parenthetically as MS.
11. In addition to DuPlessis's own discussions of the influence of midrash on *Drafts*, other critics have noted the connection between the practice and the poetry. See Patrick Pritchett, "Review of *Drafts 1–38, Toll*," *Jacket* 22 (May 2003), no pagination, http://jacketmagazine.com/22/prit-dupless.html, and Walter Kalaidjian, *The Edge of Modernism: American Poetry and the Traumatic Past* (Baltimore: Johns Hopkins University Press, 2006).
12. David Stern, "Midrash and the Language of Exegesis: A Study of Vayikra Rabbah, Chapter 1," in *Midrash and Literature*, ed. Geoffrey H. Hartman and Sanford Budick (New Haven: Yale University Press, 1986), 105.
13. DuPlessis, *Drafts 1–38, Toll* (Middletown, CT: Wesleyan University Press, 2001), 186. Hereafter cited parenthetically as T.

14. David Stern, "Moses-cide: Midrash and Contemporary Literary Criticism," review of *The Slayers of Moses: The Emergence of Rabbinic Interpretation in Modern Literary Theory* by Susan A. Handelman, *Prooftexts* 4 (1984), 203.

15. Jacob Neusner, *What Is Midrash? and A Midrash Reader*, 2nd printing (Atlanta: Scholars Press, 1994), 23. Hereafter cited parenthetically as WM.

16. Neusner gives many examples of this multiplicity (WM 258–9).

17. David Stern, "Midrash and Indeterminacy," *Critical Inquiry* 15.1 (1988), 137.

18. Irving Jacobs, *The Midrashic Process: Tradition and Interpretation in Rabbinic Judaism* (Cambridge: Cambridge University Press, 1995), 4.

19. Ibid., 4.

20. Susan Handelman, *The Slayers of Moses: The Emergence of Rabbinic Interpretation in Modern Literary Theory* (Albany: SUNY Press, 1982), 30.

21. Ibid., 49.

22. Ibid., 65.

23. Ibid., 65.

24. Stern, "Midrash and Indeterminacy," 153.

25. Ibid., 155.

26. Ibid., 156.

27. Emmanuel Levinas, *In the Time of the Nations*, trans. Michael B. Smith (London: Athlone, 1994), 112.

28. Ibid., 112.

29. Ira F. Stone, *Reading Levinas/Reading Talmud* (Philadelphia: Jewish Publication Society, 1998), ix.

30. For further analysis of these elements of Levinas's work, see Edith Wyschogrod, "Language and Alterity in the Thought of Levinas," in *The Cambridge Companion to Levinas*, ed. Simon Critchley and Robert Bernasconi (Cambridge: Cambridge University Press, 2002), 188–205.

31. Rachel Blau DuPlessis, *Drafts: Drafts 39–57, Pledge, with Draft, Unnumbered: Précis* (Cambridge: Salt Publishing, 2004), 219, hereafter cited parenthetically as D.

32. Rachel Blau DuPlessis, *Surge: Drafts 96–114* (Norfolk: Salt Publishing, 2013), 2.

33. Rachel Blau DuPlessis, *Torques: Drafts 58–76* (Cambridge: Salt Publishing, 2007), 21–30.

34. DuPlessis, *Blue Studios*, 210.

35. Ibid., 210.

36. Ibid., 242.

37. Ibid., 238.

38. The theory and practice of Language poetry is beyond the scope of this study; for two useful bibliographies of primary and secondary material on the movement, see Oren Izenberg, *Being Numerous: Poetry and the Ground of Social Life* (Cambridge: Harvard University Press, 2011), 216 n. 2 and Andrew Epstein, "'There Is No Content Here, Only Dailiness': Poetry as Critique of Everyday Life in Ron Silliman's *Ketjak*," *Contemporary Literature* 51.4 (2010), 742 n. 6.

39. For the publication history of *Ketjak*, see Epstein, "There Is No Content Here," 740, n. 3.
40. Ibid., 749. Epstein also points out that the poem doesn't follow the rules perfectly, but that Silliman opted to include these errors and departures in the final published poem.
41. Ron Silliman, *Age of Huts (compleat)* (Berkeley: University of California Press, 2007), 3.
42. Silliman, "The New Sentence," 90.
43. Ibid., 92.
44. Epstein, "There Is No Content Here," 753.
45. Izenberg, *Being Numerous*, 162.
46. Ibid., 161.
47. Other poems by Silliman are much more directly structurally coupled to the environment, such as "BART," a poem consisting of one long sentence that uses a ride on the Bay Area's public transit system as a challenge for writing in real time. But here, too, the poem resists emergent, second-order effects, remaining closely tied to the immediacy of the moment and the grammatical spaces created by the comma (not the period). See *Age of Huts (compleat)*, 300–11.
48. Kalaidjian's reading of DuPlessis in terms of the "urgent, post-Auschwitz question of the ethics of poetic form" is an important parallel to the analysis offered in this concluding section (*The Edge of Modernism*, 89).
49. Adorno, "Cultural Criticism and Society," 34.
50. DuPlessis, *Pitch*, 131.
51. Ibid., 131.
52. Stern, "Midrash and Indeterminacy," 134.

CHAPTER 6

1. Nathaniel Mackey, *Discrepant Engagement: Dissonance, Cross-Culturality, and Experimental Writing* (Cambridge: University of Cambridge Press, 1993), 231–2. Hereafter cited parenthetically as DE.
2. The term "diaspora" must be deployed with caution. Here, I use it as a general placeholder for the hybrid, multiple histories of Black music that Mackey employs. For the complexities of the term, see in particular Paul Gilroy, *The Black Atlantic: Modernity and Double Consciousness* (Cambridge: Harvard University Press, 1993), 205–12 and Brent Hayes Edwards, "The Uses of Diaspora," *Social Text* 66 (2001), 45–73.
3. Nathaniel Mackey, *From a Broken Bottle Traces of Perfume Still Emanate*, Vols. 1–3 (New York: New Directions, 2010), 423. Hereafter cited parenthetically as FBB.
4. The phrase comes from the title of Paul Naylor's *Poetic Investigations: Singing the Holes in History* (Evanston, IL: Northwestern University Press, 1999).

5. Anthony Reed, *Freedom Time: The Poetics and Politics of Black Experimental Writing* (Baltimore: Johns Hopkins University Press, 2014), 18. Reed's analysis of Mackey shares many of my interests: futurity, poetic form, social critique, and the need for alternative models of time.

6. On the role of music in Mackey's work, see in particular Reed, *Freedom Time*, 171–206; Brent Hayes Edwards, "Notes on Poetics Regarding Mackey's Song," *Callaloo* 23.2 (2000), 572–91; Aldon Lynn Nielson, "N + 1: Before-the-Fact Reading in Nathaniel Mackey's Postcontemporary Music," *Callaloo* 23.2 (2000), 796–806; and Robert Zamsky, "A Poetics of Radical Musicality: Nathaniel Mackey's '-mu' Series," *Arizona Quarterly* 62.1 (2006): 113–40.

7. Gilroy, *The Black Atlantic*, 4.

8. Spencer Brown, *Laws of Form*, 3.

9. Ibid., v.

10. Nathaniel Mackey, "Wringing the Word," *World Literature Today* 68.4 (1994), 734. I was directed to this quotation by Edwards, "Notes on Poetics," 572.

11. The critical analysis of Mackey's use of music often emphasizes the way music structures the work while also initiating change. For Zamsky, Mackey's work "constantly unfolds within our ears, shimmering with acoustic resonances even as it equally expands with allusive complexity" ("A Poetics of Radical Musicality," 117), while for J. Edward Mallot, music establishes a "tiered process of becoming – even in repeated performances of the same piece – rather than a fixed, static identity" ("Sacrificial Limbs, Lambs, Iambs, and I Ams: Nathaniel Mackey's Mythology of Loss," *Contemporary Literature* 45.1 [2004], 149).

12. Edwards, "Notes on Poetics," 572.

13. Megan Simpson, "Trickster Poetics: Multiculturalism and Collectivity in Nathaniel Mackey's *Song of the Andoumboulou*," *MELUS* 28.4 (2003), 39.

14. Nathaniel Mackey, *School of Udhra* (San Francisco: City Lights, 1993), 68. Hereafter cited parenthetically as SU.

15. Nathaniel Mackey, *Eroding Witness* (Urbana: University of Illinois Press, 1985), 33. Hereafter cited parenthetically as EW.

16. Benjamin, "Theses," 255.

17. Nathaniel Mackey, *Splay Anthem* (New York: New Directions, 2006), ix. Hereafter cited parenthetically as SA.

18. Simpson, "Trickster Poetics," 95.

19. The thinly veiled link between N. and Nathaniel Mackey is fairly obvious; Aldon Lynn Nielsen further notes the pun on "Nate" in the novel title's *Emanate* (Nielson, "N + 1," 797).

20. Nathaniel Mackey, *Paracritical Hinge: Essays, Talks, Notes, Interviews* (Madison: University of Wisconsin Press, 2005), 295.

21. Edwards, "Notes on Poetics," 585.

22. Norman Finkelstein, "Nathaniel Mackey and the Unity of All Rites," *Contemporary Literature* 49.1 (2008), 25.

23. Zamsky, "A Poetics of Radical Musicality," 119, 122.

24. Nathaniel Mackey, *Nod House* (New York: New Directions, 2011), 83.

25. Ibid., 80.

26. The most extensive collection of Mackey's performances available online can be found at *PennSound*, Center for Programs in Contemporary Writing, University of Pennsylvania, (2016) http://writing.upenn.edu/pennsound.
27. Simon Jarvis, "The Melodics of Long Poems," 619.
28. Jameson is careful to note that postmodernism is not the only art of his time but is instead a "cultural dominant" (*Postmodernism, or, The Cultural Logic of Late Capitalism* [Durham: Duke University Press, 1991], 6. Hereafter cited parenthetically as PCL).
29. Francis Fukuyama, *The End of History and the Last Man* (New York: Free Press, 1992).
30. Varela et al., *Embodied Mind*, 156. For a more extensive discussion of Varela on this point, see Chapter 1.
31. Nathaniel Mackey, *Whatsaid Serif* (San Francisco: City Lights, 1998), p. 85. Hereafter cited parenthetically as WSS.
32. Walter Benjamin, *The Arcades Project*, ed. Rolf Tiedemann, trans. Howard Eiland and Kevin McLaughlin (Cambridge, MA: Belknap, 2002), 471.
33. Hannah Arendt, "Introduction: Walter Benjamin: 1892–1940," in Benjamin, *Illuminations* (New York: Schocken, 1969), 48.
34. Benjamin, "Theses," 263.
35. Ibid., 264. Philosophies of history are themselves historically and culturally conditioned, of course, with complex variations even within a single culture. To take Western thought as a broad example, Karl Löwith contrasts the Judeo-Christian messianic view of history with the Greek model of nonprogressive history, arguing that modernity is "a more or less inconsistent compound of both traditions" (*Meaning in History* [Chicago: University of Chicago Press, 1949], 19). Indeed, Benjamin's own challenging synthesis of Marxist and mystical language might be read as one such "inconsistent compound." I am grateful to an anonymous reader of this text for calling Löwith's work to my attention.
36. Benjamin, "Theses," 255.
37. Joseph Allen, "Nathaniel Mackey's Unit Structures," in *Black Orpheus: Music in African American Fiction from the Harlem Renaissance to Toni Morrison*, ed. Saadi A. Simawe (New York: Garland, 2009), 209.
38. Mackey, *Bass Cathedral* (New York: New Directions, 2008), 89–90.
39. Ibid., 90.
40. For "periplum," see Pound, *ABC of Reading*, 43–4; for "mappemunde," see Olson, *Maximus Poems*, 257.
41. Quoted in Naylor, *Poetic Investigations*, 143.
42. Erin Fehskens, "Accounts Unpaid, Accounts Untold: M. NourbeSe Philip's *Zong!* and the Catalogue," *Callaloo* 35.2 (2012), 409.
43. For a thorough historical and theoretical analysis of the *Zong* case, see Ian Baucom, *Specters of the Atlantic: Finance Capital, Slavery, and the Philosophy of History* (Durham: Duke University Press, 2005).
44. M. NourbeSe Philip, *Zong!* (Middletown, CT: Wesleyan University Press, 2008), 3.
45. Ibid., 63.

46. For an analysis of Walcott's relationship to Homer, see Rei Terada, *Derek Walcott's Poetry: American Mimicry* (Boston: Northeastern University Press, 1992), 183–212.
47. Derek Walcott, *Omeros* (New York: Farrar, Straus & Giroux, 1990), 14. As an alternative to the ghost in Walcott, see Jahan Ramzani's reading of the wound in *Omeros* as "a resonant site of interethnic connection" (*The Hybrid Muse: Postcolonial Poetry in English* [Chicago: University of Chicago Press, 2001], 50).
48. Srila Nayak, "'Nothing in that Other Kingdom': Fashioning a Return to Africa in *Omeros*," *Ariel* 44.2–3 (2014), 7.
49. Isabella Zoppi, "*Omeros*, Derek Walcott, and the Contemporary Epic Poem," *Callaloo* 22.2 (1999), 513–15.
50. Oppen, *New Collected Poems*, 166–7.
51. Finkelstein, "Unity of All Rites," 27.
52. Jeffery Gray, *Mastery's End: Travel and Postwar American Poetry* (Athens: University of Georgia Press, 2005), 50.
53. Ibid., 50.

CHAPTER 7

1. Alan Liu, "Friending the Past: The Sense of History and Social Computing," *New Literary History* 42 (2011), 19.
2. Marjorie Perloff, *Unoriginal Genius: Poetry by Other Means in the New Century* (Chicago: University of Chicago Press, 2010), xi.
3. "2011 Year in Review: Tweets Per Second," *Twitter.com* (2011), no pagination, https://yearinreview.twitter.com/en/tps.html. To put these figures in perspective: Twitter users produced roughly 700 manuscript pages per second after Beyoncé's announcement, or 42,000 pages a minute.
4. The existence of PRISM was first reported by Glen Greenwald and Ewan MacAskil; see "NSA Prism Program Taps in to User Data of Apple, Google and Others," *The Guardian* (6 June 2013), no pagination, www.theguardian.com/world/2013/jun/06/us-tech-giants-nsa-data. On Target's pregnancy predictors, see Kashmir Hill, "How Target Figured Out a Teen Girl Was Pregnant before Her Father Did," *Forbes* (16 February 2012), no pagination, www.forbes.com/sites/kashmirhill/2012/02/16/how-target-figured-out-a-teen-girl-was-pregnant-before-her-father-did/#6beab88f34c6.
5. Jerome McGann, *Radiant Textuality: Literature after the World Wide Web* (New York: Palgrave, 2001), xi.
6. Adalaide Morris, "New Media Poetics: As We May Think/How to Write," in *New Media Poetics: Contexts, Technotexts, and Theories*, eds. Adalaide Morris and Thomas Swiss (Cambridge: MIT Press), 2.
7. Ibid., 2.
8. Liu, "Friending the Past," 1.
9. Ibid., 20.

10. Plato, "Phaedrus," trans. Alexander Nehamas and Paul Woodruff, in *Complete Works of Plato*, ed. John M. Cooper (Indianapolis: Hackett, 1997), 275a.
11. Liu, "Friending the Past," 22.
12. Ibid., 24–25. Liu's *The Laws of Cool: Knowledge Work and the Culture of Information* (Chicago: University of Chicago Press, 2004) offers a more extensive analysis of the role the arts and humanities might play in the information age.
13. Brian Reed, *Nobody's Business: Twenty-First Century Avant-Garde Poetics* (Ithaca: Cornell University Press, 2013), 156.
14. A useful introduction to conceptual poetry is the anthology edited by Craig Dworkin and Goldsmith, *Against Expression* (Evanston, IL: Northwestern University Press, 2011).
15. Kenneth Goldsmith, *Uncreative Writing: Managing Language in the Digital Age* (New York: Columbia University Press, 2011), 24–5.
16. Ibid., 3, 100.
17. Ibid., 28.
18. Reed, *Nobody's Business*, 126.
19. This parallel between conceptualism's self-presentation and the language of neoliberalism was suggested by Joshua Clover's paper "Poetry, Marx, and the Long Crisis," presented at the 2014 Modern Language Association convention in Chicago, IL, January 10, 2014.
20. Perloff, *Unoriginal Genius*, 161.
21. Ibid., 164.
22. Ibid., 169.
23. Reed, *Nobody's Business*, 86.
24. Ibid., 86–7.
25. Goldsmith, *Uncreative Writing*, 9.
26. Ibid., 85.
27. Ibid., 28.
28. Goldsmith's taste became the subject of vociferous criticism after his piece "The Body of Michael Brown." This work, which Goldsmith read live at Brown University, was an edited and rearranged version of the autopsy report prepared for Michael Brown, the 18-year-old black man killed in Ferguson, Missouri, by Darren Wilson, a white police officer. C. A. Conrad's "Kenneth Goldsmith Says He's an Outlaw" archives many of the pointed criticisms that Goldsmith received from the poetry community (on *Harriet: A Poetry Blog* [Poetry Foundation: 1 June 2015], no pagination, www.poetryfoundation.org/harriet/2015/06/kenneth-goldsmith-says-he-is-an-outlaw).
29. For another reading of Spahr's work in relationship to network theory, see Sianne Ngai, "Network Aesthetics: Juliana Spahr's *The Transformation* and Bruno Latour's *Reassembling the Social*" in *American Literature's Aesthetic Dimensions*, ed. Cindy Weinstein and Christopher Looby (New York: Columbia University Press, 2012), 367–92.
30. Juliana Spahr, *This Connection of Everyone with Lungs* (Berkeley: University of California Press, 2005), 3–4. Hereafter cited parenthetically in the text as CEL.

31. For more on breath in Spahr, see Lisa Sirganian's *Modernism's Other Work: The Art Object's Political Life* (Oxford: Oxford University Press, 2012), 168–84.

32. Charles Altieri, "The Place of Rhetoric in Contemporary American Poetics: Jennifer Moxley and Juliana Spahr," *Chicago Review* 56.2–3 (2011), 137.

33. For more on the lyric elements in Spahr's work, see Heather Milne, "Dearly Beloveds: The Politics of Intimacy in Juliana Spahr's *This Connection of Everyone with Lungs*" *Mosaic* 47.2 (2014), 203–18.

34. For one summary and critical reinterpretation of the recent lyric debates in American poetics, see Jennifer Ashton, "Labor and the Lyric: The Politics of Self-Expression in Contemporary American Poetry," *American Literary History* 25.1 (2013), 217–30.

35. McHale, "Poetry as Prosthesis," 24.

36. Ibid., 28.

37. Donna Haraway, *Simians, Cyborgs, and Women: The Reinvention of Nature* (New York: Routledge, 1991), 149.

38. Ibid., 150.

39. Ibid., 154.

Bibliography

"2011 Year in Review: Tweets Per Second," *Twitter.com* (2011), no pagination, https://yearinreview.twitter.com/en/tps.html.

Abrams, M. H., *Natural Supernaturalism: Tradition and Revolution in Romantic Literature* (New York: Norton, 1971).

Adams, Henry, *The Education of Henry Adams* (New York: Library of America, 2009).

Adorno, Theodor, "Cultural Criticism and Society," in *Prisms* (1967), trans. Samuel and Shierry Weber (Cambridge: MIT Press, 1997), 17–34.

Alexander, Michael, *The Poetic Achievement of Ezra Pound* (Berkeley: University of California Press, 1981).

Allen, Joseph, "Nathaniel Mackey's Unit Structures," in *Black Orpheus: Music in African American Fiction from the Harlem Renaissance to Toni Morrison*, ed. Saadi A. Simawe (New York: Garland, 2009), 205–29.

Althusser, Louis, "Ideology and Ideological State Apparatuses," trans. Ben Brewster, in *Critical Theory Since Plato*, ed. Hazard Adams and Leroy Searle, 3rd ed (Boston: Thomson Wadsworth, 2005), 1297–308.

Altieri, Charles, "The Place of Rhetoric in Contemporary American Poetics: Jennifer Moxley and Juliana Spahr," *Chicago Review* 56.2–3 (2011), 127–45.

"Spectacular Antispectacle: Ecstasy and Nationality in Whitman and His Heirs," *American Literary History* 11.1 (1999), 34–62.

Ammons, A. R., *Tape for the Turn of the Year* (New York: Norton, 1993).

Arendt, Hannah, "Introduction: Walter Benjamin: 1892–1940," in Walter Benjamin, *Illuminations* (New York: Schocken, 1969), 1–55.

Aristotle, "Poetics," trans. by Ingram Bywater, in *The Basic Works of Aristotle*, ed. Richard McKeon (New York: Modern Library, 2001), 1453–87.

Ashton, Jennifer, "Labor and the Lyric: The Politics of Self-Expression in Contemporary American Poetry," *American Literary History* 25.1 (2013), 217–30.

Attridge, Derek, *The Singularity of Literature* (London: Routledge, 2004).

Badiou, Alain, "The Event as Trans-Being," in *Theoretical Writings*, eds. and trans. Ray Brassier and Alberto Toscano (London: Continuum, 2004), 97–102.

Baker, Peter, *Obdurate Brilliance: Exteriority and the Modern Long Poem* (Gainsville: University of Florida Press, 1991).

Barbour, Philip L., "Introduction," in *The Complete Works of Captain John Smith*, ed. Philip L. Barbour, vol. 2 (Chapel Hill: University of North Carolina Press, 1986), 27–32.

Baucom, Ian, *Specters of the Atlantic: Finance Capital, Slavery, and the Philosophy of History* (Durham: Duke University Press, 2005).

Benjamin, Walter, *The Arcades Project*, ed. Rolf Tiedemann, trans. Howard Eiland and Kevin McLaughlin (Cambridge, MA: Belknap, 2002).

"Theses on the Philosophy of History," trans. Harry Zohn, in *Illuminations* (New York: Schocken, 1969), 253–64.

The Work of Art in the Age of Its Technological Reproducibility, and Other Writings on Media, ed. Michael W. Jennings, Brigid Doherty, and Thomas Y. Levin (Cambridge: Belknap Press, 2008).

Bernstein, Michael André, *The Tale of the Tribe: Ezra Pound and the Modern Verse Epic* (Princeton: Princeton University Press, 1980).

Best, Stephen, "Well, That Was Obvious," response to *Denotatively, Technically, Literally*, special issue of *Representations* 125 (2014), no pagination, www.representations.org/responses.

Best, Stephen and Sharon Marcus, "Surface Reading: An Introduction," *Representations* 108 (2009), 1–21.

Blaser, Robin, "The Violets: Charles Olson and Alfred North Whitehead," in *The Fire: Collected Essays of Robert Blaser*, ed. Miriam Nichols (Berkeley: University of California Press, 2006), 196–228.

Bollobás, Enikó, *Charles Olson* (New York: Twayne, 1992).

Bram, Shahar, *Charles Olson and Alfred North Whitehead: An Essay on Poetry* (Lewisburg, PA: Bucknell UP, 2004).

Breitwieser, Mitchell, "Who Speaks in Whitman's Poems?," in *The American Renaissance: New Dimensions* eds. Harry R. Garvin and Peter C. Carafiol, *Bucknell Review* 28.1 (London and Toronto: Associated University Press, 1983), 121–43.

Brooks, Cleanth, *The Well Wrought Urn* (New York: Harcourt, Brace, 1947).

Brunner, Edward, *Cold War Poetry: The Social Text in the Fifties Poem* (Urbana-Champaign: University of Illinois Press, 2004).

Burnham, Jack, "System Esthetics," *ArtForum* (September 1968), 30–5.

Bush, Ronald, *The Genesis of Ezra Pound's Cantos* (Princeton: Princeton University Press, 1976).

"Modernism, Fascism, and the Composition of Ezra Pound's Pisan Cantos" *Modernism/Modernity* 2.3 (1995), 69–87.

Butterick, George, "Charles Olson Photographs," Charles Olson Research Collection, University of Connecticut Libraries, http://charlesolson.uconn.edu/Photographs/selectphotos.cfm?SeriesID=6.

A Guide to The Maximus Poems *of Charles Olson* (Berkeley: University of California Press, 1978).

Byrd, Don, *Charles Olson's Maximus* (Urbana: University of Illinois Press, 1980).

"The Emergence of the Cyborg and the End of the Classical Tradition: The Crisis of Alfred North Whitehead's Process and Reality" *Configurations* 13 (2005), 95–116.

Casillo, Robert, *The Genealogy of Demons: Anti-Semitism, Fascism, and the Myths of Ezra Pound* (Evanston, IL: Northwestern University Press, 1988).

Castoriadis, Cornelius, *Figures of the Thinkable*, trans. Helen Arnold (Stanford: Stanford University Press, 2007).

Chomsky, Noam, *Aspects of the Theory of Syntax* (Cambridge: MIT Press, 1969).

Clarke, Bruce and Mark B. N. Hansen, "Introduction: Neocybernetic Emergence," in *Emergence and Embodiment: New Essays on Second-Order Systems Theory*, eds. Bruce Clarke and Mark B. N. Hansen (Durham: Duke University Press, 2009), 1–25.

Clover, Joshua, "Poetry, Marx, and the Long Crisis," presented at the Modern Language Association Convention, Chicago, IL, January 10, 2014.

Coleridge, Samuel Taylor, *Coleridge's Criticism of Shakespeare: A Selection*, ed. R. A. Foakes (London: Athlone Press, 1989).

Conrad, C. A., "Kenneth Goldsmith Says He's an Outlaw," *Harriet: A Poetry Blog* (Poetry Foundation: 1 June 2015), no pagination, www.poetryfoundation.org/harriet/2015/06/kenneth-goldsmith-says-he-is-an-outlaw.

Conte, Joseph M., *Unending Design: The Forms of Postmodern Poetry* (Ithaca: Cornell University Press, 1991).

Cookson, William, *A Guide to the Cantos of Ezra Pound* (London: Croom Helm, 1985).

Csikós, Ella, "Emergence and Reference in Whitehead's *Process and Reality*" *Semiotica* 170 (2008), 49–61.

Davenport, Guy, *Cities on Hills: a Study of I–XXX of Ezra Pound's Cantos* (Ann Arbor: UMI Research Press, 1983).

De Man, Paul, *The Rhetoric of Romanticism* (New York: Columbia University Press, 1984).

Derrida, Jacques, "The Laws of Genre," trans. Avital Ronell, *Critical Inquiry* 7.1 (1980), 55–81.

Of Grammatology, trans. Gayatri Chakravorty Spivak (Baltimore: Johns Hopkins University Press, 1974).

The Post Card: From Socrates to Freud and Beyond, trans. Alan Bass (Chicago: University of Chicago Press, 1987).

Dewey, Anne Day, *Beyond Maximus: The Construction of Public Voice in Black Mountain Poetry* (Stanford: Stanford University Press, 2007).

Dickie, Margaret, *On the Modernist Long Poem* (Iowa City: University of Iowa Press, 1986).

Duncan, Robert, *Fictive Certainties* (New York: New Directions, 1955).

DuPlessis, Rachel Blau, *Blue Studios: Poetry and Its Cultural Work* (Tuscaloosa: University of Alabama Press, 2006).

"Considering the long poem: genre problems," *Readings Webjournal* 4 (2009), no pagination, www.bbk.ac.uk/readings/issues/issue4/duplessis_on_Consideringthelongpoemgenreproblems.

Drafts 1–38, Toll (Middletown, CT: Wesleyan University Press, 2001).

Drafts: Drafts 39–57, Pledge, with Draft, Unnumbered: Précis (Cambridge: Salt Publishing, 2004).

"Manifests," *Diacritics* 26.3–4 (1996), 31–53.

"Midrashic Sensibilities: Secular Judaism and Radical Poetics (A personal essay in several chapters)," in *Radical Poetics and Secular Jewish Culture*, eds. Stephen Paul Miller and Daniel Morris (Tuscaloosa: University of Alabama Press, 2010), 199–224.

"Notes on Silliman and Poesis," *Journal of Poetics Research* 2 (February 2015), no pagination, http://poeticsresearch.com/article/rachel-blau-duplessis-notes-on-silliman-and-poesis-2.

"*Pater*-daughter: Male Modernists and Female Readers," in *The Pink Guitar: Writing as Feminist Practice* (New York: Routledge, 1990), 41–67.

Pitch: Drafts 77–95 (London: Salt Publishing, 2010).

Purple Passages: Pound, Eliot, Zukofsky, Olson, Creeley, and the Ends of Patriarchal Poetry (Iowa City: University of Iowa Press, 2012).

Surge: Drafts 96–114 (Norfolk: Salt Publishing, 2013).

Torques: Drafts 58–76 (Cambridge: Salt Publishing, 2007).

Dworkin, Craig and Kenneth Goldsmith, *Against Expression* (Evanston, IL: Northwestern UP, 2011).

"Economy," Oxford English Dictionary Online (Oxford University Press, March 2015).

Edwards, Brett Hayes, "Notes on Poetics Regarding Mackey's *Song*," *Callaloo* 23.2 (2000), 572–91.

"The Uses of Diaspora," *Social Text* 66 (2001), 45–73.

Eliot, T. S., "Tradition and the Individual Talent," *The Sacred Wood* (London: Methuen, 1920), 47–59.

The Waste Land: A Facsimile and Transcript of the Original Drafts, ed. Valerie Eliot (New York: Harcourt Brace Jovanovich, 1971).

The Waste Land and Other Writings (New York: Modern Library, 2002).

Emerson, Ralph Waldo, "The Poet," in *Essays and Lectures* (New York, Library of America, 1983), 447–68.

Epstein, Andrew, "'There Is No Content Here, Only Dailiness': Poetry as Critique of Everyday Life in Ron Silliman's *Ketjak*," *Contemporary Literature* 51.4 (2010), 736–76.

Fehskens, Erin, "Accounts Unpaid, Accounts Untold: M. NourbeSe Philip's *Zong!* and the Catalogue," *Callaloo* 35.2 (2012), 407–24.

Felski, Rita, "Latour and Literary Studies," *PMLA* 130.3 (2015), 737–42.

Uses of Literature (London: Blackwell, 2008).

Finkelstein, Norman, "Nathaniel Mackey and the Unity of all Rites," *Contemporary Literature* 49.1 (2008), 24–55.

Folsom, Ed, *Whitman Making Books, Books Making Whitman: A Catalog and Commentary* (Iowa City: Obermann Center for Advanced Studies, University of Iowa: 2005).

Frank, Joseph, *The Idea of Spatial Form* (New Brunswick: Rutgers University Press, 1991).

Fredman, Stephen, *The Grounding of American Poetry: Charles Olson and the Emersonian Tradition* (Cambridge: Cambridge University Press, 1993).

Froula, Christine, *To Write Paradise: Style and Error in Pound's Cantos* (New Haven: Yale University Press, 1984).

Fukuyama, Francis, *The End of History and the Last Man* (New York: Free Press, 1992).

Gabriel, Daniel, *Hart Crane and the Modernist Epic: Canon and Genre Formation in Crane, Pound, Eliot, and Williams* (New York: Palgrave Macmillan, 2007).

Gardner, Thomas, *Discovering Ourselves in Whitman: The Contemporary American Long Poem* (Urbana: University of Illinois Press, 1989).

Genoways, Ted, *Walt Whitman and the Civil War: America's Poet During the Lost Years of 1860–1862* (Berkeley: University of California Press, 2009).

Geoghegan, Bernard Dionysius, "From Information Theory to French Theory: Jakobson, Lévi-Strauss, and the Cybernetic Apparatus," *Critical Inquiry* 38.1 (2011), 96–126.

George, Rosemary, *The Politics of Home: Postcolonial Relocations and Twentieth-Century Fiction* (Cambridge: Cambridge University Press, 1996).

Gilroy, Paul, *The Black Atlantic: Modernity and Double Consciousness* (Cambridge: Harvard University Press, 1993).

Ginsberg, Allen, *Howl and Other Poems* (San Francisco: City Lights, 1956).

Gioia, Ted, *The Imperfect Art: Reflections on Jazz and Modern Culture* (Oxford: Oxford University Press, 1988).

Goble, Mark, *Beautiful Circuits: Modernism and the Mediated Life* (New York: Columbia University Press, 2010).

Goldsmith, Kenneth, *Uncreative Writing: Managing Language in the Digital Age* (New York: Columbia University Press, 2011).

Gray, Jeffery, *Mastery's End: Travel and Postwar American Poetry* (Athens: University of Georgia Press, 2005).

Greenberg, Clement, "Avant-Garde and Kitsch" (1939), *Art and Culture: Critical Essays* (Boston: Beacon, 1965), 3–21.

Greenwald, Glen and Ewan MacAskil, "NSA Prism program taps in to user data of Apple, Google and others," *The Guardian* (6 June 2013), no pagination, www.theguardian.com/world/2013/jun/06/us-tech-giants-nsa-data.

Grieve-Carlson, Gary, "Charles Olson and the Poetics of Postmodern History," in *Olson's Prose*, ed. Gary Grieve-Carlson (Newcastle upon Tyne, England: Cambridge Scholars Press, 2007), 89–120.

Grossman, Allen, "The Poetics of Union in Whitman and Lincoln: An Inquiry toward the Relationship of Art and Policy," in *The American Renaissance Reconsidered*, ed. Walter Benn Michaels and Donald E. Pease, *The English Institute* n.s. 9 (Baltimore: Johns Hopkins University Press, 1985), 183–208.

Gümüşbaş, Bariş, "Charles Olson's Poetical Economy," *Journal of American Studies of Turkey* 5 (1997), 81–9.

Hall, Donald, "Ezra Pound: An Interview," in *Ezra Pound's Cantos: A Casebook*, ed. Peter Makin (Oxford: Oxford University Press, 2006), 251–60.

Handelman, Susan, *The Slayers of Moses: The Emergence of Rabbinic Interpretation in Modern Literary Theory* (Albany: SUNY Press, 1982).

Hansen, Mark B. N., "System-Environment Hybrids," *Emergence and Embodiment: New Essays on Second-Order Systems Theory*, eds. Bruce Clarke and Mark B. N. Hansen (Durham: Duke University Press, 2009), 113–42.

Haraway, Donna, *Simians, Cyborgs, and Women: The Reinvention of Nature* (New York: Routledge, 1991).

Harris, W. C., "Whitman's *Leaves of Grass* and the Problem of the One and the Many," *Arizona Quarterly* 56.3 (2000), 29–61.

Hayles, N. Katherine, *How We Became Posthuman: Virtual Bodies in Cybernetics, Literature, and Informatics* (Chicago: University of Chicago Press, 1999).

    My Mother Was a Computer: Digital Subjects and Literary Texts (Chicago: University of Chicago Press, 2005).

    Writing Machines (Cambridge: MIT Press, 2002).

Heims, Steve Joshua, *The Cybernetics Group* (Cambridge, MIT Press: 1991).

Hejinian, Lyn, *My Life and My Life in the Nineties* (Middletown, CT: Wesleyan UP, 2013).

    Introductory note to "The Rejection of Closure" (1985) (Poetry Foundation: 2015), no pagination, www.poetryfoundation.org/learning/essay/237870?page=1.

    Writing Is an Aid to Memory (Los Angeles: Sun & Moon, 1996).

Herrnstein Smith, Barbara, *Poetic Closure: A Study of How Poems End* (Chicago: University of Chicago Press, 1968).

Heyrman, Christine Leigh, *Commerce and Culture: The Maritime Communities of Colonial Massachusetts, 1690–1750* (New York: Norton, 1984).

Hill, Kashmir, "How Target Figured Out a Teen Girl Was Pregnant before Her Father Did," *Forbes* (16 February 2012), no pagination, www.forbes.com/sites/kashmirhill/2012/02/16/how-target-figured-out-a-teen-girl-was-pregnant-before-her-father-did/#6beab88f34c6.

Hoeynck, Joshua, "Introduction," *The Principle of Measure in Composition by Field: Projective Verse II*, by Charles Olson, ed. Joshua Hoeynck (Tucson: Chax Press, 2010), 9–13.

Holland, John, *Emergence: From Chaos to Order* (Reading, MA: Perseus, 1998).

Holley, Margaret, "The Model Stanza: The Organic Origin of Moore's Syllabic Verse," *Twentieth Century Literature* 30.2–3 (1984), 181–91.

Izenberg, Oren, *Being Numerous: Poetry and the Ground of Social Life* (Cambridge: Harvard University Press, 2011).

Jackson, Virginia, *Dickinson's Misery: A Theory of Lyric Reading* (Princeton: Princeton University Press, 2005).

Jacobs, Irving, *The Midrashic Process: Tradition and Interpretation in Rabbinic Judaism* (Cambridge: Cambridge University Press, 1995).

Jakobson, Roman and Claude Lévi-Strauss, "Baudelaire's 'Les Chats,'" *Language in Literature*, ed. Krystyna Pomorska and Stephen Rudy (Cambridge: Belknap, 1987), 180–97.

Jameson, Frederic, *A Singular Modernity* (London: Verso, 2002).

    Postmodernism, or, The Cultural Logic of Late Capitalism (Durham: Duke University Press, 1991).

Jarvis, Robin, *Wordsworth, Milton, and the Theory of Poetic Relations* (London: Macmillan, 1991).

Jarvis, Simon, "The Melodics of Long Poems," *Textual Practice* 24.4 (2010), 607–21.

Johnson, Steven, *Emergence: The Connected Lives of Ants, Brains, Cities, and Software* (New York: Scribner, 2001).

Johnston, Kenneth R., *Wordsworth and The Recluse* (New Haven: Yale University Press, 1984).

Kaag, John, *Thinking through the Imagination: Aesthetics in Human Cognition* (New York: Fordham University Press, 2014).

Kalaidjian, Walter, *The Edge of Modernism: American Poetry and the Traumatic Past* (Baltimore: Johns Hopkins UP, 2006).

Kant, Immanuel, *Critique of Judgment*, trans. J. H. Bernard (New York: Prometheus, 2000).

Karlson, Fred, "Syntactic Recursion and Iteration," in *Recursion and Human Language*, ed. Harry van der Hulst (Berlin: De Gruyter Mouton, 2010), 43–68.

Kateb, George, "Walt Whitman and the Culture of Democracy," *Political Theory* 18.4 (1990), 545–71.

Katsaros, Laure, *New York-Paris: Whitman, Baudelaire, and the Hybrid City* (Ann Arbor: University of Michigan Press, 2012).

Keller, Lynn, *Forms of Expansion: Recent Long Poems by Women* (Chicago: University of Chicago Press, 1997).

Kenner, Hugh, "Leucothea's Bikini: Mimetic Homage," in *Ezra Pound: Perspectives*, ed. Noel Stock (Chicago: Henry Regnery, 1965), 25–40.

The Pound Era (Berkeley: University of California Press, 1971).

Kepner, Diane, "From Spears to Leaves: Walt Whitman's Theory of Nature in 'Song of Myself,'" *American Literature* 51.2 (1979), 179–204.

Killingsworth, M. Jimmie, *Walt Whitman and the Earth: A Study in Ecopoetics* (Iowa City: University of Iowa Press, 2004).

Landgraf, Edgar, *Improvisation as Art: Conceptual Challenges, Historical Perspectives*, (New York: Continuum, 2011).

Lawson, Andrew, *Walt Whitman and the Class Struggle* (Iowa City: University of Iowa Press, 2006).

Levinas, Emmanuel, *In the Time of the Nations*, trans. Michael B. Smith (London: Athlone, 1994).

Levine, Caroline, *Forms: Whole, Rhythm, Hierarchy, Network* (Princeton: Princeton University Press, 2015).

Levinson, Marjorie, "Lyric: The Idea of This Invention," unpublished manuscript, University of Michigan (2015).

"What Is New Formalism?" *PMLA* 122.2 (2007), 558–69.

Lewis, Wyndham, ed., *Blast* 1 (1914) (Santa Rosa: Black Sparrow Press, 2002).

Liu, Alan, "Friending the Past: The Sense of History and Social Computing," *New Literary History* 42 (2011), 1–30.

The Laws of Cool: Knowledge Work and the Culture of Information (Chicago: University of Chicago Press, 2004).

Liu, Lydia H., *The Freudian Robot: Digital Media and the Future of the Unconscious* (Chicago: University of Chicago Press, 2010).

Love, Heather A., "Cybernetic Modernism and the Feedback Loop: Ezra Pound's Poetics of Transmission" *Modernism/Modernity* 23.1 (2016), 89–111.

Lowell, Robert, *Life Studies* (New York: Farrar, Straus, and Cudahy, 1959).

  Notebook (New York: FSG Classics, 1995).

Löwith, Karl, *Meaning in History* (Chicago: University of Chicago Press, 1949).

Luhmann, Niklas, *Art as a Social System*, trans. Eva M. Knodt (Stanford: Stanford University Press, 2000).

  Introduction to Systems Theory, trans. Peter Gilgen (Cambridge: Polity, 2013).

Mackey, Nathaniel, *Bass Cathedral* (New York: New Directions, 2008).

  Blue Fasa (New York: New Directions, 2015).

  Discrepant Engagement: Dissonance, Cross-Culturality, and Experimental Writing (Cambridge: University of Cambridge Press, 1993).

  Eroding Witness (Urbana: University of Illinois Press, 1985).

  From a Broken Bottle Traces of Perfume Still Emanate, Vols. 1–3 (New York: New Directions, 2010).

  Nod House (New York: New Directions, 2011).

  Outer Pradesh (Anomalous Press, 2014).

  Paracritical Hinge: Essays, Talks, Notes, Interviews (Madison: University of Wisconsin Press, 2005).

  School of Udhra (San Francisco: City Lights, 1993).

  Splay Anthem (New York: New Directions, 2006).

  Whatsaid Serif (San Francisco: City Lights: 1998).

  "Wringing the Word," *World Literature Today* 68.4 (1994), 733–40.

Maharaj, Ayon, "Why Poetry Matters: The Transpersonal Force of Lyric Experience in Ezra Pound's *The Pisan Cantos*" *Arizona Quarterly* 66.4 (2010), 71–92.

Mallot, J. Edward, "Sacrificial Limbs, Lambs, Iambs, and I Ams: Nathaniel Mackey's Mythology of Loss," *Contemporary Literature* 45.1 (2004), 135–64.

Mancuso, Girolamo, "The Ideogrammic Method in The Cantos," trans. Peter Makin, in *Ezra Pound's Cantos: A Casebook*, ed. Peter Makin (Oxford: Oxford University Press, 2006), 65–80.

Mancuso, Luke, "Leaves of Grass, 1871–1872 Edition," in *Walt Whitman: An Encyclopedia*, eds. J. R. LeMaster and Donald D. Kummings (New York: Garland, 1998), 368–72.

Marinetti, F. T., "Manifesto of Futurism," (1909), trans. R. W. Flint and Arthur A. Coppotelli, in *Manifesto: A Century of Isms*, ed. Mary Ann Caws (Lincoln: University of Nebraska Press, 2001), 187–9.

Maturana, Humberto and Francisco Varela, *Autopoiesis and Cognition: The Realization of the Living* (Dordrecht: D. Reidel, 1980).

Mayer, Bernadette, "Sonnet: you jerk you didn't call me . . . ," in *A Bernadette Mayer Reader* (New York: New Directions, 1992), 93.

McConnell, Frank, *The Confessional Imagination: A Reading of Wordsworth's Prelude* (Baltimore: Johns Hopkins University Press, 1974)

McGann, Jerome, *Radiant Textuality: Literature After the World Wide Web* (New York: Palgrave, 2001).

The Textualist Condition (Princeton: Princeton University Press, 1991).

Towards a Literature of Knowledge (Oxford: Clarendon, 1989).

McHale, Brian, "Beginning to Think about Narrative in Poetry" *Narrative* 17.1 (2009), 11–27.

The Obligation Toward the Difficult Whole: Postmodernist Long Poems (Tuscaloosa: University of Alabama Press, 2004).

"Poetry as Prosthesis," *Poetics Today* 21.1 (2000), 1–32.

Mellor, Anne K., "Writing the Self/Self Writing: William Wordsworth's Prelude," *William Wordsworth's The Prelude: A Casebook*, ed. Stephen Gill (Oxford: Oxford University Press, 2006), 293–304.

Miller, Cristanne, "Drum Taps: Revisions and Reconciliations," *Walt Whitman Quarterly Review* 26.4 (2009), 171–96.

Miller, James E., *The American Quest for a Supreme Fiction: Whitman's Legacy in the Personal Epic* (Chicago: University of Chicago Press, 1979).

Miller, John H. and Scott E. Page, *Complex Adaptive Systems: An Introduction to Computational Models of Social Life* (Princeton: Princeton University Press, 2007).

Miller, Matt, *Collage of Myself: Walt Whitman and the Making of Leaves of Grass* (Lincoln: University of Nebraska Press, 2010).

Milne, Heather, "Dearly Beloveds: The Politics of Intimacy in Juliana Spahr's *This Connection of Everyone with Lungs*," *Mosaic* 47.2 (2014), 203–218.

Moody, A. David, *Ezra Pound: Poet. A Portrait of the Man and His Work. I: The Young Genius 1885–1920* (Oxford and New York: Oxford University Press, 2007).

Moretti, Franco, *Modern Epic: The World-System from Goethe to García Márquez*, trans. Quintin Hoare (New York: Verso, 1996).

"On Literary Evolution," in *Signs Taken For Wonders: Essays in the Sociology of Literary Forms*, revised edition, trans. Susan Fischer, David Forgacs, and David Miller (London: Verso, 1983), 262–78.

Morowitz, Harold, *The Emergence of Everything: How the World Became Complex* (Oxford: Oxford UP, 2002).

Morris, Adalaide, "New Media Poetics: As We May Think/How to Write," in *New Media Poetics: Contexts, Technotexts, and Theories*, eds. Adalaide Morris and Thomas Swiss (Cambridge: MIT Press), 1–46.

Morris, Roy Jr., *The Better Angel: Walt Whitman in the Civil War* (Oxford: Oxford University Press, 2000).

Nayak, Srila, "'Nothing in that Other Kingdom': Fashioning a Return to Africa in *Omeros*," *Ariel* 44.2–3 (2014), 1–28.

Naylor, Paul, *Poetic Investigations: Singing the Holes in History* (Evanston, IL: Northwestern University Press, 1999).

Neusner, Jacob, *What Is Midrash? and A Midrash Reader*, 2nd printing (Atlanta: Scholars Press, 1994).

Ngai, Sianne, "Network Aesthetics: Juliana Spahr's *The Transformation* and Bruno Latour's *Reassembling the Social*" in *American Literature's Aesthetic*

Dimensions, eds. Cindy Weinstein and Christopher Looby (New York: Columbia University Press, 2012), 367–92.

Nicholls, Peter, *Ezra Pound: Politics, Economics and Writing* (London: Macmillan, 1984).

Nichols, Miriam, *Radical Affections: Essays on the Poetics of Outside* (Tuscaloosa: University of Alabama Press, 2010).

Nielson, Aldon Lynn, "N + 1: Before-the-Fact Reading in Nathaniel Mackey's Postcontemporary Music," *Callaloo* 23.2 (2000), 796–806.

Nikolova, Olga, "Ezra Pound's Cantos De Luxe," *Modernism/Modernity* 15.1 (2008), 155–77.

Olson, Charles, *Collected Prose*, eds. Donald Allen and Benjamin Friedlander (Berkeley: University of California Press, 1997).

   The Maximus Poems, ed. George F. Butterick (Berkeley: University of California Press, 1983).

   The Principle of Measure in Composition by Field: Projective Verse II (Tucson: Chax Press, 2010).

   The Special View of History, ed. Ann Charters (Berkeley, CA: Oyez, 1970).

Oppen, George, *New Collected Poems* (New York: New Directions, 2002).

Paul, Sherman, *Olson's Push: Origin, Black Mountain, and Recent American Poetry* (Baton Rouge: Louisiana State University Press, 1978).

"Para-, prefix," Oxford English Dictionary Online (Oxford University Press, March 2015).

PennSound, Center for Programs in Contemporary Writing, University of Pennsylvania (2016), http://writing.upenn.edu/pennsound.

Perloff, Marjorie, *Unoriginal Genius: Poetry by Other Means in the New Century* (Chicago: University of Chicago Press, 2010).

   The Poetics of Indeterminacy: Rimbaud to Cage (Princeton: Princeton University Press, 1981).

Philip, M. NourbeSe, *Zong!* (Middletown, CT: Wesleyan University Press, 2008).

Plato, "Phaedrus," trans. Alexander Nehamas and Paul Woodruff, *Complete Works of Plato*, ed. John M. Cooper (Indianapolis: Hackett, 1997), 506–56.

Poe, Edgar Allan, "The Poetic Principle," in *Selected Poetry and Prose of Edgar Allan Poe*, ed. T. O. Mabbott (New York: Modern Library, 1951), 383–403.

Pound, Ezra, *ABC of Reading* (New York: New Directions, 1960).

   The Cantos (New York: New Directions, 1996).

   Selected Poems (New York: New Directions, 1957).

Pressman, Jessica, "Machine Poetics and Reading Machines: William Poundstone's Electronic Literature and Bob Brown's Readies," *American Literary History* 23.4 (2011), 767–94.

Price, Kenneth M., *To Walt Whitman, America* (Chapel Hill: University of North Carolina Press, 2004).

Pritchett, Patrick, "Review of *Drafts 1–38, Toll*," *Jacket* 22 (May 2003), no pagination, http://jacketmagazine.com/22/prit-dupless.html.

Prynne, J. H., "Poetic Thought," *Textual Practice* 24.4 (2010), 595–606.

Rainey, Lawrence, "Introduction," in *A Poem Containing History: Textual Studies in The Cantos*, ed. Lawrence Rainey (Ann Arbor: University of Michigan Press, 1997), 1–17.

  Ezra Pound and the Monument of Culture: Text, History, and the Malatesta Cantos (Chicago: University of Chicago Press, 1991).

Ramzani, Jahan, *The Hybrid Muse: Postcolonial Poetry in English* (Chicago: University of Chicago Press, 2001).

Redman, Tim, *Ezra Pound and Italian Fascism* (Cambridge: Cambridge University Press, 1991).

Reed, Anthony, *Freedom Time: The Poetics and Politics of Black Experimental Writing* (Baltimore: Johns Hopkins University Press, 2014).

Reed, Brian, *Nobody's Business: Twenty-First Century Avant-Garde Poetics* (Ithaca: Cornell University Press, 2013).

Riddel, Joseph, "'Neo-Nietzschean Clatter' – Speculation and/on Pound's Poetic Image," in *Ezra Pound: Tactics*, ed. Ian F. A. Bell (London: Vision, 1982), 187–220.

Robertson, Michael, *Worshipping Walt: The Whitman Disciples* (Princeton: Princeton University Press, 2008).

Rosenthal, M. L. and Sally M. Gall, *Modern Poetic Sequence: The Genius of Modern Poetry* (New York: Oxford University Press, 1986).

Rukeyser, Muriel, *The Life of Poetry* (Ashfield, MA: Paris Press, 1996).

Saint-Amour, Paul K., "*Ulysses* Pianola," *PMLA* 130.1 (2015), 15–36.

Sanders, Frederick K., *John Adams Speaking: Pound's Sources for the Adams Cantos* (Orono: University of Maine Press, 1975).

Scroggins, Mark, *The Poem of a Life: A Biography of Louis Zukofsky* (Berkeley: Counterpoint, 2007).

Sicari, Stephen, *Pound's Epic Ambition: Dante and the Modern World* (Albany: State University of New York Press, 1991).

Silliman, Ron, *Age of Huts (compleat)* (Berkeley: University of California Press, 2007).

  "The New Sentence," in *The New Sentence* (New York: Roof, 1987), 63–93.

Simpson, Megan, "Trickster Poetics: Multiculturalism and Collectivity in Nathaniel Mackey's *Song of the Andoumboulou*," *MELUS* 28.4 (2003), 35–54.

Sirganian, Lisa, *Modernism's Other Work: The Art Object's Political Life* (Oxford: Oxford University Press, 2012).

Smith, John, *The Complete Works of Captain John Smith*, ed. Philip L. Barbour, vol. 2 (Chapel Hill: University of North Carolina Press, 1986).

Spahr, Juliana, *This Connection of Everyone with Lungs* (Berkeley: University of California Press, 2005).

Spencer Brown, George, *Laws of Form* (London: George Allen and Unwin, 1969).

Spivak, Gayatri Chakravorty, *An Aesthetic Education in the Era of Globalization* (Cambridge: Harvard University Press, 2012).

Stern, David, "Midrash and Indeterminacy," *Critical Inquiry* 15.1 (1988), 132–61.

"Midrash and the Language of Exegesis: A Study of Vayikra Rabbah, Chapter 1," in *Midrash and Literature*, ed. Geoffrey H. Hartman and Sanford Budick (New Haven: Yale University Press, 1986), 105–24.

"Moses-cide: Midrash and Contemporary Literary Criticism," review of *The Slayers of Moses: The Emergence of Rabbinic Interpretation in Modern Literary Theory* by Susan A. Handelman, *Prooftexts* 4 (1984), 193–213.

Stevens, Wallace, "Notes Toward a Supreme Fiction," in *The Palm at the End of the Mind* (New York: Vintage, 1972), 207–34.

Stone, Ira F., *Reading Levinas/Reading Talmud* (Philadelphia: Jewish Publication Society, 1998).

Terada, Rei, *Derek Walcott's Poetry: American Mimicry* (Boston: Northeastern University Press, 1992).

Terrell, Carroll, *A Companion to The Cantos of Ezra Pound* (Berkeley: University of California Press, 1993).

Thomas, M. Wynn, *Transatlantic Connections: Whitman U.S., Whitman U.K.* (Iowa City: University of Iowa Press, 2005).

Tynyanov, Yuri. "On Literary Evolution," trans. C. A. Luplow, in *The Critical Tradition*, ed. David H. Richter (Boston: Bedford/St. Martins, 1998), 727–35.

Vanderborg, Susan "'Who Can Say Who Are Citizens?': Causal Mythology in Charles Olson's Polis," *Modern Language Quarterly* 59.3 (1998), 363–84.

Varela, Francisco, Evan Thompson, and Eleanor Rosch, *The Embodied Mind: Cognitive Science and Human Experience* (Cambridge: MIT Press, 1993).

Vickery, Ann, "From Being Drafted to a Draft of Being: Rachel Blau DuPlessis and the Reconceptualisation of the Feminist Avant-Garde," in *Avant-Post*, ed. Louis Armand (Prague: Literaria Pragensia, 2006), 138–40.

von Hallberg, Robert, *Charles Olson: The Scholar's Art* (Cambridge: Harvard University Press, 1978).

Walcott, Derek, *Omeros* (New York: Farrar, Straus & Giroux, 1990).

Walker, Jeffery, *Bardic Ethos and the American Epic Poem: Whitman, Pound, Crane, Williams, Olson* (Baton Rouge: Louisiana State University Press, 1989).

Walt Whitman Archive, ed. Ed Folsom and Kenneth M. Price, Center for Digital Research in the Humanities (Lincoln: University of Nebraska-Lincoln, 2016), www.whitmanarchive.org.

Warren, James Perrin, *Walt Whitman's Language Experiment* (University Park: Pennsylvania State University Press, 1990).

Watten, Barrett, "New Meaning and Poetic Vocabulary: From Coleridge to Jackson Mac Low," *Poetics Today* 18.2 (1997), 147–86.

Weber, Andreas and Francisco Varela, "Life after Kant: Natural Purposes and the Autopoietic Foundations of Biological Individuality," *Phenomenology and the Cognitive Sciences* 1 (2002), 97–125.

Whitehead, Alfred North, *Modes of Thought* (New York: Macmillan, 1938).

Whitman, Walt, *An American Primer* (Cambridge: 1904).

Poetry and Prose (New York: Library of America, 1996).

Wiener, Norbert, *Cybernetics, or Control and Communication in the Animal and the Machine*, 2nd ed. (Cambridge: MIT Press, 1961).

Williams, William Carlos, "Author's Introduction to *The Wedge*" (1944), in *Selected Essays of William Carlos Williams* (New York: New Directions, 1969), 255–7.

Wilson, Ivy, ed., *Whitman Noir: Black America and the Good Gray Poet* (Iowa City: University of Iowa Press, 2014).

Wimsatt, W. K. and Monroe C. Beardsley, "The Intentional Fallacy" (1954), in *The Critical Tradition*, ed. David H. Richter, 3rd ed. (Boston: Bedford/St. Martins, 2007), 801–18

Wohl, Robert, *A Passion for Wings: Aviation and the Western Imagination, 1908–1918* (New Haven: Yale University Press, 1994).

Wolfe, Cary, "The Idea of Observation at Key West, or, Systems Theory, Poetry, and Form beyond Formalism," *New Literary History* 39.2 (2008), 259–76.

Wolfram, Stephen, *A New Kind of Science* (Champaign, IL: Wolfram Media, 2002).

Wordsworth, William, *The Prelude 1799, 1805, 1850*, ed. Jonathan Wordsworth, M. H. Abrams, and Stephen Gill (New York: Norton, 1979).

Wyschogrod, Edith, "Language and Alterity in the Thought of Levinas," in *The Cambridge Companion to Levinas*, eds. Simon Critchley and Robert Bernasconi (Cambridge: Cambridge UP, 2002), 188–205.

Zamsky, Robert, "A Poetics of Radical Musicality: Nathaniel Mackey's '-mu' Series," *Arizona Quarterly* 62.1 (2006), 113–40.

Zoppi, Isabella, "Omeros, Derek Walcott, and the Contemporary Epic Poem," *Callaloo* 22.2 (1999), 509–28.

Index

Recent Books in This Series